NAPOLEON CROSSING THE ALPS.

THE

CAMP-FIRES

OF

NAPOLEON:

COMPRISING

THE MOST BRILLIANT ACHIEVEMENTS

OF THE

EMPEROR AND HIS MARSHALS.

BY HENRY C. WATSON.

PHILADELPHIA:
PORTER & COATES,

PREFACE.

THE vivid pictures of war, however ensanguined, have a wonderful attraction for the mass of men. They stir the heart like a trumpet. No narratives are so generally perused with avidity as those of "feats of broils and battles;" for in them, in spite of many disgusting features, there is always something to excite a pleasing thrill. We love excitement, and it seems that it is to war, and the descriptions of its varied scenes of danger, during which the faculties of the combatants are roused to extraordinary strength, that most look for the gratification of their natural desires. We have heard of many persons who, in the abstract, condemn all wars as brutal and degrading to humanity, peruse, with unwearied attention, narratives of the campaigns of great generals, and dwell upon their details with evident manifestations of delight. The passion is irresistible.

In this work, the author has endeavored to present to the mental eye, more vividly than the so-termed dignity of ordinary history permits, the most striking scenes and remarkable personages of Napoleon's astonishing career of glory—to show the greatest warrior of any age in the field, and at the nightly bivouacs—upon the fertile plains of Piedmont—in the shadow of the Egyptian pyramids—amid the forests of Germany, and on the frozen plains of Russia—surrounded by his galaxy of splendid generals, his military family—to illustrate a passage in the history of Europe, which, for stirring scenes and powerful characters, has, perhaps, no parallel. From the camp-fire at Toulon, where the young lieutenant of artillery gave the first impression of his wonderful genius, till the terrible night of darkness and death following the battle of Waterloo, the career of Napoleon is traced by his bivouacs; and around each watch-fire is grouped the incidents of the conflicts which there occurred. The salient points in the life of the great warrior are, therefore, illumined, so as to fix them in the memory.

Who can know the incidents of that career of glory without astonishment? We find a genius, under the smile of fortune, rising from the ranks of the people to the summit of despotic power—surpassing the generalship of Hannibal—the statesmanship of Cæsar, and performing exploits, which, before his time, were placed among the impossible. There is imperishable interest attached to every event in the life of such a character; and, therefore, no work which honestly aims to illustrate them can be considered superfluous.

It is hoped that the numerous engravings will add to the attractions of the book, and render its word-pictures clearer and more perfect to the mind. Their value is so well established, that the time is approaching when few historical works will be published without such illustrations.

CONTENTS.

MARSHAL JUNOT.

THE CAMP-FIRE AT TOULON.

IT was the night of the 19th of December, 1793. A sky of darkness, unbroken by the twinkling of a single star, arched over the town and harbor of Toulon. But on the rugged heights of Balagrier and L'Equillette, where the English had vainly constructed their "Little Gibraltar," the watch-fires of the French beseigers were redly burning; sending up showers of sparks, which looked like rising stars against the intense blackness of the heavens. It was the 19th of December, and the fate of Toulon, which for four months had lingered in the balance, was decided. Britons, Spaniards, Neapolitans and French—a garrison of the enemies of the republic—had fought in vain. The "Little Gibraltar," which commanded the town and harbor was in the hands of the French; their troops were even forcing their way into the town, and consternation had seized those who dared to oppose the decrees of the Committee of Safety, as well as those who had so promptly tendered them aid. The evacuation of Toulon had been hurriedly resolved; and now, as the red gleam of the watch-fires and the blaze of the thundering artillery shone upon the dark waters of the bay, crowds of trembling people could be seen embarking in vessels of all kinds, glad to avail themselves of the protection of the English fleet, to escape the bloody revenge of the triumphant republicans.

The batteries of the "Little Gibraltar," were already sending a shower of death upon the hostile fleet in the roadstead. On a rock, by a small blazing fire, and just above a battery, a form could be dimly seen through the smoke of the guns, which was destined to rise as a terrible image before the eyes of Europe, as it stood now, the conqueror of the foes of France, at Toulon. It was a slender form, on which the costume of a commandant of artillery hung loosely. But the inexorable resolution of the pale face, and the keen, quick flashes of the eagle eyes, caused those who gazed to forget all but awe and wonder before this genius of war. Occasionally, between the reports of the heavy guns, could be heard the shrill voice of command, which none refused to obey—it would be obeyed. Those eyes had seen where to strike, and that voice had commanded, the blow which brought Toulon to the feet of the republic. The commander was Napoleon Bonaparte, the young Corsican—the pet of Paoli—the child cradled amid the civil wars of his native island—who had made the cannon his toy—and who had been educated to war at the military school of Brienne. A subordinate, he had compelled his superior officers to bow before the oracles of his genius. One after another they had yielded, till the last, General Dugommier, a brave old warrior, acknowledged his artillery officer as the conqueror of Toulon.

That was a proud moment for the young Napoleon. He knew that the triumph was secured, and that to him, alone, it was due; for his plan had prevailed against the ignorant and imbecile schemes of the republic's generals, and his devices for rousing an irresistible enthusiasm in the troops, — such as naming a battery in a desperate position, the battery "*des hommes sans peur*," had rendered the execution of that plan complete. And now the enemy were preparing for flight—precipitate flight.

"A cooler aim — cut down a flag, brave Junot!" commands the shrill voice, amid the thunder of the guns, and the dusky, slovenly looking artillery man on the right of the battery, fronting Napoleon, steadily watches for a moment when the red glare shall show him a portion of the fleet in the roadstead. A glimpse of the cross of St. George! Loud thunders the gun, and at the next vivid glare, the flag falls; and amid the roar of the storm of death rises the cheer of the artillery men.

"Well done, Junot!" exclaimed the shrill voice. The slovenly man who brought down the cross of St. George was Andoche Junot, afterwards Marshal of France and Duke d'Abrantes, whose cool courage had more than once won the commendation of the commandant during this memorable siege.

But now occurred a scene which caused the fire of the "Little Gibraltar," to slacken. Even as Napoleon spoke to Junot, he discovered a spreading flame in the harbor, and in a few moments, great tongues of fire licked the air in front of the town, and lit up the scene for miles around with a terrible brilliancy. The English and Spaniards, under the direction of Sir Sydney Smith, had set fire to the arsenal, the stores, and the French ships which they could not remove. The rising flames, growing redder and redder, seemed at length like the glowing crater of a volcano, amid which could be seen the masts and yards of the burning vessels, and the advance of the republican troops who were attempting to force their way into the town. The waters of the bay resembled streams of lava flowing from the mountains and hills around the town, which, themselves glowed like living coals. The Jacobins in the town now arose to take revenge upon the flying royalists. Horrid screams and yells, cries and entreaties rang upon the air like sounds from the infernal regions, while in the midst of all could be heard the swelling chorus of the Marseillais. The guns of Malbosquet were turned upon the town, and their thunder increased the uproar of this terrible scene. Suddenly, a tremendous explosion, as if a mountain had been shattered to its base by a bolt from heaven, shocked the air, and even caused the stern men under the eye of Napoleon to tremble. Hundreds of barrels of powder had exploded, and high above the harbor, the air was filled with the blazing fragments, which descended even among the batteries of the "Little Gibraltar," causing the men to spring about to save themselves from the fire. Again that awful shock was given, a second magazine had exploded, and again the air seemed fairly alive with soaring fires, which threatened destruction when they fell. Fragments fell at the very feet of Napoleon, but he stood still, as a statue of resolution, a man without fear. His eyes were fixed upon the British fleet, which, by the red glare of earth and sky, could be seen slowly making sail, the decks of the vessels being crowded with fugitives. Once more he commanded the artillery to fire; and before the fleet got beyond the range of the guns, it received a shower of balls. The triumph was now complete.

Wearied officers and men now threw themselves upon the ground to rest, beside the fire. But to most of them, sleep could not come, with such a scene of terror, conflagration and tears before them. Napoleon, however, surveyed the harbor and town, for a few moments, and then, stretching himself upon the ground, commanded himself to slumber,—a faculty which he possessed through life—an evidence of his astonishing force of will.

The day dawned with a pale, ashen light. The roll of the drums, resounding among the hills, roused the triumphant soldiers of the republic; and as they gazed upon the smouldering ruins of the arsenal, and the bay strewn with the black fragments of the ships destroyed, they would have cursed their enemy; but they remembered their conquest, and pitied the destructive spite. Cheer after cheer rent the air. The artillery men crowded round their young chief, and with clamorous congratulations, gave him the first evidence of that enthusiastic affection, which, years afterwards, caused them to yearn to die in his service—to pave with their bodies his path to victory. What thoughts—what feelings burned within that young conqueror's breast none could know; for his stern, bronze countenance expressed nothing but his concentred strength of resolution. The same day, General Dugommier sent intelligence of the capture of Toulon to the Committee of Public Safety, and in the despatch he particularly recommended Napoleon for promotion, in these remarkable words,—"Promote him, or he will promote himself."

THE CAMP-FIRE AT MONTE NOTTE.

THE pure, bright moon shone with serene majesty in the soft, dark blue of the Italian sky, dimming the light of the silver stars, in her own calm glory. The rugged heights of Monte Notte, with here and there a tower and wall, or a row of trees upon its broken ascent, and the two small villages at its base, surrounded with groves and vineyards, were revealed with scarce the variation of a shadow. They would have seemed to sleep beneath the soothing influence of the night, but for the numerous red fires, which burned here and there along the mountain side, and at intervals for the distance of half a mile from its base; and the occasional booming of a gun, with its grumbling echoes. At a considerable distance in front could be seen the lights of the redoubts upon the heights of Monte Legino, which throughout the day, under the command of the indomitable Colonel Rampon, had withstood the furious assaults of the Austrians under d'Argenteau, the commander preferring to perish rather than capitulate. His resolution had saved the plans of Bonaparte from receiving a check, and now the young general of the French felt sure of his game.

Around the watch-fires to which we have alluded were gathered the half-fed, half-clothed, but enthusiastic troops of the divisions commanded by La Harpe and Cervoni, who had united and marched to this strong position in the rear of Monte Legino, in accordance with the plans of Bonaparte. The general-in-chief was with them, for near this place he anticipated the triumph of his wonderful combinations, and the defeat of the Austrians. Most of the principal officers were quartered in the villages, resting from the fatigues of a rapid march. But the time was too critical for Bonaparte to think of sleep. He was abroad among those camp-fires, accompanied by the brave and active Swiss, La Harpe, that faithful and untiring friend, Michael Duroc, then aid-de-camp to the young general, and several other officers of distinction. As he walked among them, he looked like a mere boy attending a throng of rough and hardy soldiers. To each group gathered round a fire, he had a pleasant and encouraging word to say, a condescension to which these war-worn veterans were unaccustomed. As he turned away from them he might have heard expressions which showed that the troops believed in his invincibility, and at all events, were prepared to suffer any hardships in his service. The wretched clothing of many of them was observed by the general, and he occasionally reminded them, that they had now an opportunity of winning not only glory, which every true soldier should seek first, but wealth and abundance, amid the fertile plains of Italy. Such words, uttered by a commander among the camp-fires of an army are calculated to have more effect in arousing its enthusiasm than the most eloquent of regular and formal addresses. At length, arriving at a fire much larger than any of the others upon the side of the mountain, Bonaparte threw himself upon the ground, and, motioning his officers to follow his example, he took out the plan of operations, which he had drawn up, and began with his usual precision, to explain how far it had been carried out, and what would be the movements of the next day. In the meantime the soldiers, grim, moustached veterans, withdrew and set about kindling another fire at a respectful distance.

"Augereau will reach this point early in the morning, and render efficient support to the troops already in position. Marching by this road on the other side of the Appenines, Massena will show himself, nearly at the same time, in d'Argenteau's rear, and then the Austrians cannot escape us. They will be surrounded on all sides by a superior force.

"Thus far it has been successful," said La Harpe. "But if Rampon had not fought so desperately at Monte Legino, the plan would have been defeated, or at least, checked for a time."

"Rampon fought bravely; but when such a plan depends upon the maintenance of a post, a good officer should prefer to die rather than yield it to the enemy," replied Bonaparte.

"Rampon fought like a hero because he knew the importance of his position," said Duroc.

"I trust Massena will be as active as the occasion demands. He has courage, perseverance, and skill; but it requires the most imminent danger to awaken his activity," said the young commander-in-chief.

"A singular man, truly," remarked Duroc.

"However," continued Bonaparte, following the train of his own reflections, "never had a commander-in-chief more reason to be proud of his general officers than myself. They are all men born to lead. With them, I have nothing to fear from the delinquency of our half-fed troops."

"Yet, general, the soldiers are in a condition calculated to depress their spirits," said La Harpe. "We officers, who chiefly fight for glory, and for the honor of our country, never murmur, although very badly treated by our government. But the majority of the soldiers in the ranks have a constant eye to their pay."

"But to make soldiers worthy of France, we must alter that;" replied Bonaparte, "one and all must be taught to fight for glory, and then our arms will be irresistible."

La Harpe shook his head. But the enthusiastic Duroc, catching the noble fire of his illustrious friend, exclaimed.

"Yes, the love of glory makes the true soldier! This will cause the troops to forget their toilsome, bare-foot marches, and their long days of hunger! And never have I seen the French soldiers more eager for conflict in defence of their country's honor, than they have been since our young general took command of the army of Italy. That first proclamation gave them a new spirit, which has been growing stronger every day. There are splendid triumphs before us, I am sure."

The face of Bonaparte expressed nothing of the emotions which must have heaved in his soul at these words. But he grasped the hand of Duroc and shook it warmly.

"My friends," said he, "it is all clear enough to me. To-morrow will be a great day for France. Old Beaulieu will begin to know his enemy. The plain before us shall be the scene of more Austrian astonishment and dismay than has been known in Italy for many years. Beaulieu supposes that I intended to file off along the coast to Genoa; whereas, here I am, ready to overwhelm his centre. Following up this victory, it will be easy to cut him off from communication with the Piedmontese."

The officers gazed with wonder and admiration upon the stripling who was thus summarily disposing of the fate of armies and countries, and while they listened to his words of conscious power, an awe crept over them, they felt themselves in the presence of a superior being; and yet among them were several men of splendid qualities,—born to command.

By this time the groups around the fires had stretched themselves upon the hard earth to repose, and the pacing of the sentinels alone disturbed the stillness of the scene, where thousands of brave warriors submitted to the conqueror, sleep. Bonaparte and his officers returned to a house in the little village of Monte Notte, which had been selected as the quarters for the night. And the army slumbered on, beneath the sweet vigil of the moon, and beside the cheerful warmth of the camp-fires until the cold, white light in the east told that the most glorious king of day, who has arisen and set upon so many fields of conflict, was about to ascend the heavens.

"Far off his coming shone,"

and the stars soared out of sight, and the moon slowly faded to vapor, as the white light turned to a golden glow.

Then was heard the roll of the reveillé. With astonishing rapidity, the French were under arms and in motion. Bonaparte and his staff rode to an elevated knoll, commanding the whole plain, and then were ordered the movements which gave to the young commander-in-chief the victory of Monte Notte. D'Argenteau, the Austrian commander, found himself attacked upon one side by the divisions of La Harpe, Cervoni and Augereau, and upon the other by Massena. Then boomed the cannon, and the rattled musketry over the plain. The Austrian infantry sustained the conflict with admirable courage. But they were surrounded by superior forces and after several charges had been made by the French, in the full confidence of victory, the discomfited d'Argenteau was compelled to retreat towards Dego. In fact, the retreat was a disorderly flight. The French made two thousand prisoners, and several hundred Austrians were left dead on the field. The centre of the Austrian army had been completely overwhelmed. Bonaparte was the victor of Monte Notte. In after years, when the imperial crown adorned his brow, the conqueror showed his contempt for ancestral distinctions by saying that he dated his title to rule from this battle.

THE CAMP-FIRE AT MONDOVI.

WHEN the conflict is at an end, and the awful silence of night descends upon the field where stark and stiff lie the mangled dead, among the broken weapons and spoils of the fight, the scene is fearfully impressive. There lie the cold forms of those, who in life were furious foes; but in death, side by side, united in their doom of darkness.

they are all clay together. The bugle and the drum, which were sounded to signal the contest, are broken beside the mutilated and bloody bodies of those who played them at the head of the marching regiments. The captain, whose gallant "forward!" roused the spirits of his men, lies where he perished, in the van. The standard-bearer still clasps a portion of that dear symbol of his country, which numbers cut from his hands, and seems to have yielded his breath, while hugging that remnant to his heart. The grim veteran of a hundred fights, to whom death has been a jeer and a mockery, and the youth, with blooming cheek and eager eye, who left his mother's cottage high in the hope of a glorious renown, are found cold and stiff together; the one with a smile of scorn curling his lip, the other with the keen agony, kindled by the rushing remembrance of the dear home lost forever, pictured in his countenance. The meek moon and the sentinel stars shining on this field of death, with a pallid light, add to its horrors, increasing the ghastly hue in the faces of the slain.

Such a scene was presented on the night of the 22nd of April, 1796, after the desperate battle of Mondovi. Near the town of that name, the dispirited army of Colli had been overtaken by two divisions of Bonaparte's army, commanded by Serrurier and Massena. Serrurier had been repulsed, but the onset of Massena was irresistible, and the enemy were attacked on both flanks at once. The cavalry of the Piedmontese over powered and drove back that of the French, but the wonderful valor of Murat, the most glorious of cavalry officers, renewed the fortune of the day, and, shortly afterwards,

Colli's army was put to flight. During the retreat, the Piedmontese suffered dreadfully, losing the best of their troops, their cannons, baggage and appointments.

Wearied with the desperate conflict, the greater portion of the victorious army encamped in and about the town of Mondovi, a body of cavalry, alone pursuing and harassing the enemy. The description of the field of battle given above, will apply to this one, with the addition of a view of the towers and spires of Mondovi, and of numerous blazing fires in the vicinity, around which the exhausted troops had sunk to repose. Bonaparte had arrived; and, now, having gathered his principal officers at a ruined building, just outside of the town, which seemed to have been an old chapel, talked over with them the achievements of the day, and what was contemplated for the morrow. The ruin consisted of four broken walls, and was entirely roofless. It was several yards square, and the floor was strewn with fragments of sculpture which had once adorned the edifice. In the centre of the floor a fire was kindled, and camp-stools were ranged around it. At some distance from the ruin, guards were placed, with orders to keep the inquisitive beyond ear-shot. This place had evidently been selected by Bonaparte, in preference to the best mansion of Mondovi, to be secure from the treachery of Italians, who might have overheard and communicated to the enemy important information.

As usual, Bonaparte had the paper containing the lines of his movements before him, and with pencil and compasses in hand, he devised and marked alterations even while he talked. Among the officers gathered around the fire, were Massena, Berthier, Serrurier, Murat and Duroc.

Next to the commander-in-chief himself, Massena had the most remarkable personal appearance of any of the group. His massive features had a somewhat Jewish cast and their general expression was extremely heavy, or rather drowsy. The eyes were half-closed, and they did not sparkle like those of the rest, when Bonaparte spoke. Yet it was well known that, when excited by the storm of battle, their flash was terrible. The expression of the mouth, was always that of an inexorable will. The whole aspect of Andrew Massena was that of a man of great powers, difficult to rouse. Napoleon himself remarked that it was only in danger that appalled most men, that Massena acquired clearness and force of thought. His want of activity was his great defect as a commander.

Serrurier was a large man, with rough, prominent features, in which strong passions and dogged determinations were plainly expressed. His dress was torn and dusty; for although repulsed by the Piedmontese, he had fought like a lion on that desperate day.

The face of Duroc was manly and prepossessing. The slightly receding forehead, prominent nose, clear, bright eyes, and firm mouth, were illumined by a bland, but determined expression, indicative of the truly heroic spirit of this faithful friend of Napoleon. By the side of Michael Duroc, could be seen the stalwart form and noble countenance of Joachim Murat, the great leader of the cavalry, whose desperate charge had decided the battle in favor of the French. His gaudy costume was arranged with scrupulous nicety, and it bore no traces of the conflict. He sat toying with his long, dark curls during the conference.

"To-morrow, we will occupy Cherasco, which is within ten leagues of the Piedmontese capital," said Bonaparte. "It has been a month of glory. Within that time, we have gained complete possession of the mountain passes and thus opened the road for our armies into Italy. We have gained three battles over forces far superior to our own; inflicted upon the enemy a loss of about twenty-five thousand men in killed, wounded, and prisoners, taken eighty pieces of cannon and twenty-one stand of colors; and almost annihilated the army of Sardinia. We can dictate a treaty at Turin."

"The fight to-day was desperate enough, however," said Murat, ever vain of his services. "The cavalry was beaten back by the Piedmontese, and General Stengel was among the slain."

"A brave man lost to France," interrupted Bonaparte.

"But I soon taught them that the French cavalry was not so easily beaten," continued Murat. "That charge decided the day."

"I am told," said Bonaparte, "that the charge was indeed brilliant. But we expect such from Murat, and we hope that, hereafter, he may have the best opportunities of displaying his valor and horsemanship at the head of the cavalry of France. You have won a high promotion. General Serrurier, you were repulsed; but you afterwards bravely sustained your reputation, and contributed much to the victory. As for you, General Massena, high as were my expectations from your valor and skill, you have astonished me. France will yet regard you as a child of victory."

Massena opened his eyes somewhat wider and nodded his thanks. "The troops," he remarked, "are sadly worn with their rapid marches, and four days' fighting. Besides, since they have been so severely treated for seizing upon what food and clothes they found along the line of march, they have suffered much for want of the common necessaries of life."

"I know—I know," replied Bonaparte; "I pity them, and hope that their wants may soon be relieved. But they must not become Goths and Vandals. What did you say was the loss of the enemy, to-day, Berthier?"

"It is estimated at about three thousand men," replied the officer addressed—an elegant looking soldier, with a frank, intelligent countenance.

"Colli is then effectually crippled," said Bonaparte "He will not dare to make a stand between us and Turin. I learn that Cherasco is an ill-defended place, but it has an important position at the confluence of the Stura and the Tanaro, and with the artillery taken from the enemy, we can soon render it defensible, should that be necessary. But at present, the prospect is that we shall in a few days conclude a peace with the king of Sardinia, and then we must pursue the Austrians, whom we shall drive beyond the Alps. But in the meantime, you, Murat, shall take some of our trophies to Paris, and proclaim the triumphs of France. A more fitting messenger of victory could not be found." At this intelligence Murat's eyes sparkled, and a smile lit up his dark features; for next to the storm of battle, this proud soldier loved to boast of victory. Next to being a lion upon the field of battle, he desired to be a lion in the saloons of Paris.

"General," said Duroc, "you may remember that when we stood upon the heights of Monte Lemoto, and beheld that glorious picture of the plains of Piedmont and Italy, you exclaimed, 'Hannibal crossed the Alps; as for us, we have gone round them!' It seems to me, with deference, that if reinforcements are not speedily sent to our aid, you will find yourself in a position more nearly resembling that of Hannibal, when, although victorious in Italy, he was deserted by Carthage. The chief difference will be, however, that Hannibal, by fortunate circumstances, was enabled to maintain his army against all the forces of Rome. But we should soon be overwhelmed by superior numbers."

"The government of France has neglected its duty," replied Bonaparte, "but I cannot believe that it will desert us altogether. If so, however, I have no doubt that we can provide for ourselves."

"For myself," said Serrurier, "I love France, but despise the present government. But for the bravery of the army, whose triumphs they have taken to themselves, the members of that government would not now hold their places."

At these words, Bonaparte raised his head, and gave a steady, piercing glance at the frank, out-spoken soldier's countenance, probably with the design of ascertaining the full depth of his meaning. But Serrurier returned glance for glance, and Bonaparte returned to the contemplation of his map. There was more in that young conqueror's look than, perhaps, any of that martial group, suspected.

The chief incidents of the fight of the day having been communicated to Bonaparte by the various officers engaged in its terrible scenes, he proceeded to award commendation where it was due; and then gave the generals orders in regard to the movements of the next day. Despatches, hurriedly written, were sent to the generals of the divisions not engaged at Mondovi, and then the conference terminated. Most of the officers retired to their respective commands; but, accompanied by Duroc and Murat, the sleepless commander-in-chief rode over the field, to gain a more accurate knowledge of the terrible character of the battle—to observe where the fight had been thickest, what corps had suffered the greatest loss, and what had the been advantages and disadvantages of the ground. In many places, it was difficult for the horses to proceed without trampling upon the groups of ghastly dead; and the reckless Murat occasionally rode directly over the corpses, while talking to the commander-in-chief. A considerable number of women, from Mondovi, were seen among the bodies, collecting many little articles of value attached to the clothing of the dead warriors. At the approach of Bonaparte and his officers they scampered away, like so many frightened vultures, upon which Murat would give chase for a short distance to increase their alarm. After a complete survey of the field, Bonaparte and his aids returned to Mondovi. The only remark the young commander-in-chief was heard to make, was, "It was a hard-won victory—Mondovi ought to be decisive." And it was decisive. At Cherasco, Sardinia submitted to the victor's terms; and thus one of the bravest of the foes of France was crushed after a campaign of very brief duration, the glories of which are thus touched upon by Bonaparte in an eloquent and powerful proclamation to his soldiers.

"Soldiers! in a fortnight you have gained six victories, taken twenty-one pair of colors, fifty-five pieces of cannon, several fortresses, and conquered the richest part of Piedmont; you have made fifteen thousand prisoners, and killed or wounded more than ten thousand men; you had hitherto been fighting for barren rocks, rendered famous by your courage, but of no service to the country; you this day compete by your services with the army of Holland and of the Rhine. Destitute of every thing, you have supplied all your wants. You have gained battles without cannon, crossed rivers without bridges, made forced marches without shoes, bivouacked without brandy, and often without bread. Republican phalanxes, the soldiers of liberty alone, could have endured what you have endured. Thanks be to you for it, soldiers!"

THE CAMP-FIRE AT THE BRIDGE OF LODI.

BEAULIEU, the veteran general of the Austrians, had been beaten and compelled to retreat before the French commander of twenty-six. The Po being crossed and the Tesino turned, Bonaparte beheld the road to Milan open before him. But he prepared to make the effort to cut off Beaulieu's retreat, and compel the Austrian army to surrender. Like Nelson, upon the sea, he thought no triumph complete unless the enemy was entirely prostrated. But to cut off the retreat of Beaulieu, it was necessary to anticipate him at the passage of the rivers. A great number of these flow from the Alps, and cross Lombardy on their way to the Po and the Adriatic. After the Po and the Tesino, come the Adda, the Oglio, the Mincio, the Adige and numerous others.

The Adda was now before Bonaparte. It is a large and deep river, although fordable in some places. The passage was to be made at the town of Lodi, an old place containing about twelve thousand inhabitants. It has old Gothic walls, but its chief defence consists in the river, which flows through it, and which is crossed by a wooden bridge, about five hundred feet in length. Having crossed the river, Beaulieu drew up twelve thousand infantry and four thousand horse on the opposite bank, posted twenty pieces of artillery so as to sweep the bridge, and lined the bank with sharp-shooters It was against all military practice to attempt the passage of a river in the face of such difficulties. But it was the military mission of Bonaparte to astonish the routine generals.

Napoleon, coming up on the 10th of May, easily drove the rear-guard of the Austrian army before him into the town, but found his further progress threatened by the tremendous fire of the pieces of cannon, stationed at the opposite end of the bridge, so as to sweep it most completely. The whole body of the enemy's infantry drawn up in a dense line, supported this appalling disposition of the artillery.

An answering battery was instantly constructed on the French side, Napoleon exposing himself in the thickest of the fire to point two of the guns with his own hands. This he effected in such a manner as to prevent the possibility of any approach on the part of the enemy to undermine or blow up the bridge. Observing, meanwhile, that Beaulieu had removed his infantry to a considerable distance backwards, to keep them out of the range of the French battery, he instantly detached his cavalry, with orders to gallop out of sight, and then ford the river, and coming suddenly upon the enemy, attack them in flank.

He now drew up a body of six thousand grenadiers in close column, under the shelter of the houses, and bade them prepare for the desperate attempt of forcing a passage across the narrow bridge, in the face of the enemy's thickly-planted artillery.

The cavalry of Napoleon had a difficult task to perform in passing the river, and he waited with anxiety for their appearance on the opposite bank. But a sudden movement in the ranks of the enemy showed him that his cavalry had arrived and charged, and he instantly gave the word. The head of the column of grenadiers wheeled to the left, and was at once upon the bridge. The whole body rushed forward with impetuosity, shouting, "Vive la Republique!" A hundred bodies rolled dead, and the advancing column faltered under the redoubled roar of the guns, and the tempest of the grape shot. At this critical moment, Lannes, Napoleon, Berthier, and L'Allemand, hurried to the front, and dashing onwards were followed by the whole column in the very mouth of the artillery. They gained the opposite side: Lannes reached the guns first, and Napoleon second. The artillerymen were killed; their guns seized; and the Austrian infantry, which had been removed too far back, not having time to come up to support the artillery, the whole army was put to flight.

The French cavalry pursued in the blazing enthusiasm of almost unprecedented victory. About two thousand Austrians were either killed or wounded, and the same number made prisoners, while twenty pieces of cannon remained in the hands of the French.

The victorious army encamped on the banks of the Adda, in the position which had been occupied by the defeated Austrians. Before night fell, Bonaparte was informed that he had failed to get between Beaulieu, and the other divisions of the Austrian army; but, aware of the terror which his daring exploit would strike into the enemy, he scarcely regretted his trifling failure of movement. The line of the Adda was carried; tremendous difficulties had been vanquished with a loss of only two hundred men, and the courage and devotion of the soldiers had been raised to the highest pitch.

The encampment upon the Adda presented a remarkable aspect. Most of the officers had the accommodation of tents, but the troops were destitute of that luxury, and their only resource for rest was to throw themselves upon the ground around their fires. These gallant men, although fatigued with the efforts of the glorious day, were too much excited by their victory to rest without some demonstration. It was a clear, beautiful moonlight night. Although filled in some places with the dead, the Adda danced merrily onward, the ripples sparkling in the moonbeams. All was quiet above; but in camp and town, there was the bustle of men to whom sleep would not come. Bonaparte had retired to his tent to partake of some refreshment, and having soon satisfied his abstemious appetite, he was about to traverse the camp, alone, to observe the spirit of his troops, as well as to ascertain the character and rank of the prisoners. In front of his tent, he was astonished to meet a small deputation of grim-visaged grenadiers, who saluted him with the title of the "Little Corporal." One of their number then stepped forward, and respectfully communicated the intelligence that they had elected him a corporal, in consideration of his gallant service in the ranks that day, and hoped that they might one day confer still higher honors upon him. Three hearty cheers were then given by the veterans, who appeared to enjoy the joke amazingly; and after they had retired, the young general was saluted in various parts of the camp as the "Little Corporal." This gaiety was characteristic of the French soldiers. Bonaparte was rather pleased with the singular mode of showing affection for his person, and admiration of his intrepidity.

The general approached a group of Hungarian prisoners without being recognised by them. They were standing near a fire, conversing, and evidently much irritated at the misfortunes of their position. He went among them and mingled in the conversation. An old officer, who spoke to him, appeared to be extremely moody. Bonaparte could not but smile at his language. "Things are going on as ill and irregular as possible," said this veteran of routine. "The French have got a young general who knows nothing of the regular rules of war; he is sometimes on our front, sometimes on our flank, sometimes on the rear. There is no supporting such a gross violation of rules." He evidently preferred to be whipped in a regular way. But it is agreed that the object of war is victory, and if rules do not secure that victory, they are of no value. Bonaparte's system appeared very extraordinary to the Austrian commanders. It was something beyond what they had learned at their German military schools.

After traversing the camp, and receiving many testimonials of the warm devotion of the troops to his person, Bonaparte returned to his tent, where he was soon joined by Berthier, Massena, Augereau, Bessieres, Duroc, Serrurier, Lannes, and others. To each and all he gave a word of compliment; but he was especially fluent in his praise of the indomitable young General Lannes, whose daring courage had attracted his attention in previous engagements as well as at the tremendous charge across the bridge of Lodi. They were, indeed, as gallant a group of officers, as ever a general had at his command—men who could as calmly reason and determine upon manœuvres in the hottest storm of battle, as during the quiet hours of this moonlight night—quick in devising, irresistible in the execution; and yet it was only yonder stripling, with the Roman features and the piercing eyes, who could give a glorious harmony to their action, bring their peculiar faculties into play, and secure their triumph. Great as they undoubtedly were, they failed to achieve great triumphs when beyond the reach of the "Little Corporal's" controlling mind. The conference was long, for there were difficulties in the arrangement of the plan for moving upon Milan, and some of the officers, particularly Massena, had objections to urge. However, Bonaparte determined according to his own views. The officers observed that there was a remarkable change in his bearing towards them. He had hitherto admitted them to complete familiarity; but they now felt constrained by his lofty manner to keep at a respectful distance. When they retired that night, some of them exchanged glances of significance; they were evidently displeased at the haughty bearing of the young commander-in-chief; yet few of them, perhaps, comprehended the change.

The fact was that the victory of Lodi had a great influence upon Napoleon's mind. He afterwards acknowledged, that neither the quelling of the sections at Paris, nor the victory of Monte Notte made him regard himself as any thing superior, but that after Lodi, for the first time, the idea dawned upon him, that he should one day be "a decisive actor," on the stage of the political world. It was Lodi which gave birth to the 18th Brumaire.

THE CAMP-FIRE AT CASTIGLIONE.

IT was at Castiglione and in its vicinity that the wonderful spirit and rapidity of Napoleon's movements were more fully displayed than at any other of his scenes of victory in Italy. The aged Beaulieu had been superseded in the command of the Austrian army, by General Wurmser, a commander of high reputation.

His army was greatly superior in numbers to that of Bonaparte. It descended from the Tyrol during the last days of July, in three divisions, commanded by Davidowich, Quasdanowitch, and Wurmser himself.

Wurmser, confident in his numbers, and calculating upon the absorption of the energies of the French army, by its endeavors to subdue Mantua, disposed his forces in the most admirable way to improve a victory; never reflecting that he might happen to be defeated. Untaught by all the previous disasters of Beaulieu, he committed the error of dividing his army, in order to cover an extent of country. His right wing was detached, with orders to occupy Brescia, and cut off the retreat of the French in the direction of Milan: his left wing was to descend the Adige, and manœuvre on Verona; while the centre, under his own command, advanced to raise the siege of Mantua. During the two first days of his approach, the French generals, after resisting to the utmost, yielded up successively, Rivoli, Brescia, and Salo; but these two days were sufficient to make Napoleon master of the plan on which Wurmser proposed to carry on the campaign, and he instantly disconcerted the whole of it, by a movement so unlike that of any ordinary general, as to defy all calculation.

In one night, (31st July,) he raised the siege of Mantua; sacrificing the whole of his artillery. The men were employed to destroy as much as the time would allow. They spiked the guns, burnt the carriages, threw the powder into the lake, and buried the balls. Augereau and Massena were stationed to defend the line of the Mincio as long as possible. Before morning the whole French army had disappeared from Mantua, and Napoleon was hurrying forward to attack the right wing of the Austrian army, before it could effect a junction with the central body of Wurmser.

The Austrian right wing was advancing in three divisions. Napoleon defeated one division at Salo, and another at Lonato. At the same time, Augereau and Massena, leaving a sufficient number of men at their posts to maintain a defence, or at least to impede the enemy, marched upon the third division at Brescia; but it had already fled in disorder towards the Tyrol. The French generals instantly countermarched to the support of their rear-guards, which had been forced by the Austrians.

Wurmser reached Mantua and was astonished to find what he believed to be a precipitate flight. He entered the city in triumph—but he was completely deceived. (August 2nd.)

Bonaparte did not halt for a moment. His troops had been constantly on the march, he had himself been all the time on horseback; he resolved to make them fight the very next morning. He had before him Bayalitsch at Lonato, and Liptai at Castiglione, presenting to both of them a front of twenty-five thousand men. He had to attack them before Wurmser should return from Mantua. Sauret had for the second time abandoned Salo; Bonaparte sent Guyeux again thither to recover the position, and to keep back Quasdanowitch. After these precautions on his left and on his rear, he resolved to march forward to Lonato with Massena, and to throw Augereau upon the heights of Castiglione, which had been abandoned on the preceding day by General Vallette. He broke that general at the head of his army, in order to make his lieutenants do their duty without flinching. On the following day, the 16th (August 3rd,) the whole army was in motion; Guyeux re-entered Salo, and this rendered any communication between Quasandowitch and the Austrian army still more impracticable. Bonaparte advanced upon Lonato; but his advanced guard was beaten back, some pieces of cannon were taken, and General Pigeon was made prisoner. Bayalitsch, proud of this success advanced with confidence, and extended his wings around the French division. He had two objects in performing this manœuvre; in the first place, to surround Bonaparte, and in the second, to extend himself on the right for the purpose of entering into communication with Quasandowitch, whose cannon he heard at Salo. Bonaparte, not alarming himself about his rear, suffered himself to be surrounded with imperturbable coolness; he placed some sharp-shooters on his exposed wings, and next took the 18th and 32d demi-brigades of infantry, ranged them in close column, gave them a regiment of dragoons to support them, and rushed headlong upon the enemy's centre, which was weakened by its extension. With this brave body of infantry he overthrew all before him, and thus broke the line of the Austrians. The latter, divided into two bodies, immediately lost their courage: one part of the division of Bayalitsch fell back in all haste towards the Mincio; but the other, which had extended itself in order to communicate with Quasandowitch, was driven towards Salo, where Guyeux was at that moment. Bonaparte caused it to be pursued without intermission, that he might place it between two fires. He let loose Junot in pursuit of it, with a regiment of cavalry. Junot dashed off at a gallop, killed six horsemen with his own hand, and fell, having received several sabre wounds. The fugitive division, entrapped between the corps at Salo and that which was pursuing it from Lonato, was routed, and lost at every step thousands of prisoners. During this successful pursuit, Bonaparte proceeded on his right to Castiglione, where Augereau had been fighting ever since the morning with admirable bravery. The heights on which Liptai's division had placed itself had now to be carried. After an obstinate combat, several times renewed, he had at length accomplished his object, and Bonaparte on his arrival found the enemy retreating on all sides. Such was the battle called the battle of Lonato, fought on the 16th (August 3rd.)

This battle produced considerable results. The French had taken twenty pieces of cannon and three thousand prisoners from the division cut off and driven back upon Salo, and they were still pursuing its scattered remnant in the mountains. They had made a thousand or fifteen hundred prisoners at Castiglione, and killed or wounded three thousand men; they had alarmed Quasandowitch, who finding the French army at Salo, and hearing it in the distance at Lonato, thought that it was every where. They had thus nearly disorganized the divisions of Bayalitsch and Liptai, which fell back upon Wurmser. That general at this moment came up with fifteen thousand men to rally the two beaten divisions, and began to draw out his lines in the plains of Castiglione.

Bonaparte now determined upon fighting a decisive battle upon the ground which the Austrian general had chosen, but as it was necessary to collect all his disposable force at Castiglione, he deferred the action until the 5th.

It was the night of the 4th of August. The weather had been excessively warm for several days, and the troops were almost exhausted by their rapid marches under a burning sun. The hostile armies were encamped close in front of each other, vertically from the line of the heights on which both supported one wing, Bonaparte having his left thereon, and Wurmser his right. A series of heights formed by the last range of the Alps extends from Chiessa to the Mincio, by Lonato, Castiglione and Solferino. At the foot of these heights was the plains on which the great battle was to be fought. Bonaparte had at most twenty-two thousand men, Serrurier's division not having come up yet; and, indeed, it had been ordered to make an effort to gain the rear of the Austrians. Wurmser had thirty thousand men under his command, and the wing of his army which was on the plain was supported by a redoubt placed upon the elevation of Medolano. It was a clear, warm night. The stars were thickly sprinkled in the arching heaven, but there was no moon, and the position of each army could only be clearly distinguished by the light of the lines of watch-fires, stretching away from the foot of the heights. In the rear of the Austrians, the low wall, and tower of the old town of Castiglione could be distinguished, forming a looming and shadowy background to a striking and imposing picture.

Around one of the fires in the vicinity of the tent of the commander-in-chief, was sitting a group of officers, among whom Bessieres, Duroc, and Augereau were the only men of renown. All ears were opened listening to Bessieres, who was giving an account of Bonaparte's wonderful exploit that day, in escaping from a surprise at Lonato. He told the story as follows:

"You know that this morning, our commander-in-chief set off for Lonato at full gallop, to personally hasten the movements of the troops. He was accompanied only by his staff and the Guides under my command. We arrived at Lonato about noon. We found that the orders of the general were already carried out; part of the troops were marching upon Castiglione, and the rest were proceeding towards Salo and Gavardo. About a thousand men remained at Lonato. Scarcely had the general entered the place, when an Austrian flag of truce presented itself, and the bearer summoned him to surrender. The general started at the summons. He could not understand how it was possible that the Austrians could be so close upon him. But the case was soon explained. The division separated in the battle of Lonato, and driven back upon Salo, had been partly captured; but a body of about four thousand five hundred men had been wandering all night in the mountains; and seeing the town almost abandoned, wanted to enter the place, in order to open for itself an outlet upon the Mincio. General Bonaparte had no time to fight a battle, or perhaps he would have done it, even with his force of one thousand men. His plan was formed with his usual quickness and decision. He ordered all the officers about him to mount their horses, and then, the bearer of the flag to be brought before him, with his eyes uncovered; for, as usual on such occasions, the officer was blindfolded. You should have seen the Austrian's astonishment when he found himself in the presence of our general and his staff. 'Unhappy man!' said General Bonaparte, 'you know not then that you are in the presence of the commander-in-chief, and that he is here with his whole army. Go tell those who sent you, that I give them five minutes to surrender, or I will put them to the sword to punish the insult which they have dared to offer me.' The astonished bearer of the flag returned with this message to his general. In the meantime, General Bonaparte prepared his small force for action. The Austrian then asked him to propose terms of capitulation. But our general, knowing the importance of immediate action, replied—'No, you must become at once prisoners of war.' The Austrian hesitated, but when General Bonaparte ordered his artillery and grenadiers to advance to the attack, the enemy surrendered; and thus, without striking a blow, four thousand infantry and five hundred cavalry surrendered themselves prisoners of war to about one thousand Frenchmen. We gained, besides, two pieces of artillery."

A general laugh followed this narrative. All agreed that it was an admirable exploit, and quite worthy of the genius of Bonaparte. At this moment, the young commander-in-chief appeared at the door of his tent.

His horse was standing near, and he was quickly mounted. "Come, Bessieres and Duroc," said he in a sharp voice, "we will go over the field." So saying, he rode away, leaving the officers addressed to follow him as soon as they could. They immediately left the group, which was now joined, however, by Lannes and Berthier, who, wearied out, sought the vacant seats to obtain a short rest.

"Who ever saw the like?" said young Lannes,—he of the tall, stout form, stern countenance, and long, fair hair, parted in the centre. "Such incessant activity! That slender 'little Corporal' would tire a host of us. In a few days he has killed five horses with fatigue. He will not entrust any of us with the execution of his important orders. He must see every thing with his own eyes, inquire into every thing, and set every body in a fever of motion by his presence. Such tremendous energy I never knew any other person to possess. I do not believe he sleeps at all. There he goes again, to make his final arrangements for the battle."

"He will wear himself out too soon, I am afraid," said Augereau.

"But he will accomplish more in one month than many men could achieve in years. His immortality is already established, and he is but twenty-six," replied Berthier.

"He will have a glorious opportunity to achieve a decisive victory to-morrow," said Lannes; "but I doubt whether the battle will be as long and as desperate as that of yesterday."

"Yesterday was indeed a day of hard fighting, for

my division here, at least," said Augereau. "My troops were completely exhausted, when Liptai's division was driven from the heights. But how did Junot get cut up in such a way?"

"I'll tell you," replied Berthier. "When the Austrian line was broken by the charge of our infantry, one division was driven towards Salo, where Guyeux was posted. General Bonaparte caused it to be pursued, in order to place it between two fires, and General Junot was let loose, with a regiment of cavalry. Junot set off at full speed. He encountered Colonel Bender with a party of his regiment of hussars, whom he charged, with his wonted bravery. But not wishing to waste his time by attacking the rear, Junot made a detour to the right, charged the regiment in front, wounded Colonel Bender and attempted to take him prisoner, when he suddenly found himself surrounded. Of course, he fought like a hero, as he is, and it is said that he killed six of the enemy with his own hand, before he was cut down, and thrown into a ditch. I suppose he will be disabled for some time, which is a real misfortune to the army, as Junot is one of the bravest and most active officers now under General Bonaparte's command."

"Yes," said the generous Lannes, "we shall miss him. He was promoted from the ranks on account of his cool bravery, and he certainly has done hónor to the judgment of our general, who first noticed his merit at the siege of Toulon."

"Still," said Augereau, "brave men are not scarce in the army of Italy. We shall conquer without Junot, I have no doubt."

Thus the group continued to converse, until General Bonaparte came up, with Massena and others, and invited them to his tent to receive their final instructions. The quick movements, and rapid, concise speech of the young conqueror indicated the unwearied activity of his mind. He had undergone tremendous exertion, but no trace of it appeared in his bearing. The restless fire of his eye was undimmed; his mind labored as vigorously and with as much precision as if he had been enjoying repose for several days; and the commander of the Guides reported that the general slept but an hour that night.

At the first peep of day, the two armies were in motion. Wurmser, impatient to attack, moved his right along the heights; Bonaparte, to favor this movement, drew back his left, formed by Massena's division; he kept his centre immovable in the plain. He soon heard Serrurier's fire. Then, while he continued to draw back his left, and Wurmser to draw out his right, he ordered the redoubt of Medolano to be attacked. At first, he directed twenty pieces of light artillery upon that redoubt, and after briskly cannonading it, he detached General Verdier, with three battalions, to storm it. That brave general advanced, supported by a regiment of calvalry, and took the redoubt. The left flank of the Austrians was thus exposed at the very moment when Serrurier, arriving at Cauriana, excited alarm upon their rear. Wurmser immediately moved part of his second line upon his right, now deprived of support, and placed it *en potence* to front the French, who were debouching from Medolano. He took the remainder of his second line to the rear, to protect Cauriana, and thus continued to make head against the enemy. But Bonaparte, seizing the opportunity with his accustomed promptness, immediately ceased to avoid engaging his left and his centre, and gave Massena and Augereau the signal which they were impatiently awaiting. Massena with the left, Augereau with the centre, rushed upon the weakened line of the Austrians, and charged it with impetuosity. Attacked so briskly on its entire front, and threatened on its left and its rear, it began to give ground. The ardour of the French increased. Wurmser seeing his army jeopardized then gave the signal for retreat. He was pursued, and some prisoners were taken. To put him completely to the rout, it would have been necessary to make much more haste, and to push him while in disorder upon the Mincio. But for six days the troops had been constantly marching and fighting; they were unable to advance further, and slept on the field of battle. Wurmser had on that day lost no more than two thousand men, but he had nevertheless lost Italy.

That night, the first time for five days, Bonaparte enjoyed the sweets of repose. The anxiety was at an end—Italy was his own.

THE CAMP-FIRE AT ARCOLA.

THE indomitable Bonaparte had nearly destroyed the army of Wurmser. The laurels of Roveredo, Bassano, and Saint George, adorned his young brow, beside those of Monte Notte, Lodi and Castiglione. Within ten days, he had carried positions, the natural difficulties of which seemed to defy human assault, killed or captured about twenty thousand men, and taken artillery and stores which were almost an encumbrance to his gallant little army. His brave officers, Massena, Augereau, Bessieres, Murat, Berthier, Lannes, and the rest, had heaped up their titles to immortal renown. To use the language of Thiers, "France was lost in admiration of the commander-in-chief of the army of Italy."

Still, Bonaparte's situation was rapidly becoming one of startling peril. Austria redoubled her efforts to recover Lombardy. A fine army was prepared from the wrecks of Wurmser, the troops from Poland and Turkey, the detachments from the Rhine, and fresh recruits. Marshal Alvinzi was appointed to the command. Bonaparte's army at this time numbered about thirty thousand men, but they were badly provided, while Alvinzi could bring sixty thousand men into the field. On the 1st of November, 1796, the Austrian commander advanced upon the Brenta. At first, the French fell back, but Bonaparte resolved to strike a blow at the onset of this new series of movements, which would break the spirit of the enemy. The action took place on the 5th, between Carmignano and Bassano, and after a hot and bloody conflict, the French were victorious. Other contests followed; but in spite of the advantages gained by Bonaparte, he found that unless a great decisive battle was fought, Italy would be lost. The troops began to murmur at the neglect with which their government treated them, and the general complained to the Directory that the majority of his best officers were either killed or disabled by wounds. But in the meantime, Bonaparte conceived a daring plan of action, which, considering the circumstances, stands unparalleled in the annals of war. He resolved to give battle, unexpectedly, amid the marshes of the Adige, where the difference in numbers would be neutralized. Then followed the tremendous battle of Arcola, which lasted seventy-two hours, and ended in the complete triumph of the French.

It was the night of the 17th of November. The sun had set upon a third day of slaughter amid the marshes and upon the plain at Arcola. But with the quiet shadows of evening, came victory to gladden the hearts of the French and their glorious general. Exhausted by the terrible conflict, both armies were to pass the night upon the plain. But the Austrians took care to be beyond the reach of the conquerors and far towards Vicenza. The French kindled their camp-fires upon the field of their triumph. It was a gloomy night. Neither moon nor star smiled in the sky; and the line of the encampments could only be traced by the fires, blazing even among the heaps of the dead, while far away over the plain the long line of Austrian fires could be distinguished. Having partaken of some slight refreshment, the French soldiers were stretched upon the ground around the fires. The majority slept. But to some, wearied as they were in body, sleep would not come, so excited were their minds by the vivid and terrible images of the conflict through which they had passed. The Guides, who had kindled their fires around a little cottage in which Bonaparte had taken quarters for the night, were among the wakeful ones. They had secured for themselves, at the order of the commander-in-chief, abundant refreshments, and now, sitting upon their camp-stools to rest their weary limbs, they discussed both the provision and the glorious achievements of the army of Italy. Their number had been considerably thinned by the great battle through which they had just passed, for they, as well as their general, had been in the thickest of the fire. But there were still Bessieres, the commander, young Lemarois, Duroc, and others of distinction; while among them was, Augereau, who, having been reared in the democratic faubourg St. Antoine, never had any scruples upon the subject of rank, outside of actual military operations. He associated with general and private upon equal terms. The others doubtless considered themselves as honoring the company with their presence; but they could not have formed a part of a more gallant group. Not an officer among them but bore marks of the terrible conflict through which they had passed. Their costume was bespattered with mud, their faces blackened with powder, and some of them had sabre wounds, which, for the time, disfigured their countenances.

"The officers of the army have suffered dreadfully, during these three days of fighting," said Augereau. "I thought that before the battle we were crippled enough in that way; but only look now. Here's General Lannes, who was wounded before he went into the conflict, and he now lies low with three more wounds. Verne, Bon, Verdier, and several others are also wounded, while General Robert and the brave Colonel Muiron, who saved General Bonaparte's life at Toulon, and covered him here again, are killed."

"This battle will long be deemed a glorious monument of the genius of Bonaparte," said Bessieres, "I say it with deference, that heroic as are his principal officers, they might have striven in vain against the superior numbers of the enemy, but for the daring and profound combinations of the general-in-chief, while much is also due to his efforts of resolute valor during the struggle."

"No one will venture to deny that," said the frank and generous Augereau. Massena merely nodded his head, but left the meaning of the nod unexplained.

"For," continued Bessieres, "consider the position of the army before the battle. Our army was greatly inferior in numbers to that of Alvinzi, as, in spite of the immense loss of the Austrians, it remains. Our hospitals were full of sick and wounded. The troops were dispirited, because of the shameful neglect with which their government treated them. A large number of our best officers were entirely disabled. Yet an address from General Bonaparte restored confidence to the army, and when, on the night of the 15th, orders were given to the troops to fall back, they obeyed with alacrity, although they believed they were retreating—a movement to which they are unaccustomed, for they supposed that some daring plan had been formed for their glory. When they had recrossed the Adige by the bridge of boats here at Ronco, they found that their confidence in their general had not been misplaced."

"See then," said Duroc, "how General Bonaparte availed himself of the advantages of the ground. What other general of this age would have thought of fighting among the marshes. Alvinzi was encamped on the road from Verona to the Brenta. Consequently when General Bonaparte reached Ronco, he found himself brought back on the flanks and nearly on the rear of the Austrians. The army was then amidst extensive marshes, traversed by two causeways, which we were ordered to occupy.

"Now mark the result of his calculations; amidst these marshes numerical advantage was neutralized; there was no deploying but upon the causeways, and on the causeways the courage of the advanced guards of the columns would decide the event. By the causeway on the left, which communicated with the road between Verona and Caldiero, he could fall upon the Austrians if they attempted to scale Verona. By the causeway on the right, which crossed the Alpon at the bridge of Arcola, and terminated at Villa Nova, he might debouch upon the rear of Alvinzi, take his artillery and baggage, and cut off his retreat. He was therefore impregnable at Ronco, and he stretched his two arms around the enemy. He had caused the gates at Verona to be shut, and had left Kilmaine there, with fifteen hundred men, to stand a first assault. This combination, so daring and so profound, struck the army, and inspired them with confidence."

"It was a grand stroke of genius," said Massena. "I was stationed on the *dike* at the left, so as to go up to Gombione and Porcil, and take the enemy in the rear, if he should march to Verona."

"And I," observed Augereau, "was despatched to the right, to debouch upon Villa Nova. But before I could advance along the right hand dike, I had to cross the Alpon by the bridge of Arcola. Some battalions of Croats were stationed along the river, and had their cannon pointed at the bridge. They received my advance guard with a rattling fire of musketry, and at first the men fell back. I rode up and did all in my power to push them on, but the fire compelled them to halt. Soon after that, I saw a party of Hungarian cavalry come to inquire into the reason of the firing among the marshes. The Austrian marshal could not understand it. He did not for a moment suppose that General Bonaparte would choose such a field of battle, at least I judge so, from his orders."

"Ha! ha!" shouted Massena, "you should have seen Rivera leading his division close along the left dike where I was posted. I permitted them to get too far on the dike to retreat, and then dashed upon them at a run. How we tumbled them into the marsh! Ha! ha! The troops shot them by scores, as they floundered in the mud and water. Ha! ha!" It was a grim laugh.

"I did the same for Mitrowski's division," said Augereau. "I then pursued, and attempted to pass the bridge, the soldiers gallantly crowding around the flag I held to cheer them on. But they could not stand that tremendous fire. Lannes, Bon, Verne, and Verdier were wounded. In spite of my utmost efforts, the column fell back, and the soldiers descended to the side of the dike, to shelter themselves from the fire."

"Then came the heroism of the 'Little Corporal,'" exclaimed Duroc, his eyes glowing with enthusiasm. "He saw from Ronco, that Alvinzi had become sensible of his danger, and was striving to prevent you, brave Guyeux, from taking him in the rear at Villa Nova. He saw that it was of the utmost importance to cross the river at Arcola immediately, if he would gain Alvinzi's rear, and thus secure great results. Did you see that glorious commander? He set off at full gallop, came near the bridge, threw himself from his horse, went to the soldiers who were crouching down by the borders of the dike, asked them if they were still the conquerors of Lodi, revived their courage by his words, and seizing a flag cried, 'Follow your general!' Hearing his voice, a number of soldiers went up to the causeway and followed him; unfortunately, the movement could not be communicated to the whole of the column, the rest of which remained behind the dike. Bonaparte advanced, carrying the flag in his hand, amidst a shower of balls and grape-shot. We all surrounded him. Lannes, who had already received two wounds from musket-shots during the battle, was struck by a third. Muiron, the general's aid-de-camp, striving to cover him with his body, fell dead at his feet. The column was nevertheless on the point of clearing the bridge, when a last discharge arrested it, and threw it back. The rear abandoned the advance. The soldiers who still remained with the general, then laid hold of him, carried him away amidst the fire and smoke, and insisted on his remounting his horse. An Austrian column debouching upon them, threw them in disorder into the marsh. Bonaparte fell in, and sunk up to the waist. As soon as the soldiers perceived his danger, 'Forward,' cried they, 'to save the general.' They ran after Belliard and Vignolles to extricate him. They pulled him out of the mud, set him upon his horse again, pressed forward and Arcola was taken.

"Was there ever a more glorious man?" And as the enthusiastic Duroc concluded his animated description of the splendid exploit, his eyes gleamed in admiration of his great friend and patron.

"Yes," said Guyeux, "Arçola was taken. But I could not get across the river in time to attack Alvinzi's rear, and thus the Austrian was enabled to deploy into the plain. The general had striven gloriously, but he had not attained his object. In my humble opinion, he might have avoided the obstacle of Arcola by throwing nis bridge over the Adige a little below Ronco.

"Aye," said Massena, "but then he would have debouched into the plain, which it was of great importance to avoid. The general had the best reasons for doing what he did, and although the success was imperfect, important results had been obtained. Alvinzi had quitted the formidable position of Caldiero; he had descended again into the plain, he no longer threatened Verona; and he had lost a great number of men in the marshes. The two dikes had become the only field of battle between the two armies, which gave the superiority to bravery. Besides, so glorious had been the conflict, that our soldiers had completely recovered their confidence, a result of immense importance, as all may perceive." This defence of Bonàparte's course did honor to the intelligence of Massena.

"But it must be admitted," said Bessieres, "that the battle of to-day surpassed all the rest in the display of strategic genius. Yesterday was glorious for us, for the bravery and perseverance of the whole army was exerted in beating the enemy from the dikes, and tumbling them into the marsh, and we destroyed an immense number of them. But to-day proved most conclusively that in strategy our general is at least the rival of the Carthagenian Hannibal. Our general saw that the long conflict had disheartened the enemy, and considerably reduced their superior numbers. He then dared to encounter them on the plain. You, General Massena, marching at the head of your column, with your hat upon the point of your sword, showed them the way to victory, and the Austrians were once more crowded into the marsh. But General Robert was repulsed at the bridge of Ronco. Yet mark the resources of the general-in-chief! Sensible of the danger, he placed the 32d in a wood of willows, which borders the right hand dike. While the enemy's column, victorious over Robert, was advancing, the 32d sallied from its ambuscade, and, of the three thousand Croates who composed it, the greater part were slain or captured. Crossing the Alpon, Bonaparte brought the whole army into the plain, in front of the Austrians. An ordinary general would now have ordered a simple charge. But the 'Little Corporal' determined upon a stratagem. A marsh, overgrown with reeds, covered the left wing of the Austrians. Hercule, *chef de battallion*, was ordered to take twenty-five guards, to march in single line through the reeds, and to make a sudden charge, with a great blast of trumpets."

"And Hercule was the very man for such a desperate service," observed Duroc.

"Precisely," said Bessieres. "Then the great charge was made by you generals, Massena and Augereau;

but the Austrians stood their ground until they heard the great blast of trumpets, when, thinking they were going to be charged by a whole division of cavalry, they fled, and the battle was decided in favor of France. Italy is our own."

"Not yet," said Massena. "Austria is stubborn. In spite of her many defeats, she will make at least one more effort to recover possession of this fair land. We have much fighting yet to do, I am sure."

"We have lost many brave men in these three fighting days," said young Lemarois. "But the enemy have suffered a loss of at least twelve thousand killed, and six thousand made prisoners, while we have taken eighteen pieces of cannon and four stand of colors."

"Trophies enough," said Augereau. "It seems to me, that whether this battle has decided the fate of Italy or not, we shall soon have a short respite from our toils, which will give us time to recruit."

The conversation continued thus till most of the officers, being overcome with fatigue, retired to their quarters. The Guides slept around their fires, in close proximity to numbers of the gallant dead, whose slumber was destined to be broken only by the arch-angel's trump.

In the meantime, the young conqueror had sought his couch for much needed repose, and so soundly did he sleep that even the glories of Arcola were forgotten for the time.

THE CAMP-FIRE AT RIVOLI.

THE chain of Monte Baldo divides the lake of Garda from the Adige. The high road winds between the Adige and the foot of the mountains, to the extent of some leagues. At Incanale the river washes the very base of the mountains, leaves no room whatever for proceeding along its bank. The road then leaves the banks of the river, rises by a zig-zag direction round the sides of the mountain, and debouches upon an extensive elevated plain, which is that of Rivoli. It overlooks the Adige on one side, and is encompassed on the other side by the amphitheatre of Monte Baldo. An army in position of this *plateau* commands the winding road by which the ascent to it is made, and sweeps by its fire both banks of the Adige to a great distance. It is very difficult to storm this *plateau* in front, since you must climb up the narrow zig-zag road before you can reach it. Therefore no one would attempt to attack it by that single way. Before arriving at Incanale, other roads lead to Monte Baldo, and ascending its long and sloping acclivities terminate at the *plateau* of Rivoli. They are not passable either for cavalry or for artillery, but they afford easy access to foot soldiers, and may be made available for carrying a considerable force in infantry upon the flanks and rear of the body defending the *plateau*.

Here the star of Napoleon was destined to shine with new glory. Alvinzi commanded the principal attack on the Tyrolese side, at the head of fifty thousand men, and advanced his head-quarters from Bassano to Roveredo. General Provera took the command of the army on the lower Adige, which was twenty thousand strong: its head-quarters were at Padua. A great many troops appeared on different points, and some spirited actions also took place in the course of the 12th and 13th; but the enemy had not fully unmasked his plans, so that the moment for adopting a decisive course had not yet arrived. On the 13th it rained very heavily, and Napoleon had not yet resolved in what direction to march, whether up or down the Adige. At ten in the evening, the accounts from Joubert, at La Corona, determined him. It was plain that the Austrians were operating with two independent corps, the principal attack being intended against Monte Baldo, the minor one on the Lower Adige. Augereau's division appeared sufficient to dispute the passage of the river with Provera; but on the Monte Baldo side the danger was imminent. There was not a moment to lose; for the enemy was about to effect a junction with his artillery and cavalry, by taking possession of the level of Rivoli; and if he could be attacked before he could gain that important point, he would be obliged to fight without artillery or cavalry. All the troops were therefore put in motion from the head-quarters at Verona, to reach Rivoli before day-break; the general-in-chief proceeded to the same point, and arrived there at two in the morning.

The weather had been rainy for several days. But now the sky was without a cloud. The moon and stars shone with a brilliancy peculiar to their light in this region. The air was keen and bitter cold. The French general, accompanied by his aids and the faithful Guides, proceeded to a projecting rock on the heights of Monte Maggone, to gain a complete view of the enemy, previous to fixing the plan of battle. And now behold the group, dismounted, and collected near the fire, Bonaparte being in advance, with glass in hand, surveying the positions of the enemy. Duroc, Lemarois, Murat, Berthier and Bessieres stood together just behind him. The whole horizon was in a blaze with the Austrian fires, and the red glare contrasted strangely with the pure white light of the moon. Bonaparte observed and talked with his customary precision and rapidity.

"Alvinzi has at least forty-five thousand men under his command. We have but twenty-two thousand; while the brave Joubert, who has so nobly maintained his position at Rivoli, has but ten thousand. The enemy has divided his force into three columns, although I see no less than five camps. The principal column, will proceed along the high road between the river and Monte Baldo, and will debouch by the winding road of Incanale. Three divisions of infantry have climbed the steep mountains, and will get to the field by descending the steps of the amphitheatre formed by this chain of heights. Another division will wind round the side of the mountains and attempt to gain our rear.

"But yonder seems to be another camp on the other side of the Adige," said Murat, pointing to a line of fires.

"True," said Bonaparte, "but that can do no damage. It can only fire a few balls across the river. It is clear, we must keep the plateau at all events. Posted there we prevent the junction of the different divisions of the enemy. We may play our artillery upon the infantry which is deprived of its cannon, and drive back the cavalry and artillery which must be crowded together in a narrow, winding road. The other divisions will not trouble us much." Thus, with lightning-like rapidity, did this matchless general conceive the plan which was to give him a glorious victory.

"I suppose we are to begin the battle at daybreak," said Duroc.

"At daybreak! Now! now is the time!" replied the French general, sharply. "Duroc! Joubert's troops have been fighting forty-eight hours, and they are now taking a little repose. They must be aroused immediately. Tell them for me, that they must not let Massena's division surpass them in endurance, and his troops have marched by night and fought by day. Order General Joubert to attack the advanced post of the Austrian infantry, drive them back, and extend his force more widely upon the plateau."

Duroc immediately spurred away to communicate the order to Joubert.

"Joubert has done well; but he should not have abandoned yonder St. Mark's Chapel. At all events, I do not believe the enemy have occupied it. Duroc is rapid in movement. The battle of Rivoli will soon commence," said the French general.

"I wish Massena was nearer the field," observed Murat.

"He will be up in time, never fear. He is indomitable. Besides, if the battle should assume a critical aspect, I will go myself to hurry up his division. Ha! Joubert is up like a roused lion, and in movement. Who leads the column? Vial—a brave officer," continued Bonaparte. At this moment, a rattling fire of musketry rang on the air, and from the height where Bonaparte stood, could be seen the rapid advance of Joubert's troops, as well as the long line of D'Ocksky's column of Croats against whom the attack was directed. Then the thunder of the artillery was heard, and clouds of smoke curled up from the plateau."

"St. Mark's Chapel is recovered," said Bessieres.

"The Austrian infantry cannot stand against the artillery, and they are falling back in a semicircle, with the heights at their rear," remarked Bonaparte.

At this moment, Liptai's division which kept the extremity of the enemy's semicircle, fell upon Joubert's left, composed of the 89th and 25th demi-brigades, surprised them, broke their lines and compelled them to retire in disorder. The 14th coming immediately after these demi-brigades formed *en crochet* to cover the rest of the line, and bravely stood their ground. The Austrians now put forth all their strength and almost overwhelmed this little band of heroes. They made desperate efforts to capture the artillery, the horses of which had all been killed. They had even reached the pieces, when a brave officer rushed forward, and exhorted the grenadiers not to allow their guns to be taken. Fifty men immediately rushed forward, repulsed the enemy, harnessed themselves to the pieces, and drew them back.

In the midst of this terrible struggle, the day began to dawn upon the field of Rivoli. Bonaparte who had watched the progress of the fight with the keenest interest, repeatedly making exclamations of surprise or admiration, now perceived the critical position of affairs. Turning to Berthier, he said quickly,

"General Berthier, I leave you in charge of my troops at the point where they are threatened. I know you and General Joubert can hold that position, no matter what the number of the enemy may be. I am going with all speed after Massena. Come, aids—Bessieres, mount and forward!" The whole party was quickly in the saddle, and away, leaving the watch-fire to smoudler and die, as the lurid blaze of battle arose upon the plain.

Massena's first troops had scarcely come up, after marching all night. Bonaparte took the 32d, already distinguished by its exploits during the campaign, and brought it to bear upon the left, so as to rally the two demi-brigades, which had given way. The intrepid Massena advanced at its head, rallied behind him the broken troops, and overthrew all before him. He repulsed the Austrians, and placed himself by the side of the 14th, which had not ceased to perform prodigies of valor. The fight was thus kept up on this point, and the army occupied the semicircle of the plateau. But the momentary check of the left wing had obliged Joubert to fall back with the right; he gave ground, and already the Austrian infantry was a second time nearing that point which Bonaparte had such an object in compelling him to abandon; in fact, the Austrian infantry was about getting up to the outlet by which the winding road of Incanale led to the plateau. At this moment, the column composed of artillery and cavalry, and preceded by several battalions of grenadiers, ascended the winding road, and with incredible efforts of bravery, repulsed the 29th. Wukassovich, from the other bank of the Adige, sent a shower of cannon balls to protect this kind of escalade. Already had the grenadiers climbed the summit of the defile, and the cavalry was debouching in their train upon the plateau. This was not all. Lusignan's column, whose fires had been seen at a distance, and who had been perceived on the left, getting to the rear of the position of the French, were now coming up to their rear, in order to cut them off from the road to Verona, and to stop Rey, who was coming from Castel-Novo with the division of reserve. Lusignan's soldiers finding themselves on the rear of the French army, already clapped their hands, and considered it as taken. Thus, on this plateau, closely pressed in front by a semicircle of infantry, pressed on the rear, on the left by a strong column, sealed on the right by the main body of the Austrian army, and galled by the cannon balls which came from the opposite bank of the Adige in the direction of this plateau, Bonaparte was alone with Joubert's and Massena's divisions, in the midst of a cloud of enemies. In fact, he was with sixteen thousand men, surrounded by forty thousand at least.

At this anxious moment, Bonaparte was not shaken; he retained all the fire of inspiration. On seeing Lusignan's Austrians, he said, "*Those are ours!*" and he allowed them to engage without giving himself any concern about their movement. The soldiers, conjecturing what their general meant, experienced the same confidence, and also repeated to one another, "*They are ours!*" Bonaparte did not concern himself with more than what was passing before him. His left was protected by the heroism of the 14th and the 32d. His right was threatened at once by the infantry which had resumed the offensive, and by the column that was scaling the plateau. He immediately directed decisive movements to be effected.

A battery of light artillery and two squadrons, under two brave officers, Leclerc and Laselle, were ordered to the outlet of which the enemy had taken possession. Joubert, who, with the extreme right, had this outlet at his back, suddenly faced about with a corps of light infantry. All charged at once. The artillery first poured a discharge upon all that had debouched; the cavalry and light infantry then charged with vigor. Joubert's horse was killed under him; he got up nowise daunted, and rushed upon the enemy with a musket in his hand. All that had debouched, grenadiers, cavalry, artillery, all were hurled pell-mell headlong down the winding road of Incanale. The confusion was awful; some pieces of cannon firing down into the defile, augmented the terror and confusion. At every step, the French killed and made prisoners.

Having cleared the plateau of the assailants who had scaled it, Bonaparte again returned to his attacks against the infantry which was ranged in semicircle before him, and set Joubert upon it with the light infantry, and Laselle with two hundred hussars. On this new attack, consternation seized that infantry, now deprived of all hope of effecting a junction with the main body; it fled in confusion. The French semicircular line then moved from right to left, drove back the Austrians against the amphitheatre of Monte Baldo, and pursued them as far as possible into the mountains. Bonaparte then returned, and proceeded to realize his prediction upon Lusignan's division. That body, on witnessing the disasters of the Austrian army, soon perceived what would be its own fate. Bonaparte, after firing upon it with grape-shot, ordered the 18th and the 75th demi-brigades to charge. These brave demi-brigades moved onwards, singing the *chant du départ,* and drove Lusignan back by the road which Rey was coming up with the reserve. The Austrian corps at first made a stand, then retreated, and came full butt upon the advanced guard of Rey's division. Terrified at this sight, it sought the clemency of the conqueror, and laid down its arms, to the number of four thousand men. Two thousand had been taken in the defile of the Adige.

It was five o'clock. The Austrian army was almost annihilated. Lusignan was taken. The infantry which had advanced from the mountains, was flying over the rugged declivities. The principal column was pent up on the bank of the river, while the subordinate division of Wukassovich was an idle spectator of the disaster, separated by the Adige from the field of battle. The French general had had several horses killed under him, and had received several slight wounds, but in spite of his constant activity and exposure, he was still ready to follow up his victory immediately. The battle of La Favorita ensued, in which the army of Provera was annihilated. In three days, twenty-three thousand men were captured. Massena's troops had marched and fought four days and nights, without any considerable intermission. The intrepid general himself, afterwards received the title of Duke of Rivoli. Mantua was at the feet of Bonaparte, and Italy was won.

BONAPARTE CROSSING THE ALPS AT TARWIS.

THE CAMP-FIRE ON THE ALPS.

ALTHOUGH Bonaparte had performed amazing, and, in some respects, unparalleled, exploits in Italy, there was a general disposition among both Frenchmen and foreigners to set up inferior commanders as his rivals. Now it was Moreau, then Massena; then Hoche, and then the young Archduke Charles, of Austria. The last mentioned had attained a high reputation by a campaign in which he triumphed over Generals Moreau and Jourdan, but his valor and skill, although great, were overrated, as Bonaparte and Massena soon rendered evident.

The Archduke took command of the Austrian army of Italy, and on the 6th of February, 1797, advanced his head-quarter to Innspruck. During that month, his engineers visited the passes of the Julien and Noric Alps, which it had been designed to fortify. Napoleon, having about fifty-three thousand troops under his command, resolved to astonish his enemy by a rapid and daring march upon the passes of the Alps before they could be fortified. He formed the plan of a campaign, the great object of which was the Austrian capital, Vienna, and the execution was as prompt as the conception was bold. The Tagliamento was passed, and the enemy completely defeated; the passes of the Alps were carried, after a tremendous struggle. Joubert beat the Austrians in the Tyrol, the Archduke's reputation was reduced to its proper dimensions, and Vienna trembled, having no means of resisting the all-conquering Bonaparte. Tarwis is the loftiest pass of the Noric Alps. It is above the clouds and is generally covered with snow and ice, which give it a desolate and terrible aspect. It overlooks Germany and Dalmatia. At this point the roads leading to Italy and Trieste separate; the road to Italy running west, and that leading to Trieste running south. At this place, Bonaparte fixed his head-quarters, shortly after the pass had been captured by the indomitable Massena. It was the last day of March. The weather was intensely cold, and and the body of troops accompanying the French general suffered severely. Bonaparte and his aids were snugly quartered in the rude chalets, which are the only habitations upon the height of Tarwis. The soldiers were grouped amid a cordon of fires, the fuel for which they had brought from a great distance below, with a vast amount of labor and difficulty. Yet they shivered beside the crackling blaze. It was a wild and startling scene. The night was cloudy—the wind, keen and furious. The red glare of the fires was reflected by walls of ice and blood-stained snow. As the soldiers wrapped themselves in their blankets, crept as close to the fires as they could get, and conversed with a French attempt at gaiety, they were surprised to see their beloved general, accompanied by Berthier and Duroc, come out of a chalet, to examine their condition, and speak a word of cheer.

"A freezing time, men; but it will be hot enough soon," he remarked to a group of veterans.

"The cold is more terrible than the Austrians, general," said one of them, with an attempt at a laugh.

"But it cannot conquer the conquerors of Italy," replied Bonaparte. Thus he went among the brave men who followed his standard, and thus he communicated his own spirit to all with whom he came in contact. After traversing the whole ground occupied by the troops, the French general returned to his quarters to repose.

Beneath a kind of shed in the rear of the chalet, several of the Guides were seated round a cheerful fire, smoking pipes and conversing of the recent actions and their thrilling incidents. Among them were Bessieres and Lemarois. The wall of the chalet, which formed the rear of the shed, served to keep off the fury of the wind, so that this place was comfortable, compared with the position of the soldiers. Besides, the hearts of these veterans had been gladdened with abundance of good eating at the chalet, and satisfaction was evident in their faces. The manly face of Bessieres, wore that expression of calm circumspection, which it never lost in the thickest of battle.

"The passage of the Tagliamento," said this brave leader, "will take rank with any similar exploit, recorded in history."

"It must be acknowledged that the archduke had posted his forces in an admirable style," said young Lemarois. "His artillery covered the level shingle of the river, and his fine cavalry, deployed on the wings, so as to be brought rapidly into service, was an admirable disposition."

"Yes," said Bessieres, "but as usual, the character of the manœuvres which defeated the Austrians throws all their dispositions into insignificance. Was there ever a general so fertile of stratagem as Bonaparte? See how quickly he determined upon a plan to diminish the vigilance of the enemy! An immense number of men might have been lost if he had attempted the passage of the river as soon as he reached its banks. But he valued the lives of his soldiers too much, to throw them away, when a simple stratagem could save them. The Austrians naturally supposed that after marching all night, he wanted rest, and when the general ordered us to halt and begin to partake of our soup, they were completely deceived. How the archduke must have opened his eyes, when he saw us get suddenly in motion at noon!"

"The disposition of our forces was so admirable that it made some of our own skilful officers open their eyes," said Lemarois. "Look at it! Guyeux's division on the left, and Bernadotte's on the right, by which arrangement the troops of Italy and the soldiers of the Rhine were brought into a noble rivalry. Then battalions of grenadiers were formed. At the head of each division was placed the light infantry, ready to disperse as sharp-shooters, then the grenadiers who were to charge, and the dragoons who were to support them. Each demi-brigade had its first battalions, deployed in line, and the two others arranged in close column on the wings of the first. The cavalry hovered on the wings. A finer disposition could not have been made."

"Crossing the river was a glorious scene!" said Bessieres. "The light infantry covered the bank with a cloud of sharp-shooters. Then the grenadiers entered the water. 'Soldiers of the Rhine!" exclaimed Bernadotte, 'the army of Italy has its eyes upon you.' Each division displayed the utmost bravery in the charge; we can make no distinction between them."

"No, indeed," observed a grim-visaged Guide, who sat next to Bessieres." Our soldiers called the troops of the Rhine *the contingent*, and treated them with the greatest contempt before the battle. A number of sabre cuts were exchanged on account of this raillery. But the contingent proved themselves worthy of any army at Tagliamento. They drove the Austrians before them like a flock of sheep.

"All acted in a manner worthy of France," said Lemarois. The archduke was routed and the line of the Tagliamento cleared in a remarkably short time."

"What is the name of that general of cavalry who was captured?" inquired one of the Guides—a burly fellow, with a good-humored cast of countenance.

"I forget his name," replied Bessieres; "but I cannot forget that he is a brave man, and that he fought with a courage and resolution which put most of his countrymen to shame.

"To be just, however," observed Lemarois, "there are many gallant officers in the Austrian army. It is not their fault if they have not a Bonaparte to bring victory to their standard. They have a large number of hearts following their flag, as intrepid as old Wurmser. But strange to say, they have never had a first class general.

"That's about the truth of the matter," commented the burly Guide.

"By the way, Jacques," said Bessieres, "it seems to be getting colder as the night advances. Put on a little more of that wood. Its bad enough fuel, though, for it smokes abominably."

Jacques was the burly Guide previously alluded to. He obeyed the order of his commander.

"The men outside ought to have plenty of provision to console them amid their sufferings on such a night. They will scarcely dare to sleep," said Lemarois.

"I saw our general out among them a short time ago," replied Bessieres. "A few sympathetic words from him will do more than any amount of provision."

"That's a fact," said the grim veteran who sat next to the commander of the Guides. "They know that he feels for them, and that he would help them if he could. See there at St. George, an outpost of Mantua, where there was a necessity for constant vigilance, to prevent Provera from surprising us, and relieving Wurmser. The general visiting one of the outposts at night, found a sentinel lying at the foot of a tree, where he had fallen fast asleep from exhaustion. He took the soldier's musket and walked backwards and forwards on sentry for more than half an hour. Suddenly the soldier started up, and was terrified at seeing General Bonaparte on duty; he expected nothing less than death. But the general spoke kindly to him, told him that after his great fatigues, he wanted sleep; but cautioned him against chosing such a time. That is the way for a general to make heroes out of soldiers. That sentinel would have risked his life at any time to give victory to General Bonaparte."

"Bonaparte is every inch of a general, a soldier and a man," said Bessieres.

"Some miserable judges wish to set up this young Archduke Charles as a rival to our general," said Lemarois. "Why, this battle of Tarwis, in which he had every thing in his favor, proves that he is not by a great deal, up to the measure of Massena."

"Have you heard the full particulars of the struggle at this pass?" inquired Bessieres. "Battles come so rapidly, that it is difficult to gain a complete knowledge of them."

"I was present when an officer of Massena's division who participated in the fight communicated the intelligence," replied Lemarois. "While we were advancing to Gradisca, General Massena pressed forward, reached this pass, and made himself master of it without much difficulty. The division of Bayalitsch, proceeding across the sources of the Izonzo to anticipate Massena at the pass, would therefore find the outlet closed. The Archduke Charles, foreseeing this result, left the rest of his army on the Friule and Carniola road, with orders to come and rejoin him behind the Alps at Klagenfurt; he then himself made the utmost haste to Villach, where numerous detachments were coming up from the Rhine, to make a fresh attack on the pass, to drive Massena from it, and to re-open the road for Bayalitsch's division. Bonaparte, on his side, left Bernadotte's division to pursue the divisions that were retreating into Carniola, and with Guyeux's and Serrurier's divisions, proceeded to harass the Bayalitsch division in its rear, in its passage through the valley of the Izonzo. Prince Charles, after rallying behind the Alps the wrecks of Lusignan and Orksay, who had lost the pass, reinforced them with six thousand grenadiers, the finest and bravest soldiers in the imperial service, and again attacked the pass, where Massena had left scarcely a detachment. He succeeded in recovering it, and posted himself here with the regiments of Lusignan and Orksay, and the six thousand grenadiers. Massena collected his whole division, in order to carry it again. Both generals were sensible of the importance of this point. Tarwis retaken, the French army would be masters of the Alps, and would make prisoners of the whole of Bayalitsch's division. Massena rushed on headlong with his brave infantry, and suffered as usual in person. Prince Charles was not less chary of himself than the republican general, and several times ran the risk of being taken by the French riflemen. Whole lines of cavalry were thrown down and broken on this frightful field of battle. At length, after having brought forward his last battalion, the Archduke Charles abandoned Tarwis to his pertinacious adversary, and found himself compelled to sacrifice Bayalitsch's division. Massena, left master of Tarwis, fell down upon that division which now came up, attacked it in front, while it was pressed in the rear by the divisions of Guyeux and Serrurier. That division had no other resource than to be made prisoners, and our army captured all the baggage, artillery and ammunition of the enemy that had followed this route. For my part, I think that a good general could have maintained this pass against a greatly superior force."

"It is a strong position, and it does not appear to me that it could be turned," observed Bessieres. "However," continued he, rising, "the pass is ours; Joubert has beaten the enemy and will soon join us; the archduke is completely beaten, and there is scarcely an obstacle in the way of a march to Vienna. These are the results of a march as daring and skilful as any ever conceived by a general. So much glory for General Bonaparte, and renown to the arms of France.

Come, Lemarois, we will enter the chalet, and strive to gain some repose. Keep up your spirits, men, and above all keep up the fire. Good night!"

And keen and swiftly blew the Alpine wind, and redly blazed the fires of Tarwis till the light of day arose from the ashes of the night. Then the French general pursued his march. He united his forces; Vienna was threatened, and the treaty of Campo Formio was extorted from Austria.

THE CAMP-FIRE ON THE NILE.

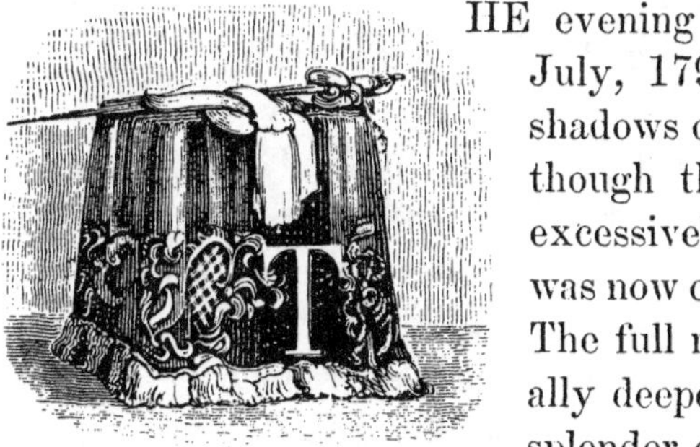

HE evening of the 21st of July, 1798, had cast its shadows on the Nile. Although the day had been excessively warm, the air was now cool and pleasant. The full moon was gradually deepening the placid splendor of her light, and giving a silvery sheen to the winding waters of the river. On an elevated terrace, in the distance, could be distinguished the bold and gorgeous minarets and gilded domes of Cairo. The villages of Bulak and Shoubra were nestled on the river banks, overlooking a vast extent of cultivated plain, rich in vineyards and grain. The great obelisk of Heliopolis stood out against the eastern sky; and the vast Lybian desert stretched away in desolation to the west. In the midst of this sea of sand, could be faintly distinguished the awful forms of the great pyramids of Ghizeh, from which that day, "forty centuries had looked down," upon the victory achieved by Bonaparte over the Mameluke tyrants of Egypt.

The French were encamped upon the banks of the Nile; and the light of their watch-fires could be seen for a great distance along the river. The victorious general was at Ghizeh, having fixed his quarters in the country-seat of Murad Bey. But although the watch-fires were burning, the soldiers of the conquering army were not gathered around them. No; the spoils of victory would not let them rest. They had suffered much in the dreary march towards Cairo, and fought bravely in overcoming the gallant cavalry of the Egyptian army, and now very naturally sought to repay themselves for their hardships and toils. The field of battle was covered with the troops, who were engaged in stripping the valuable articles from the bodies of the slain Mamelukes. Among the spoils thus obtained were splendid shawls, weapons of fine workmanship, purses, some of which contained as many as two and three hundred pieces of gold; for the Mamelukes carried all their ready money on their persons. More than a thousand of these Egyptian warriors had been drowned in the Nile; and even now, by the light of the moon, the French troops were engaged in dragging for the bodies, to swell the amount of their booty. A more indefatigable set of spoil-seekers never won a victory.

The Mamelukes had sixty vessels on the Nile, containing the bulk of their riches. In consequence of the unexpected result of the battle, they lost all hope of saving them, and set them on fire. The great blaze suddenly rising to the sky, caused the French troops to pause in the midst of their search for valuables. They knew the contents of those vessels, and they beheld the gradual destruction of those vast treasures with feelings of disappointment not easily delineated. During the whole night, through the volumes of smoke and flame, the French could perceive the forms of the minarets and buildings of Cairo and the City of the Dead; and the red glare was even gloriously reflected by the Pyramids. To increase the terrors of the scene, the wild and treacherous populace of Cairo, learning the disasters of their countrymen, set fire to the splendid palaces of the Beys, and these great edifices blazed and crackled up against the sky throughout the night.

About nine, in the evening, Bonaparte, accompanied by Berthier, Desaix, Lannes, Regnier, and nearly all his principal officers, and even a number of the privates, entered the country-house of Murad Bey, at Ghizeh. This residence presented a magnificent appearance at a distance, and a close inspection disclosed many additional beauties. But it was a point of some difficulty at first to make it serve for a lodging, or to comprehend the distribution of the apartments. But what chiefly struck the officers with surprise, was the great quantity of cushions and divans covered with the finest damasks and Lyons silks, and ornamented with gold fringe. For the first time, they found the luxury and arts of Europe in Egypt—the cradle of luxury and arts. Bonaparte and his staff explored this singular structure in every direction. The gardens were full of magnificent trees, but without avenues, and not unlike the gardens in some of the nunneries of Italy. The soldiers were much elated at the discovery of large arbors of vines, burdened with the finest grapes in the world. The rapid vintage excited the laughter of the French generals, who, themselves, joined in the scramble for the delicious fruit.

In the meantime, the two divisions of Bon and Menou, which had remained behind in an entrenched camp, were equally well supplied. Among the baggage taken, had been found a great number of canteens full of preserves, both of confectionary and sweetmeats, besides carpets, porcelain, vases of perfume, and a multitude of little elegancies used by the Mamelukes. All these luxuries had been purchased by the oppression of the mass of the Egyptians, and it was but a stroke of justice which took them from the oppressor.

The French troops, who had murmured much while traversing the hot sands of the desert, now fell in love with Egypt, and began to hope for a career of easy conquest and rare enjoyment. Their general was pleased at their change of tone, and permitted them to revel amidst the fruits of their labor and endurance.

Bonaparte and his officers spent the greater part of the night in exploring the residence of Murad Bey. Towards morning they reclined upon its luxurious couches, and while the conflagration raged without, and the soldiers were revelling among the spoil, these veteran officers indulged in repose. A short time previous these gallant men had shared Bonaparte's doubt and anxiety as he stood upon the deck of a vessel, in the harbor of Alexandria, viewing the shores of the land of the Pharoahs. Now they could sleep in the confidence of continued victory.

On the 20th of July, the young conqueror of the Pyramids, entered Grand Cairo, receiving the humble submission of the Shieks and the shouts of the thronging populace. The capital of Egypt was in the power of the French.

THE CAMP-FIRE AT MOUNT TABOR.

IN Lower Galilee, to the north-east of the great plain of Esdraelon, rises an eminence rendered intensely interesting by memories sacred and profane. It is Mount Tabor. Although surrounded by chains of mountains on nearly all sides, it is the only one that stands entirely aloof from its neighbors. The figure of the mount approaches that of a semi-sphere, and presents a regular appearance. Its ground figure is usually described as round; and, indeed, seems to be perfectly so to those coming from the midst of the great plain, or from the sea of Galilee. But, in reality, it is really somewhat longer from east to west than broad, so that its true figure is oval. The height of this mountain has never been subjected to actual measurement. It appears, however, that it occupies three hours to travel round the base of the mountain; that an hour is generally required to reach the summit by a circuitous path, and that the plain upon the top of the eminence is seldom traversed in less time than half an hour.

The mountain is inaccessible except on the north, where the ascent offers so little difficulty that there are few parts which suggest to the traveler the prudence or necessity of dismounting from his horse. This remarkable mountain offers so rare a combination of the bold and beautiful, that pilgrims of all ages have expatiated upon its glories with untiring wonder and delight. The trees of various species, and the bushes always green, with which it is invested, and the small groves with which it is crowned, contribute no less than its figure to its perfect beauty. Ounces, wild boars, gazelles, and hares, are among the animals which find shelter in its more wooded parts; while the trees are tenanted by "birds of every wing," whose warblings and motions beguile the fatigues of the ascent. "The path," says Mr. Stephens, "wound around the mountain, and gave us a view from all its different sides, every step presenting something new, and more and more beautiful, until all was completely forgotten and lost in the exceeding loveliness of the view from the summit. Stripped of every association, and considered merely as an elevation commanding a view of unknown valleys and mountains, I never saw a mountain which, for beauty of scene, better repaid the toil of ascending it."

The view it commands is magnificent. To the north, in successive ranges, are the mountains of Galilee, backed by the mighty Lebanon; and Safet, as always, stands out in prominent relief. To the north-east is the Mount of Beatitudes, with its peculiar outline and interesting associations; behind which rise Great Hermon, and the whole chain of Anti-Lebanon. To the east are the hills of the Haouran, and the country of the Gadarenes, below which the eye catches a glimpse of the Lake of Tiberius, while to the south-east it crosses the valley of the Jordan, and rests on the high land of Bashan. Due south rise the mountains of Gilboa, and behind them those of Samaria, stretching far to the west. On the south-south-west the villages of Endor and Nain are seen on the Little Hermon. Mount Carmel and the Bay of Acre appear on the north-west; and towards them flows, through the fertile plains of Esdraelon, "that great river, the River Kishon," now dwindled into a little stream. Each feature in this prospect is beautiful: the eye and mind are delighted; and, by a combination of objects and associations, unusual to fallen man, earthly scenes, which more than satisfy the external sense, elevate the soul to heavenly contemplations.

The beautiful upper plain is inclosed by a wall,—probably the same which was built by Josephus, when Governor of Galilee,—and contains some ruins, which are probably those of the two monasteries, which, according to William of Tyre, were built here by Godfrey of Bouillon, in the place of others of earlier date which the Moslems had destroyed. The plain has at different times been under cultivation; but when, from oppression or fear, abandoned by the cultivator, it becomes a table of rich grass and wild flowers, which send forth a most refreshing and luxurious odor. In summer the dews fall copiously on Tabor, and a strong wind blows over it all day.

Tabor is chiefly interesting to the Christian, however, as the supposed scene of the Transfiguration, when Christ appeared in glory, with Moses, and Elias. To the reader of profane history and the student of the career of Napoleon Bonaparte, it is also rendered interesting as the scene of a decisive victory gained by the French general over some of the bravest forces of the East.

It was the night of the 16th of April. The victorious French had encamped at the foot of Mount Tabor. The evening had set in calmly and beautifully, above a plain heaped with the dead of the annihilated army, but the deep shadows of night had scarcely descended, before the French general-in-chief ordered all the villages of the Naplousians to be set on fire; and although they were distant, their red light was so glaring, that it illumined the field of battle and the camp of the victors, and rendered evident many ghastly features of the scene.

At the tent of General Kleber were assembled that gallant officer, Junot, Murat and Bon. Bonaparte was in his tent, surrounded by his faithful Guides. Just outside of the line of tents the watch-fires were brightly burning, and the sentinels paced up and down with solemn tread. Kleber, and his brothers in glory, were seated on camp-stools around a table, on which were several bottles of wine. After Napoleon himself, Kleber was the most remarkable man of the army of Egypt. See him there, with his large and powerful frame—his great head of shaggy hair, his quick, piercing eyes, prominent features, and slovenly costume. Great-souled Jean Baptiste Kleber! The revolution found him a peaceful architect. He entered the ranks as a grenadier, and rose to be esteemed a military genius indispensable to France, and a commander as humane and generous as he was brave and skilful. Always peevish, he yet was guilty of no bitterness of action—mean conduct was with him an impossibility. Opposite Kleber sat Andoche Junot. His mild, pleasant, handsome features expressed nothing of the indomitable spirit which he ever displayed in action; but his eyes were quick and intelligent. His costume was much cut and soiled by the desperate service he had performed during the last two days. Murat was as usual finely dressed. He seemed weary, and drank deeply to revive his spirits. Most terrible had been the slaughter of his sabres that day on the banks of the Jordan. General Bon had nothing remarkable in his appearance. The expression of his sun-burned countenance was that of firmness, united with intelligence and promptitude.

"I wonder how things go on at Acre," said Junot.

"Bad as usual," replied Kleber. "The place cannot be taken, that is evident. It was clear to me long ago, that Sidney Smith, and the engineer Philippeaux have stimulated the troops to extraordinary exertions. They repulse every assault; and as we have no siege trains, where is our chance for taking the town. Nowhere, nowhere—and so I told General Bonaparte—the stubborn specimen of lean genius. We shall waste our army before the walls of that place, and gain nothing; whereas, if the siege were raised, we might yet do much for Egypt.

"Then here must end our general's grand project for striking a blow at the English dominion in Asia," observed Bon.

"Aye," said Kleber, "and it was folly to entertain such projects after the destruction of our fleet at Aboukir, by that confounded Englishman, Nelson. The most we could hope to do after that was to consolidate our empire in Egypt, and that would have been no ordinary task. But this 'Little Corporal,' will not listen to any one."

"The march to El Arisch, across that burning desert was bad enough; but I'm afraid that we shall have the same thing to do again, under worse circumstances," said Murat.

"But this battle has won us glories enough to atone for many hardships," remarked Junot. "At first the prospect was desperate enough."

"You, Junot, have certainly increased your reputation," said Bon. "The advanced guard which you commanded consisted of, at most, but five hundred men.

Yet with that force you dared to encounter the enemy on the 8th, and not only covered the field with their dead, but took five stand of colors, and came off with but little loss."

"Very well, but that is scarcely worthy of mention when we consider the long and successful defence made by Kleber's whole division on the ground."

"If I had not arrived too late last night, I might have surprised the Turkish army, and then that long defence would have been unnecessary. I designed to attemp the surprise," said Kleber.

"The number of the enemy surprised me this morning, when they were drawn up in battle array," said Junot. "Fifteen thousand infantry occupied the village of Fouli, and more than twelve thousand horse were drawn up in the plain, while we had scarcely three thousand infantry in square."

"They made an imposing show, but they were met with such steady bravery, and such a blaze of fire, that their ranks seemed to melt away like mist before the sun," said Kleber. "However, it was well that General Bonaparte came up. The furious charges of the Turkish cavalry had begun to make an impression on my ranks, and it is probable enough they might have been broken in the course of the afternoon, if the general-in-chief had not brought up your division, Bon, and made those admirable dispositions, which placed the enemy between two fires, and soon put them to the rout. A tremendous fire discharged from three points of the triangle, sent the Mamelukes away in heaps. We took the village of Fouli—yes, Fouli, you call it—

and then Murat finished the enemy by putting them to soak in the waters of the Jordan. It has been â glorious day."

"Six thousand French have destroyed an army which the Naplousians stated could no more be numbered than the stars in the heavens and the sands on the seashore," observed Junot. "Well, we may fail in the conquest of the East, but this victory cannot be forgotten."

"Besides glory," said Kleber, "it may be as well to mention that the booty taken is worth considerable. The Turkish camp was well supplied with both necessaries and luxuries. We have taken four hundred camels, and the other booty is sufficient to satisfy our soldiers."

"And see," said Bon, "the Naplousians will have reason to remember us," and he pulled aside the canvass of the tent and pointed to the red light of the burning villages.

At this moment, General Bonaparte appeared at the door of the tent, in company with Bessieres. The young general looked much worn and fatigued. His figure was stouter than it had been during the campaign of Italy; but his stern countenance still showed the hollow cheeks and sunken eyes, caused by the constant and powerful workings of his genius. His costume was much soiled, and its appearance indicated his want of attention to such matters during the press of the business of life and death. He held some papers in his hand.

"Generals, I hope I do not interrupt your conversation. But business like ours admits of no delay. I set off at day-break for Acre, where I am determined to press the siege with renewed vigor. I have reason to dread that a large Turkish army will soon be landed near the mouth of the Nile, and if Acre is to be taken at all, we must accomplish the feat very speedily; and it must be taken," said Bonaparte, in his emphatic way.

"Must be taken," said Kleber, always outspoken. "My opinion is that the siege will cost us many valuable lives, and yet not be successful. Every day increases the difficulties of our safe return to Cairo."

"Yes, yes," said Bonaparte, impatiently, "but it will not do to let this Englishman, Sidney Smith, and his Turks, baffle the conquerors of Italy and Egypt. General Kleber, you will lead your division back to Acre; and you, General Bon, will follow. We have annihilated our foes in this quarter, and have nothing more to fear from them. Hasten your march to Acre, and, doubtless, with a few more determined efforts, that town will be in our hands." So saying, he bowed, and hurried out of the tent.

"A man destined to do great things; but destined to be mistaken in his present enterprise," observed Kleber.

Murat now proposed a ride over the field of battle, before retiring to repose. The others agreed, and all were soon mounted, and cantering away along the line of the camp-fires, and among the heaps of the dead. A large number of the French soldiers were engaged in searching for valuables among the bodies of the

NAPOLEON AT ACRE.

Mamelukes, and to the inquiries of the generals, they responded that they were reaping a full harvest. Around the line occupied by the troops of Kleber's division, was seen the wall of carcasses which had served as a protection to those gallant men, when they had become extremely fatigued by the struggle against the overwhelming numbers of the enemy. The light of the burning villages, and the watch-fires, was quite sufficient to enable them to pursue their spoil-seeking occupation. After riding over the whole field, the generals separated, and each sought his tent to stretch himself for repose, and to dream of the glorious incidents of the victory of Mount Tabor.

THE CAMP-FIRE AT ABOUKIR.

THE battle of Aboukir, was, perhaps, the only instance in the history of war, in which a hostile army was utterly annihilated by an inferior force. The victory, therefore, was one of the most splendid which Bonaparte ever achieved. The Turkish army, conveyed by the squadron of Sir Sidney Smith, anchored in Aboukir Bay on the 11th of July, 1799.

The place fixed upon by the English for their landing, was the peninsula which defends this road, and which bears the same name. This narrow peninsula runs out between the sea and Lake Madieh, and has a fort at its extremity. Bonaparte had ordered Marmont, who commanded at Alexandria, to improve the defences of the fort, and to destroy the village of Aboukir, situated around it. But, instead of destroying the village, he thought it better to keep the place in order to lodge the soldiers there; and it had merely been surrounded by a redoubt to protect it on the land side. But the redoubt not joining on both sides the sea, did not present the appearance of a close work, and put the fort on the same footing as a simple field-work. The Turks, in fact, landed with great boldness, attacked the intrenchments sword in hand, carried them, and made themselves masters of the village of Aboukir, putting the garrison to the sword. The village being taken, the fort could no longer hold out, and it was obliged to surrender. Marmont, who commanded at Alexandria, had issued forth, at the head of twelve hundred men, to hasten to the assistance of the troops at Aboukir. But learning that the Turks had landed in considerable numbers, he durst not attempt to drive them into the sea by a bold attack. He returned to Alexandria, and left them to quietly take up their position on the peninsula of Aboukir.

The Turks amounted to nearly eighteen thousand infantry. These were not the miserable Fellahs who had composed the infantry of the Mamelukes; but brave janizaries, carrying a musket without bayonet, slinging it at their back after firing, and rushing pistol and sword in hand upon the enemy. They had a numerous and well-served artillery, and were under the direction of English officers. They had no cavalry, for they had not brought more than three hundred horses; but they expected Murad Bey, who was to leave Upper Egypt, proceed along the desert, cross the oasis, and throw himself into Aboukir with two or three thousand Mamelukes.

When Bonaparte was informed of the particulars of the landing, he left Cairo instantly, and made from that city to Alexandria one of those extraordinary marches of which he had given so many instances in Italy. He took with him the divisions of Lannes, Bon, and Murat. He had ordered Desaix to evacuate Upper Egypt, and Kleber and Regnier, who were in the Delta, to bring themselves nearer Aboukir. He had chosen the point of Birket, midway between Alexandria and Aboukir, in order to concentrate his forces thither, and to manœuvre according to circumstances. He was very fearful lest an English army had landed with the Turks.

Murad Bey, according to the plan settled with Mustapha Pacha, had tried a descent into Lower Egypt; but being met and beaten by Murat, he had been obliged to regain the desert. There was now nothing left but the Turkish army to fight, destitute as it was of cavalry, but yet encamped behind intrenchments, and disposed to stand its ground there with its usual pertinacity. Bonaparte, after inspecting Alexandria and the admirable works executed by Colonel Cretin.

and after reprimanding Marmont, his lieutenant, who had not dared to attack the Turks at the moment of landing, left Alexandria on the 6th Thermidor, (July 24th. Next day, the 7th, he was at the entrance of the peninsula. His plan was to inclose the Turkish army by intrenchments, and to await the arrival of all his divisions, for all he had with him were no more than the divisions of Lannes, Bon, and Murat, about six thousand men. But on observing the arrangements made by the Turks, he altered his intentions, and resolved to attack them immediately, hoping to inclose them in the village of Aboukir, and to overwhelm them with bombs and howitzers.

The Turks occupied the furthest end of the peninsula, which is very narrow. They were covered by two lines of intrenchments. Half a league in advance of the village of Aboukir, where their camp was, they had occupied two round sand-hills, supported the one on the sea, the other on Lake Madieh, and thus forming their right and left. In the centre of these two hillocks was a village, which they had likewise kept. They had one thousand men on the hillock to the right, two thousand on the hillock to the left, and three or four thousand men in the village. Such was their first line. The second was at the village of Aboukir itself. It consisted of the redoubt constructed by the French, and was connected with the sea by two trenches. It was there that they had stationed their principal camp and the bulk of their forces.

Bonaparte made his arrangements with his usual promptitude and decision. He ordered General Desstaing, with some battalions, to march to the hill on the left, where one thousand Turks were posted; Lannes to march to that on the right, where the two thousand others were; and Murat, who was at the centre, to make the cavalry file on the rear of the two hillocks. These arrangements were executed with great precision. Destaing marched to the hillock on the left, and boldly climbed it; Murat contrived to get at its rear with a troop of cavalry. The Turks, when they saw this, abandoned their post, fell in with the cavalry, which cut them in pieces, and drove them into the sea, into which they chose rather to throw themselves than to surrender. The same operation was executed on the right. Lannes attacked the two thousand Mamelukes, Murat got at their rear; and they were in like manner cut to pieces and driven into the sea. Destaing and Lannes then moved towards the centre, formed by a village, and attacked it in front. The Turks there defended themselves bravely, relying upon assistance from the second line. A column in fact was detached from the camp of Aboukir; but Murat, who had already filed upon the rear of the village, cut this column in pieces, and drove it back into Aboukir. Destaing's infantry and that of Lannes entered the village at the charge step, driving the Turks out of it, who were dispersed in all directions, and who obstinately refusing to surrender, had no other retreat than the sea, wherein they were drowned.

Already four or five thousand had perished in this manner. The first line was carried; Bonaparte's object was accomplished, and now, inclosing the Turks in Aboukir, he could bombard them while waiting for the arrival of Kleber and Regnier. But he desired to make the most of his success, and to complete his victory that very moment. After giving his troops a little breathing time, he marched upon the second line. The division under Lanusse, which had been left as a reserve, supported Lannes and Destaing. The redoubt which covered Aboukir was difficult to carry; it had within it nine or ten thousand Turks. On the right, a trench joined it to the sea; on the left, another trench brought it further out; but was not continued quite to Lake Madieh. The open space was occupied by the enemy, and swept by the fire of numerous gun-boats. Bonaparte, having accustomed his soldiers to defy the most formidable obstacles, sent them upon the enemy's position. His divisions of infantry marched upon the front and the right of the redoubt. The cavalry, concealed in a wood of palm-trees, had to make the attack on the left, and then to cross, under the fire of the gun-boats, the open space between the redoubt and Lake Madieh. The charge was made; Lannes and Destaing urged forward their brave infantry. The 32d marched with their pieces on their arms towards the intrenchments, and the 18th got at the rear of the intrenchments on the extreme right. The enemy, without waiting for them, advanced to meet them. They fought hand to hand. The Turkish soldiers, having fired their pieces and their two pistols, drew their flashing sabres. They endeavored to grasp the bayonets, but received them in their flanks before they could lay hold of them. Thus a great slaughter took place in the intrenchments. The 18th was on the point of getting into the redoubt, when a tremendous fire of artillery repulsed it, and sent it back to the foot of the works. The gallant Leturcq fell gloriously, by desiring to be the last to retire; Fugieres lost an arm. Murat on his part had advanced with his cavalry, with a view to clear the space between the fire of the redoubt and Lake Madieh. Several times he had dashed forward, and had turned back the enemy; but taken between the two fires of the redoubt, and that of the gun-boats, he had been obliged to fall back on the rear. Some of his horse-soldiers had advanced to the ditches of the redoubt. The efforts of so many brave fellows appeared likely to be entirely unavailable. Bonaparte looked coolly on this carnage, waiting for a favorable moment to return to the charge. Fortunately the Turks, as they usually did, quitted the intrenchments for the purpose of cutting off the heads of the slain. Bonaparte seized this opportunity, launched forth two battalions, one of the 22d, the other of the 69th, which marched upon the intrenchments and carried them. On the right, the 18th also took advantage of this opportunity, and entered the redoubt. Murat, on his side, ordered a fresh charge. One of his divisions of cavalry traversed that most exposed space between the intrenchments and the lake, and made his way into the village of Aboukir. The Turks, affrighted, fled on all sides, and a horrible slaughter of them ensued. They were pressed by the point of the bayonet and driven into the sea. Murat, at the head of his heroes, penetrated into the camp of Mustapha Pacha. The latter, in a fit of despair, snatched up a pistol and fired it at Murat, whom he wounded slightly. Murat struck off two of his fingers and sent him prisoner to Bonaparte. Such of the Turks as were not killed or drowned retired into the fort of Aboukir.*

The proud army of the Turks was thus completely overwhelmed, as if it had been entirely buried by an avalanche. No wonder that the enthusiastic Kleber, after witnessing the manœuvres that gained this splendid victory, clasped Bonaparte in his arms, and exclaimed, "General, you are as great as the world itself."

It was the second night after the battle. The army was encamped upon the field. Bonaparte was alone in his tent. That day he had contrived to obtain from Sir Sidney Smith a file of papers from Europe, from which he eagerly sought information as to the condition and prospects of France. He had dismissed all his officers, and now, as they were either carousing in their tents, or wandering among the camp-fires of the troops, he sat in his tent to obtain that information which was destined to lead to such great and decisive plans. See him, as he sits there, with his eyes keenly fixed upon the papers, and an occasional smile lighting up his features of bronze! He learns the calamities which have visited the armies of France, and then the smile is turned to a terrible frown, and he exclaims, passionately,

"The imbeciles! the imbeciles! Why was I not there?"

He perused the accounts of the overthrow of the French armies in Italy and Germany; he saw that all

* Thiers.

that he had gained for France, had been lost; he knew that these disasters would not have occurred if he had retained a European command; and he felt more strongly than ever that he was destined to retrieve the condition of affairs, to bind victory once more to the tri-color standard. Perhaps, also, his mind perceived the opportunity for gratifying the aspirations of a selfish ambition, and that this perception caused the frown to melt once more into a smile—a smile of triumph. He saw that the disasters attending the French arms had rendered the Directory unpopular, and that power was within the reach of any bold, decisive man, who would dare to attempt the overthrow of that government; and he had faith enough in himself to decide that he was the very man for the crisis. Long he read, and long he pondered. Cæsar deliberated upon the banks of the Rubicon. At length he started up. The die was cast. He would return to France and strike for the supreme authority. Having once decided upon his movements, no man could have taken his measures with more promptitude. He resolved to sail secretly for Europe. He wrote a dispatch to Admiral Gantheaume, directing him to get the Muiron and Carrere frigates ready for sea. He determined that as Kleber was very popular with the army, that general should be left in command. There could be no doubt of Kleber's vigor, activity and skill. Bonaparte then sat down, and, with astonishing rapidity and precision, drew up a long list of instructions for the new commander-in-chief. He then sent word to Berthier, Lannes, Murat, Andreossy, Marmont, Berthollet, and

Monge, that he wished to see them in his tent. It was late. But they came, without exception, at his summons. Kleber and Menou were then at Cairo, or they, also, would have been invited to this important conference. In a few words, Bonaparte communicated his sudden resolution to those officers he had assembled around him. They were surprised, but when he told them that he wished them to go with him, they were glad; for in spite of the glory achieved in Egypt, they were anxious to return to France. Berthier had been suffering for some time from depression of spirits, owing to a long standing matrimonial engagement; and he fairly leaped from his seat when he heard of the intention of the general-in-chief. Monge, that circumspect votary of science, hinted that there was the greatest danger of the whole party being captured by the English cruisers, which were exceedingly vigilant in the Mediterranean. The only reply was the brief and emphatic "I must incur the risk." The officers cast significant glances at each other, but it was extremely doubtful if they fathomed his designs.

"I have received ill news from Europe, my friends," said Bonaparte, turning over his papers, and seemingly attending to several matters at once. "The Austrians and Muscovites have gained the superiority. That which we won with so much toil has been lost, and France is threatened with the invasion of her territory. We are wanted in Europe, and in spite of winds, waves, and English cruisers, we must go thither."

Soon afterwards the conference was broken up, and the general-in-chief was again alone in his tent—nay, not alone, for the images of ambition were fast crowding around him, and they were companions whom he valued more than the ordinary human realities of the camp. And there this all-daring, all-achieving soldier sat till the peep of day, perfecting his plans, the ultimate reach of which was a throne above thrones; for it was his habit of mind never to form a design which did not extend to the farthest point. In war, it was the conquest of a world at which he aimed; in politics, consul nor king could satisfy the cravings of his soul—he would be an emperor. Doubtless, his Rubicon was at Aboukir, and there the die was cast which determined him to be master of France.

CAMP-FIRE IN THE VALLEY OF AOSTA.

WE are now to behold Bonaparte as First Consul of France—as the successful rival of the Carthagenian Hannibal in the prodigious exploit of leading an army over the lofty and wintry Alps—and as the conqueror of his old enemies the Austrians.

The time was May, 1800. At Paris, Bonaparte had formed the plan of the most astonishing of his campaigns, with a precision so wonderful that it pointed to the very spot on which the decisive battle should be fought. While the intrepid Massena defended Genoa with unwearied energy, and Moreau engaged the attention of the Austrians on the line of the Danube, the First Consul had created a third army, caused the passes of the Alps to be explored, determined to take that of the Great St. Bernard, and achieved the passage as far as the vale of Aosta, where an unexpected obstacle was found in the fortress of Bard.

The valley of Aosta is traversed by a river which receives all the waters of the St. Bernard, and carries them into the Po, under the name of Dora-Baltea. As it approaches Bard, the valley narrows; the road lying between the base of the mountains and the bed of the river becomes gradually more contracted, until at length, a rock, which seems to have fallen from the neighboring crags into the middle of the valley, almost entirely blocks it. The river then runs on one side of the rock, and the road proceeds on the other. This road lined with houses composes all the town of Bard. On the top of the rock stands a fort, impregnable by its position, though ill-constructed, which sweeps with its fire, on the right, the whole course of the Dora-Baltea, and on the left, the long street forming the little town of Bard. Drawbridges close the entrance and the outlet of this single street. A garrison, small in number, but well commanded, occupied this fort.

The brave and persevering Lannes commanded the advanced division of the French. He was not a man to be easily stopped. He immediately put forward a few companies of grenadiers, who broke down the drawbridge, and, in the face of a sweeping fire, entered Bard. The commandant of the fort then poured a storm of shot and shell upon the town, but was soon induced to cease, by a feeling of compassion for the inhabitants. Lannes stationed his division out of the town and under cover; but it was impossible to pass the materiel of the army under the fire of the fort. He then reported to General Berthier, who, coming up, was dismayed at the unexpected obstacle. General Marescot, the skilful engineer of the army, was then brought forward.

He examined the fort, and declared it nearly impregnable, not on account of its construction, which was indifferent, but from its position, which was entirely isolated. The escarpment of the rock did not admit escalading, and the walls, though not covered by an embankment, could not be battered in breach, as there was no possibility of establishing a battery in a position suitable for breaching them. Nevertheless, it was possible, by strength of arm, to hoist a few guns of small calibre to the top of the neighboring heights. Berthier gave orders to this end. The soldiers, who were used to the most difficult undertakings, went to work eagerly to hoist up two four-pounders, and even two eight-pounders. These they in fact succeeded in elevating to the mountain of Albaredo, which overlooks the rock and fort of Bard; and a plunging fire, suddenly opened, greatly surprised the garrison, which, nevertheless, did not lose courage, but replied, and soon dismounted one of the guns, which were of too feeble a calibre to be useful.

Marescot declared that there was no hope of taking the fort, and that some other means must be devised for overcoming this obstruction. Berthier, in great alarm, instantly counter-ordered all the columns as they successively came up; suspended the march of the men and the artillery all along the line, in order to prevent them from involving themselves further, should it be necessary, after all, to retreat. An instant panic circulated to the rear, and all the men thought themselves arrested in this glorious enterprise. Berthier sent courier after courier to the First Consul, to inform him of this unexpected disappointment.

The latter tarried still at Martigny, not meaning to pass over the St. Bernard, until he had seen, with his own eyes, the last of the artillery sent forward. But this announcement of an obstacle, considered insurmountable at first, made a terrible impression on him; but he recovered quickly, and refused positively to admit the possibility of a retreat. Nothing in the world should reduce him to such an extremity. He thought that, if one of the loftiest mountains in the world had failed to arrest his progress, a secondary rock could not be capable of vanquishing his courage and his genius. The fort, said he to himself, might be taken by bold courage; if it could not be taken, it still could be turned. Besides, if the infantry and the cavalry could pass by it, with but a few four-pounders, they could then proceed to Ivrea at the mouth of the gorge, and wait until their heavy guns could follow them. And if the heavy guns could not pass by the obstacle which had arisen; and if, in order to get any, that of the enemy must be taken, the French infantry were brave and numerous enough to assail the Austrians and take their cannon. Moreover, he studied his maps again and again, questioned a number of Italian officers; and learning from these that many other roads led from Aosta to the neighboring valleys, he wrote letter after letter to Berthier, forbidding him to stop the progress of the army, and pointing out to him, with wonderful precision, what reconnoissances should be made around the fort of Bard. He would not allow himself to see any serious danger, except from the arrival of a hostile corps, shutting up the debouch of Ivrea; he instructed Berthier to send Lannes as far as Ivrea, by the path of Albaredo, and make him take a stronger position there, which should be safe from the Austrian artillery and cavalry. When Lannes guards the entrance of the valley, added the First Consul, whatever may happen, it is of little consequence, the only result may be a loss of time. We have enough provisions to subsist ourselves awhile, and one way or other we shall succeed in avoiding or overcoming the obstacles which now delay us.

These instructions having been sent to Berthier, he addressed his last orders to General Moncey, who should debouch by the St. Gothard; to General Chabran, who should come down by the Little St. Bernard, directly in front of the fort of Bard; and then, at last, resolved to cross the Alps in person. Before he set forth, he received news from the Var, informing him that on the 14th of May—the 24th of Floreal—the Baron de Melas was still at Nice. As it was now the 20th of May, it could not reasonably be supposed, that the Austrian general, in the space of six days, could have marched from Nice to Ivrea. It was then on the 20th of May, before daylight, that he set out to pass the defile. His aid-de-camp Duroc, and his secretary Bourrienne, accompanied him.

Behold him now ascending the rugged and difficult St. Bernard, the rocks and precipices around him, and above, the towering summits of perpetual snow! He is mounted on a mule, conducted by a young, hardy mountaineer. The grey great coat, which he always wore during his campaigns of sleepless activity, is buttoned closely around him. His cheeks are fuller than when we saw him in Egypt; but he has the same pale, olive complexion, the same firm-set mouth, the same steady, piercing eyes, and the same air of constant thought. Occasionally he turns to address a remark to Duroc or Bourrienne; and he has many questions to ask of those officers he meets upon the road. But, strange to say, he converses the longest with that simple-hearted mountaineer who leads his mule. The young guide unrolls his little catalogue of troubles, to which the First Consul listens as he would to a pastoral romance. The great man learns that the mountaineer is much grieved, because, for want of a little money, he is unable to marry one of the maidens of the valley who has won his heart. Thus proceeding, the party at length arrived at the monastery of St. Bernard, where the benevolent monks displayed much pleasure at seeing the illustrious general. He alighted; but before he partook of any refreshment, he wrote a brief note, which he handed to his guide, and told him to give it without delay to the administrator of the army, who had remained on the other side of the St. Bernard. In the evening, when the young mountaineer reached St. Pierre, he learned how great a person he had conducted, and also that the First Consul had given him a house and a field, as the means of marrying the girl of his heart. A delightful pastoral episode in the great warrior's stormy career.

Bonaparte halted a short time with the monks, thanked them for the care shown to his troops, made them a noble gift, and then pursued his route. The descent of St. Bernard was made very rapidly, the First Consul descending on a sledge, which glided down the glacier with almost fearful swiftness. The party arrived the same evening at Etroubles. The following morning, having spent some time in examining the park of artillery and the provisions, he started for Aosta and Bard.

The night of the 23d of May was clear, bright and cold, in the valley of Aosta. Just beyond the town of Bard—a long, narrow line of old, picturesque houses—were encamped the troops of Lannes's division, the line of the encampment being indicated by the watch-fires. In front of the large tent which had been erected as the quarters of the First Consul, stood Bonaparte, Berthier, Marescot, Lannes, Duroc, and Bourrienne. Marescot stood next to the illustrious commander-in-chief, who was examining the fort and its surroundings with a glass.

"The report was perfectly correct; that is a serious obstacle," said the First Consul. "But I have no doubt that we, who surmounted the difficulties of the St. Bernard, will conquer this rocky position, either by taking or turning it."

"The only hope of capturing the fort, is by an escalade, on the outer ramparts, as you will perceive," remarked Marescot.

"True, we can place a battery on the heights of Albaredo; but that will produce but little effect," replied Bonaparte.

"The fire of the fort sweeps the whole course of the river, and that long street of the town," observed Berthier.

"We have made reconnoissances to the left, along the sinuous flanks of the Albaredo mountain, and found a path, which through vast dangers, more terrible than those of the St. Bernard, rejoins the great road below the fort at St. Donaz," said Marescot.

"Can it be made practicable for infantry, cavalry, and a few light guns?" quickly inquired Bonaparte.

"I think it can. With about fifteen hundred workmen, it could soon be greatly altered," replied Marescot.

"Enough; you shall have the workmen, and the infantry, cavalry, and four-pounders shall be sent by that road," said the First Consul, decisively.

"The artillery horses may be sent by the same road, and the only remaining difficulty will be to get the heavy guns along beyond this fort," remarked Duroc.

A short time previous, the officers of the advanced division had been appalled by an unexpected obstruction. But difficulties of all kinds seemed to vanish before the First Consul's burning faith in possibility. No thought of retreat was now entertained.

"Come in, Marescot, and Bourrienne. Generals, you

shall hear from me either in the course of the night, or at dawn," said Bonaparte, and he entered his tent, followed by Marescot and Bourrienne. Lannes and Duroc followed General Berthier to his tent, where they were soon seated and engaged in conversation.

"Come, Lannes, as this is the first time we have met since we were at Dijon, let us know the particulars of your march over Mount St. Bernard," said Duroc.

Lannes was much better fitted for doing a great thing than giving an account of it, and it required a short period of hard thinking to bring his ideas to the proper point. However, he commenced.

"The march was no exploit of which an officer should boast. You saw that I had under my command six regiments of excellent troops—there are none better in the army. To them belongs all the glory; for they were heavily laden with provisions and ammunition, and their task was one of great difficulty and hardship. We started from St. Pierre, about midnight, in order to get over the mountain before the period of danger from tumbling avalanches. We calculated it would require eight hours to reach the summit of the pass, and two hours to descend to St. Remy. The troops went to their work in high spirits. Burdened as they were, they scaled the craggy paths, singing among the precipices, and talking gaily, as if they were certain they were marching to new victories in Italy. The labor of the foot soldiers was not near so great as that of the cavalry. The horsemen marched on foot, leading their animals. In this, there was no danger while ascending;

but when they came to the descent, the narrowness of the paths obliged each man to walk before his horse, so that each was exposed at each tumble of his animal to be dragged headlong down a precipice."

"Did any of the men perish in that way?" inquired Duroc.

"Yes, several," replied Lannes, "and about a dozen horses. The horse is not a sure-footed animal. Near daybreak, we arrived at the hospital, where the First Consul had ordered the monks to provide an agreeable surprise for the troops, in the shape of refreshment. Every soldier received a ration of bread, cheese, and wine. We did not stop longer than was required to dispatch this breakfast, and pursuing our march, we reached St. Remy, without any other accidents than those I have mentioned. While the other divisions of the army were advancing, I received orders from the First Consul to push forward to Aosta, then to Ivrea, and by taking that town, secure the entrance to the plains of Piedmont. On the 16th and 17th, I marched upon Aosta. There I found some Croatians, whom I drove down the valley. I reached Chatillon on the 18th, and routed a battalion of the enemy found there, capturing a goodly number of them. I then marched on down the valley, thinking that I would soon be upon the fertile plains of Italy, when this confounded fort suddenly appeared, and checked my march."

"We have had a difficult task upon the other side of the mountain," said Duroc. "You know that it was arranged that each day one division of the army should pass over. The materiel had to be transported with each division. The provisions and the ammunition were easily sent forward, for they could be divided into small packages. But the heavier articles which could not be divided and reduced, caused us a vast amount of trouble. In spite of the liberal expenditure of money, a sufficient number of mules could not be obtained. The transportation of the artillery was the most difficult task of all.

"The gun-carriages and caissons had been dismounted, and loaded on the backs of mules. The cannon themselves yet remained. For the twelve pounders and howitzers, the difficulty was much greater than was at first supposed. The sledges with rollers, which had been constructed in the arsenals, were wholly useless. Another mode was suggested, and immediately adopted; and it proved successful. This was to split pine trunks into two parts, hollow them out, secure a gun between them, and drag the pieces thus protected along the slippery ravines. Thanks to wise precautions, no shock could occur to injure them. Mules were attached to these strange loads, and succeeded in bringing a few pieces to the top of the defile. But the descent was more difficult: it was only to be achieved by manual exertion, and by incurring imminent risk; as the pieces had to be restrained and checked from rolling down the precipices. Unfortunately, at this juncture, the mules began to fail; the muleteers, too, who were now required in great numbers, became exhausted, and in consequence fresh means must be resorted to. A price as high as a thousand francs was offered to the neighboring peasants, for dragging a gun from St. Pierre to

St. Remy. One hundred men were required for one cannon, one day to bring it up, and one day to let it down. Several hundred peasants presented themselves, and, under the direction of artillerists, transported a few pieces.

"But not even the allurement of such gain could induce them to maintain this effort. All disappeared ere long, and although officers were sent out to seek them, lavishing money, so as to bring them back, it was in vain; and it became necessary to call on the soldiers of the several divisions to drag their own artillery themselves. It seemed that nothing could be asked, too arduous, of these devoted soldiers. The money which the exhausted peasants would no longer earn, was offered as a stimulus; but they refused it to a man, exclaiming that it was a point of honor for all troops to save their cannon; and they took charge of the abandoned pieces. Parties, each of a hundred men, leaving the ranks successively, dragged them, each in their turn. Their bands struck up lively tunes in the more difficult defiles, and animated them to surmount these novel obstacles. Arrived at the mountain top, they found refreshments prepared for them by the monks, and took some brief repose, as a preparation for greater and more perilous efforts to be exerted in descending. Thus the divisions of Chambarlhac and Monnier were seen toiling at their own artillery; and as the advanced hour of the day did not permit them to descend, they preferred bivouacking in the snow, to abandoning their cannon. Fortunately the sky was clear; nor had they to endure bad weather, in addition to the hard toils of the way."

"I am aware of much that you have been telling us," said Berthier, "having been unceasingly employed in receiving the stores, and superintending the artillery mounted again. The troops have fully communicated their toils and sufferings, but they have borne up under them with astonishing courage and fortitude. Their faithful performance of duty has enabled the First Consul to execute a grand campaign, which places him above all the generals of antiquity."

"The campaign is not yet decided. We must fight at least one great battle, and the prospect is not favorable to our getting near the Austrians in time to take them by surprise," said Lannes.

"I think not," replied Duroc. "The First Consul will either take or turn this fort within a few days at the farthest. I have no doubt of it—and the Austrians will be as much astonished as if we had dropped from the clouds. The campaign will cover us with glory."

Here Bourrienne entered the tent, and communicated to the generals the plan which the First Consul had formed, which was as follows:

He resolved to make his infantry, cavalry, and the four-pounders, proceed by the path of Albaredo, which would be possible, after repairs. All the troops should be sent to take possession of the outlets of the mountains before Ivrea; and the First Consul, meanwhile, would attempt an attack on the fort, or find some means of avoiding its obstruction, by sending his artillery through one of the neighboring defiles. He ordered General Lecchi, commanding the Italians, to proceed on the left, advancing by the road to Grassoney in the alley of the Sesia, which extended to the Simplon and the Lago Maggiore. This movement was intended to clear the road of the Simplon, to form a junction with the detachment which was coming down it, and lastly to examine all the paths practicable to wheeled carriages.

After some further conversation, the generals separated for the night.

The next day, it was apparent that the conqueror of Italy was present, and among the French. All was activity and resolution. The First Consul directed his mind to the fort of Bard.

The single street, which composed this town, was in possession of the French, but only passable, if passable at all, under such a storm of fire as would make it impossible to move artillery that way, even if the distance had been only five or six hundred yards. The commandant was summoned; but replied, with the firmness of a man who appreciated fully the importance of the post intrusted to his courage. Force, therefore, alone, could make them masters of the passage. The artillery, which had been placed in battery on the heights of Albaredo, produced no great effect; an escalade was attempted on the outer ramparts of the fort; but some brave grenadiers and an excellent officer, Dufour, were killed or wounded to no purpose. At this time the troops were defiling by the path of Albaredo; for fifteen hundred workmen had wrought the necessary repairs on it. Places that were too narrow they had enlarged by mounds of the earth; declivities too sudden they had eased, by cutting steps for the feet; trunks of trees they had thrown across other places, to form bridges over ravines, which were too broad to be leaped.

The army defiled man by man in succession, the cavaliers leading their horses by the bridles. The Austrian officer commanding in the fort of Bard, seeing the columns thus march past, was in despair that he could not stop their progress; he, therefore, sent a message to M. de Melas, informing him that he had seen the passage of a whole army of infantry and cavalry, without having any means to prevent it; but pledged his head that they should arrive without a single piece of cannon. During this time, the artillerymen made one of the boldest of attempts. This was, under the cloud of night, to carry a piece of cannon under the very fire of the fort. Unfortunately, the enemy, aroused by the noise, threw down fire-pots, which made the whole road light as day, enabling him by that means to sweep it with a hail-storm of deadly missiles. Out of thirteen gunners who had run the risk of taking this piece forward, seven were killed or wounded. There was in that enough to discourage hardy spirits; yet it was not long ere another way, ingenious, but still very perilous, was devised. The street was strewn with straw and litter; tow was fastened around all the cannon, to prevent the slightest resonance of those huge metallic masses on their carriages; the horses were taken out, and the bold artillerists, dragging them with their own hands, were so daring as to carry them under the batteries of the fort, along the street of Bard. These means succeeded to perfection. The enemy, who occasionally fired as a precaution, wounded a few of the gunners;

but soon, in spite of this fire, all the heavy artillery was transported through the defile; and this formidable obstruction, which had given the First Consul more anxiety than the St. Bernard itself, was now entirely overcome.

The Alps were passed, and victory already hovered over the banner of Bonaparte.

THE CAMP-FIRE AT MARENGO.

THE victory of Marengo was the crowning glory of a campaign unsurpassed in the annals of war, as regards the display of daring genius and profound combination. It was a stroke which changed the face of affairs in Europe, and raised the conqueror to the imperial height of his ambition.

The immense plain of Marengo extends between the

Scrivia and the Bormida. In this place, the Po retreats from the Appenine, and leaves a vast space, across which the Bormida and the Tanaro roll their waters, now become less rapid, till meeting near Alessandria, they flow on together into the bed of the Po. The road, leading along the foot of the Appenines to Tortona, departs from it abreast of this place, turns to the right, passes the Scrivia, and opens into a vast plain. The stream it crosses at a first village, called San Giuliano, runs forward to a second, named Marengo, and at length crosses the Bormida, and terminates at the celebrated fortress of Alessandria.

On the 13th of June, 1800, that army which had surmounted the crags and snows of the Alps, debouched into the plain. Here Bonaparte expected to find the Austrians; but his cavalry scoured the plain without finding a single corps, and the First Consul then concluded that Melas had escaped. He then ordered the wise and valiant Desaix, who had joined him a few days previous, to march upon Rivolta and Novi with a single division, that of Boudet, in order to check Melas, if he had gone from Alessandria to Genoa. But the division of Monnier, which was Desaix's second, he retained at head-quarters. Victor was left at the town of Marengo, with two divisions; Lannes, the indomitable Lannes, fresh from the glorious field of Montebello, was left with one division on the plain, and Murat, with his cavalry, was retained at the side of the general-in-chief, with the splendid Consular Guard.

But the First Consul had been deceived. Melas had not escaped; he expected to fight at Marengo, and had adopted measures to advance upon the French army.

The French, marching from Placentia and the Scrivia, would first come upon San Giuliano, and afterward, at three quarters of a league farther, upon Marengo, which almost touches the Bormida, and forms the principal outlet which the Austrian army had to conquer, in order to issue from Alessandria. Between San Giuliano and Marengo extends, in a right line, the road which was to be disputed; and on each side, wide spreads the plain covered with fields of wheat and vineyards. Below Marengo, to the right of the French, and left of the Austrians, lay Castel-Ceriolo, a large borough, through which General Ott intended to pass, in order to turn the corps of General Victor, stationed in Marengo. It was, therefore, upon Marengo that the principal attack of the Austrians would be directed, as this village commanded the entrance of the plain.

At day-break, the Austrian army passed the two bridges of the Bormida. But its movement was slow, because it had but one bridge-head, from which to debouch. O'Reilly passed first, and encountered the division of Gardanne, which General Victor, after having occupied Marengo, had led forward. This division was formed only of the 101st and 44th demi-brigades. O'Reilly, supported by a numerous artillery, and with double the force of his opponent, compelled him to fall back, and shut himself up in Marengo. Fortunately, he did not throw himself into the place after him, but waited till the centre, under General Haddick, should come to his support. The slowness of their march across the defile formed by the bridges, cost the Austrians two or three hours. At length Generals Haddick and Kaim deployed their forces in the rear of O'Reilly, and General Ott passed the same bridges on his way to Castel-Ceriolo.

Thus commenced the great battle of Marengo. The advance, under Gardanne, was obliged to fall back upon Victor. Victor held his position during two hours against the enormous force opposed to him. He was obliged to vacate Marengo, but retook it; and this occurred twice or thrice. Napoleon now ordered Lannes to advance to the support of Victor; but after a long and obstinate contest, the cavalry of Elsnitz suddenly appeared upon the right of Lannes, and both lines were compelled to retreat. The Austrians had fought the battle admirably. The infantry had opened an attack on every point of the French line, while the cavalry debouched across the bridge which the French had failed to destroy, and assailed the right of their army with such fury and rapidity, that it was thrown into complete disorder. The attack was successful every where; the centre of the French was penetrated, the left routed, and another desperate charge of the cavalry would have terminated the battle. The order for this, however, was not given; but the retreating French were still in the utmost peril. Napoleon had been collecting reserves between Garafolo and Marengo, and now sent orders for his army to retreat towards these reserves, and rally round his guard, which he stationed in the rear of the village of Marengo, and placed himself at their head. The soldiers could all see the First Consul, with his staff, surrounded by the two hundred grenadiers of the guard, in the midst of the immense plain. The sight revived their hopes. The right wing, under Lannes, quickly rallied; the centre, reinforced by the scattered troops of the left, recovered its strength; the left wing no longer existed; its scattered remains fled in disorder, pursued by the Austrians. The battle continued to rage, and was obstinately disputed; but the main body of the French army, which still remained in order of battle, was continually, though very slowly, retreating. The First Consul had now dispatched his aid-de-camp, Bruyere, to Desaix, with an urgent message to hasten to the field of battle. Desaix, on his part, had been arrested in his march upon Novi, by the repeated discharges of distant artillery: he had in consequence made a halt, and dispatched Savary, then his aid-de-camp, with a body of fifty horse, to gallop with all possible haste to Novi, and ascertain the state of affairs there, according to the orders of the First Consul, while he kept his division fresh and ready for action. Savary found all quiet at Novi; and returning to Desaix, after the lapse of about two hours, with this intelligence, was next sent to the First Consul. He spurred his horse across the country, in the direction of the fire and smoke, and fortunately met Bruyere, who was taking the same short cut to find Desaix. Giving him the necessary directions, Savary hastened to the First Consul. He found him in the midst of his guard, who stood their ground, on the field of battle; forming a solid body in the face of the enemy's fire, the dismounted grenadiers stationed in front, and the place of each man who fell being instantly supplied from the ranks behind. Maps were spread open before Napoleon: he was planning the movement which decided the action. Savary made his report, and told him of Desaix's position. "At what hour did you leave him?" said the First Consul, pulling out his watch. Having been informed, he continued, "Well, he cannot be far off; go, and tell him to form in that direction (pointing with his hand to a particular spot:) let him quit the main road, and make way for all those wounded men, who would only embarrass him, and perhaps draw his own soldiers after them." It was now three o'clock in the afternoon.

The aged Melas, believing the victory his own, had retired from the field, and left General Zach in command. At this critical moment, the division of Desaix appeared upon the plain. Outstripping the troops, this glorious lieutenant galloped up to the First Consul. He said the battle was lost, but there was yet time to gain another. Bonaparte immediately set about availing himself of the resources brought up by his beloved general.

Desaix's three demi-brigades were formed in front of San-Giuliano, a little way to the right of the main road. The 30th deployed in line, the 9th and 59th in close column, on the wings of the former. A slight undulation of ground concealed them from the enemy. On the right, rallying and somewhat recovered, were the shattered relics of Chambarlhac's and Gardanne's divisions under General Victor. To their right, in the plain, Lannes, whose retreat had been stopped; next to him the Consular Guard, and next again to that, Carra Saint-Cyr, who had maintained himself as near as possible to Castel-Ceriolo. In this position the army formed a long oblique line, from San-Giuliano to Castel-Ceriolo. In an interval between Desaix and Lannes, but somewhat more in the rear, was stationed Kellerman, with his cavalry. A battery of twelve pieces, the sole remains of the whole artillery of the army, was spread out in front of Desaix's line.

These dispositions made, the First Consul passed on horseback along the lines of his soldiers, speaking to several corps. "My friends," said he to them, "you have retreated far enough; recollect that I am in the habit of sleeping on the field of battle." After having re-animated his troops, who were re-assured by the arrival of their reserves, and burning to avenge the events of the morning, he gave the signal. The charge was beaten along the whole length of the lines.

The Austrians, who were rather in order of march than of battle, kept the high road. The column directed by M. de Zach came first; a little behind it came the centre, half deployed on the plain and facing Lannes. General Marmont suddenly unmasked his twelve pieces of cannon. A heavy discharge of grape-shot fell upon the head of the column, which was completely taken by surprise, and suspecting nothing less than further resistance, for they thought the French decidedly on their retreat. They had not yet recovered from their surprise, when Desaix put the 9th light infantry in movement. "Go and inform the First Consul," said he, to his aid-de camp, Savary, "that I am charging, and that I must be supported by the cavalry." Desaix, on horseback, charged in person at the head of his demi-brigade. He led it over the slight inequality of ground which concealed him from the view of the Austrians, and made them aware of his presence by a discharge of musketry at point blank distance. The Austrians poured in an answering volley; and Desaix fell on the instant, pierced by a bullet in the breast. "Conceal my death," said he to General Boudet, who was his chief of division, for it might, he thought, produce a panic among his men. Useless precaution of the young hero. He was seen to fall, and his soldiers, like those of Turenne, clamorously demanded to be led forward to avenge the death of their leader. The 9th light infantry, which on that day gained for itself the title of "*The Incomparable*," a distinction which it bore to the conclusion of the war; the 9th light infantry, after pouring its fire upon the enemy, formed in column, and fell upon the deep mass of the Austrians. At the sight, the two first regiments that led the march, surprised and confounded, fell back in disorder upon the second line, and disappeared amidst its ranks. Lattermann's column of grenadiers were now at the head, and received the shock as chosen troops might be expected to receive it. They were firm. The struggle extended to the two sides of the main road. The 9th light infantry was supported to the right by Victor's troops, which had rallied; to the left, by the 30th and 59th demi-brigades of Boudet's division, which followed the movement. Lattermann's grenadiers were defending themselves stoutly, though hard pressed, when suddenly a storm burst on their heads. General Kellermann, who, at the instance of Desaix, had received orders to charge, set off at full gallop, and passing between Lannes and Desaix, placed part of his squadron *en potence* to make head against the Austrian cavalry, whom he saw before him, and then, with the remainder, threw himself on the flank of the column of grenadiers, already assailed in front by Boudet's infantry. By this charge, which was executed with extraordinary vigor, the column was cut in two. Kellermann's dragoons sabred it to the right and left, till, pressed on every side, the unfortunate grenadiers threw down their arms. Two thousand of them surrendered themselves prisoners. At their head, General Zach himself was compelled to give up his sword, and in this manner the Austrians were deprived of any leader until the battle ended. But Kellermann did not stop here; he dashed on the dragoons of Lichtenstein and broke them! These recoiled in disorder on the centre of the Austrians, as it was forming in the plain, in front of Lannes, and there caused some confusion. At this moment Lannes advanced, pressed vigorously on the Austrians' centre, which was shaken, while the grenadiers of the Consular Guard and of Carra Saint-Cyr again bore down upon Castel-Ceriolo, from which they were not far distant. Along the whole line from San-Giuliano to Castel-Ceriolo, the French had now resumed the offensive; they marched forward, drunk with joy and enthusiasm, at seeing the victory again returning to their hands. Surprise and discouragement had passed to the side of the Austrians.

From the Giuliano to Castel-Ceriolo, the oblique line

of the French advancing at charging pace, pushed the enemy back, and compelled them to strive to escape by way of the bridges over the Bormida.

The slaughter of the Austrians was dreadful. Their army was thus thrown into the utmost confusion in a moment; and the victory, which had seemed quite secure to them at three o'clock, was completely won by the French at six. The pursuit continued far into the night, the mixed deaths and mangling upon the dark bridges being one confused and crowded horror; while the whole of the Austrians who had remained on the left bank were taken prisoners, or driven with headlong devastation into the Bormida. The waters ran a deep red with the blood of horses and of men, and presented in some parts a clotted surface of their mangled remains. Several entire battalions surrendered at discretion, and General Zach and all his staff were made prisoners.

The greater part of the French army encamped on the field of battle.

It was now about seven o'clock in the evening. The storm of conflict was hushed; but the ghastly burden of the field was revealed in all its horror by the glare of the watch-fires, and the light of the moon. The mangled dead were lying in heaps where the struggle had been most desperate; and the Bormida was a river of blood. Near the village of San Giuliano, a single officer could be seen walking among the bodies of the slain, leading his horse. For some time it seemed as if his search would be vain. Many of the bodies had been completely stripped by the enemy, and their features were mangled so that it was almost impossible to recognise them. Suddenly, however, Savary halted. In the midst of a circle of bodies, was stretched the manly form of Desaix, which the aid-de-camp recognised by the long, flowing hair which fell upon the neck, and the noble expression of the countenance, which had not altered in the agonies of death. The young man knelt down and wept over that form, like a child; for he had learned to look up to the heroic general as a father. He loved Desaix with that noble devotion which only the highest qualities can excite, and which is so admirable as to make us proud of our human nature. Savary gave free vent to his grief, and then, wrapping his cloak around the body, he lifted it upon his horse, and slowly returned with it to head-quarters. As he passed the watch-fires, the troops, who were in the highest spirits in consequence of the unexpected victory, recognised the body of Desaix, ceased their talk, and respectfully uncovered. At length, Savary brought his melancholy burden to the head-quarters of General Bonaparte, at Torre-di-Garofolo. Leaving the body in charge of some soldiers, he entered the old mansion, which had been selected for head-quarters, and was ushered into the presence of the First Consul. Bonaparte was seated amidst his principal officers, talking over the thrilling incidents of the day, and complimenting those who had particularly distinguished themselves, and there was scarcely one who did not bear sanguine marks of the fight.

"Your business, sir?" said Bonaparte, as Savary appeared.

"Your excellency, I have found the body of General Desaix, and brought it here to await your orders."

"Ah! Desaix!" interrupted Bonaparte in a tone full of sad feeling. He then appeared to indulge in mournful reflection, and there was a silence of a few minutes. He then continued, "This victory would have been, indeed, glorious, could I this evening embrace Desaix. I was going to make him a minister of war. I would have made him a prince, had I been able. As mild and modest in manners as he was firm and heroic in battle, he deserves a monument from France. You, and Rapp, are faithful aids.

"General Desaix was our father," said Savary.

"I will take you both for my aids."

This Savary was afterwards Duke of Rovigo. He was faithful to Napoleon to the end, and General Rapp deserves the same praise.

The First Consul now gave directions to Savary as to the immediate disposal of the body of Desaix. He designed that it should be embalmed as soon as possible, and placed in a fitting sarcophagus. Having received full and accurate directions, Savary retired.

"Most of you will recollect the critical position of affairs when Desaix arrived on the field," said the First Consul. "His coming was a happy thought. You all know the worth of his opinion. You drew around him and informed him of the events of the day. Yet most of you advised a retreat. I demurred, and asked the counsel of General Desaix. He cast his eye over the field, and then, taking out his watch and looking at the hour, replied, 'Yes, the battle is completely lost;

but it is only three o'clock. There is yet time to gain another.' These words encouraged me, and I immediately ordered those movements which gave us the victory. What is the loss of the enemy, according to your estimate, M. de Bourrienne?"

"In my opinion, they have lost about one-third of their army, which, before the battle, consisted of about twenty-eight thousand men. Besides that, General Haddick is killed, and a large number of their best generals are disabled by severe wounds. General Zach is a prisoner," replied the secretary.

"Aye; then they have paid a portion of their debt," said Bonaparte.

"But," said Victor, "our staff has suffered also; Generals Mainomy, Rivaud, Mahler, and Champeaux are wounded, and it is believed that Champeaux has received his mortal stroke."

"We have lost about one-fourth of the army, estimating it at twenty-eight thousand men," observed Bourrienne.

"But we have gained a great victory, and the Austrians are completely prostrated," said Bonaparte, quickly. "Let us now talk of our triumph. Little Kellermann made a fine charge—he did it just at the right time—we owe him much; see what trifles decide these affairs!"

Just then, General Kellermann, a young-looking man, of short stature and rather thin, but possessing a manly countenance, entered the room. Strange to say, the First Consul immediately changed his tone. As the gallant young general, whose charge had decided the day, approached the table at which Bonaparte was writing, he said, coldly, "You made a pretty good charge," and as a set off to this coldness, he turned to Bessieres, who commanded the horse grenadiers of the guard, and said to him audibly, "Bessieres, the guard has covered itself with glory." Kellermann bit his lips, and his eyes flashed; but in spite of reports to the contrary, he said nothing, and soon after retired from the room. The reason of the treatment extended to him by the First Consul has never been developed. It certainly does no credit to the general-in-chief. Kellermann had charged with about five hundred heavy cavalry. It was this handful of brave men who had cut in two the Austrian column. The guard made no charge till night-fall. Yet Kellermann was never raised to the rank of marshal.

Turning to Lannes, who seemed suffering from fatigue, the First Consul said,

"You ought to be fatigued, General Lannes. Never were witnessed efforts of bravery beyond those you have shown this day. I saw you, with your four demi-brigades. The enemy poured a storm of grape from eighty pieces of artillery upon your troops; yet you protracted your retreating fight three-quarters of a league for two whole hours. Every battle adds to the glory of the hero of Montebello."

Lannes was pleased at receiving praise from Bonaparte, who was the god of his idolatry. Yet it was nothing more than his due. A short time previous, he had defeated the Austrians at Montebello, in a long, bloody, hand-to-hand struggle, against greatly superior numbers, and yet he had almost surpassed the achievements of that desperate fight, when, to use his own terrific expression, "the bones were cracking in his division like hail upon a sky-light," by his unparalleled retreat at Marengo.

"I knew that so long as I maintained the right," said Lannes, "the army preserved a sure line of retreat by Sale towards the banks of the Po. I compelled the Austrians to fight, and lose a man for every inch of ground. I blew up the caissons I could not bring off."

It was late when the generals retired to their respective quarters, to sleep upon the laurels of Marengo. Even then the cavalry which had pursued the enemy had not all returned. The vanquished were allowed no repose. The First Consul slept but little that night. He knew that he should hear from the enemy, the next morning, and sat up, with his secretary Bourrienne, to fix upon the precise terms he should grant. He was not mistaken. The watch-fires of the victorious French had not been long extinguished, before Prince Lichtenstein, bearing a flag of truce, reached head-quarters. Hegotiations for a capitulation were commenced, and the convention of Alessandria was signed on the 15th of June.

It was agreed, in the first place, that there should be a suspension of arms in Italy, until such time as an answer should be received from Vienna. Should the convention be accepted, the Austrians were free to retire, with the honors of war, beyond the line of the Mincio. They bound themselves, in withdrawing, to restore to the French all the strongholds which they occupied. The castles of Tortona, Alessandria, Milan, Arona, and Placentia, were to be surrendered between the 16th and 20th of June—27th Prairial, and 1st of Messidor—the castles of Ceva aud Savona, the strongholds of Coni and Genoa, between the 16th and the 24th, and the fort of Urbia, on the 26th of June. The Austrian army was to be divided into three columns, which were to withdraw one after the other, and proportionally to the delivery of the strongholds. The immense military stores accumulated by M. de Melas, in Italy, were to be divided into two parts; the artillery of the Italian foundries was granted to the French army; the artillery of the Austrian foundries to the imperial army. The Imperialists, after having evacuated Lombardy as far as the Mincio, were to fall back behind the following line:—the Mincio, La Fossa, Maestra, the left bank of the Po, from Borgo-Forte to the mouth of that river, on the Adriatic. Peschiera and Mantua were to remain in possession of the Austrian army. It was stated, without explanation, that the detachment of this army, then actually in Tuscany, should continue to occupy that province. There could be no allusion made, in this capitulation, to the States of the Pope, or those of the King of Naples, because these potentates were strangers to the affairs of upper Italy. Should this convention not receive the emperor's ratification, ten days' notice was to be given of the resumption of hostilities. In the meantime, no detachment on the one side or the other, should be sent into Germany.

It is said that the First Consul was strongly affected

at the sight of the field of Marengo, on which so many brave men had fallen. Under the influence of these feelings he wrote a remakable letter to the Emperor of Austria.

"It is on the field of battle," said he to him, "amid the sufferings of a multitude of wounded, and surrounded by fifteen thousand corpses, that I beseech your majesty to listen to the voice of humanity, and not to suffer two brave nations to cut each other's throats for interests not their own. It is my part to press this on your majesty, being upon the very theatre of war. Your majesty's heart cannot feel it so keenly as does mine."

He then argued with peculiar eloquence for the cause of peace, and fortunately the conqueror of Marengo could contend with much grace for the restoration of tranquillity. He conquered the peace, and returned to Paris, to receive the homage of an admiring populace, who were now willing to concede to him the imperial crown.

THE CAMP-FIRE AT ULM.

FIVE years of peace, following the battle of Marengo, had enabled Napoleon Bonaparte to do much for France, and more for his own elevation. Under his wise and vigorous administration, the country made wonderful progress.

But the price she paid was first the Consulship for Life, and finally the imperial crown. Napoleon now appears as Emperor of France. His old brothers-in-arms, are Marshals. His beloved Josephine is an Empress. Besides, he has cherished designs of placing his brothers upon the thrones of Europe. Yet the man who has achieved all this greatness, is only thirty-eight years of age.

But now, (1805) the peace of Europe is again disturbed. The treaty of Amiens is alleged by both parties to have been violated, and once more vast armies traverse the fertile fields seeking for conflict. A coalition against Napoleon has been formed by Great Britain, Austria, and Russia. Napoleon has formed the plan of a campaign on a gigantic scale, and has executed a part of the proposed scheme with a rapidity and precision that has astonished the enemy. By a brilliant series of manœuvres, he has completely surrounded the Austrian army, commanded by General Mack, in the city of Ulm, (October 13.) In several great actions, the French had already captured twenty thousand Austrian troops, and Napoleon now has the satisfaction of knowing that thirty thousand more are within his reach.

On the 13th, Napoleon (who expected that Mack would rouse himself with one last effort to avoid a surrender) made an exciting address to the troops, on the bridge of the Lech, amid the most intense cold, the ground being covered with snow, and the troops sunk to their knees in mud. He warned them to expect a great battle, and explained to them the desperate condition of the enemy. He was answered with acclamations, and repeated shouts of "Vive l'Empereur." In listening to his exciting words, the soldiers forgot their fatigues and privations, and were impatient to rush into the fight.

Bernadotte entered Munich on the 14th of October, taking eight hundred prisoners. On the same day, Marshal Ney forced the strong position of Elchingen, taking three thousand prisoners and many pieces of cannon; and the Emperor's head-quarters were fixed there, in the evening. The French soldiers were in a state of great excitement from these rapid successes, and were with difficulty restrained.

From the height of the Abbey of Elchingen, Napoleon now beheld the city of Ulm at his feet, commanded on every side by his cannon; his victorious troops ready for the assault, and the great Austrian army cooped up within the walls. He expected a desperate sally, and prepared the soldiers for a general engagement; but four days passed without any movement whatever. Meanwhile, his own troops clamored for the assault, but he chose to wait in vigilant patience for the result. A scene of horrible carnage and the probable destruction of a fine city would have been the consequences of his acting differently; being what he would have called "unnecessary evils," and therefore criminal in his eyes. The weather continued dreadful; the rain fell incessantly, and the soldiers were often up to their knees in mud. The Emperor only kept his feet out of the water in his bivouac, by means of a plank. He was in this situation when Prince Maurice

Lichtenstein was brought before him, with a flag of truce from General Mack. The looks of the prince evidently showed that he did not expect to have found the Emperor there in person; otherwise it is probable he would not have brought such a proposition as that which he delivered. He came commissioned to treat for the evacuation of Ulm, with permission for the Austrian army to return to Vienna. The Emperor could not help smiling as he listened to him. "I have not forgotten Marengo," he replied; "I suffered M. de Melas to go, and in two months Moreau had to fight his troops, in spite of the most solemn promises to conclude peace. You will be forced to surrender, for want of provisions, in eight days. The Russians have scarcely reached Bohemia. There is the capitulation of your general at Memingen, his whole garrison becoming prisoners of war: carry it to General Mack; I will accept no other conditions." The same evening General Mack sent his surrender to the Emperor, and on the following morning the capitulation was signed.

On the 20th of October, the French army was drawn up on the heights, overlooking the fine city of Ulm, to receive the surrender, according to the conditions. The rain had ceased, and the sky was bright and clear. The dress and accoutrements of the French troops, and especially those of the cavalry, shone resplendent in the sun. The Emperor was posted on a slight eminence in front of the centre of his army. He had caused a large fire to be kindled there, for the air was intensely cold. A short distance in the rear, that faithful Mameluke who always accompanied Napoleon after the Egyptian campaign, held the bridle of a restless horse. His gaudy, Asiatic costume, was in singular contrast with that of the French soldiers. The French marshals and generals were grouped in the vicinity of the fire. Among them were the commanding forms of Ney, Lannes, Murat, Davoust, Duroc, Bernadotte, Bessiere, Soult and Dupont—a brotherhood of daring valor. The calm, immovable countenance of Marshal Soult was in strange contrast with the more vivacious faces near him, and bespoke the cool, steady mind of that skilful general. The Emperor stood, as usual, with his hands behind him, and his head slightly bent. His figure had grown stout, and had a decided tendency to corpulency. The countenance was stern, but the eyes were unquiet, and his mind was evidently very busy, as usual. In every lineament could be traced that keen, daring genius, which had raised the lieutenant of artillery to an imperial throne.

It was a glorious day for the French. Their drums beat, and their bands poured forth the swelling strains of triumph. The gates of Ulm were opened; and then the long line of white uniforms marked the egress of the Austrians. They advanced in silence, becoming the dejection of the vanquished, filed off slowly, and went, corps by corps, to lay down their arms upon the plain between them and the heights on which the French army appeared. The ceremony lasted the whole day. In the morning, General Mack and his principal officers, to the number of sixteen, advanced to meet the conqueror at the fire near which he stood. He received the conquered generals with respect, and addressed many remarks to them; but the officers were too deeply humiliated to reply. To General Mack, he said—

"I must complain of the iniquitous proceeding of your government, in coming without any declaration of war to *seize me by the throat.* The Aulic Council would have done better, if, instead of mixing up Asiatic hordes in European quarrels, it had joined with me to repel Russian encroachment." Mack bowed, but made no reply.

During the interview, a general officer, more remarkable for his petulance than his wit, repeated aloud an expression as coming from one of the soldiers, throwing ridicule upon the vanquished. Napoleon, whose ear was quick to catch the words, immediately sent Savary to tell the officer to retire, saying then to those near him, "He must have little respect for himself, who insults men in misfortune!"

All the officers were allowed to return home, on giving their word of honor not to serve against France until a general exchange of prisoners should take place. The men were to be marched into France, to be distributed throughout the agricultural districts of the country, where their work in the field might supply the place of that of the conscripts required for the army. The unfortunate Mack was immediately consigned to a dungeon on the charge of treachery, upon his return to Vienna.

The capitulation of Ulm gave Napoleon the remainder of the Austrian army, which had numbered fifty thousand men. The campaign was, perhaps, unexampled in the annals of war. Of the French army, scarcely fifteen hundred men were killed and wounded; while the enemy had lost an immense number of men in battle, fifty thousand excellent troops by capitulation, two hundred cannon, ninety flags, and a large number of horses. Such were the glorious results of Napoleon's skilful manœuvres and rapid movements.

The Emperor slept that night at Elchingen. Joy pervaded the French camp. The troops were now more strongly convinced than ever, that their Emperor was invincible.

BATTLE OF AUSTERLITZ.

THE CAMP-FIRE AT AUSTERLITZ.

THE victory of Austerlitz is considered by many competent judges as the most splendid triumph ever gained by Napoleon; and the "sun of Austerlitz," is a watchword with the French soldiery to the present day. The scene of this great battle is in the vicinity of the small seignoral town of Austerlitz, situated on the Littawa, in Moravia.

Napoleon, with that military tact which he had received from nature, and which he had so greatly improved by experience, had adopted, among other positions which he might have taken about Brunn, one which could not fail to insure to him the most important results, under the supposition that he should be attacked—a supposition which had become a certainty.

The mountains of Moravia, which connect the mountains of Bohemia with those of Hungary, subside successively towards the Danube, so completely that near that river Moravia presents but one wide plain. In the environs of Brunn, the capital of the province, they are not of greater altitude than high hills, and are covered with dark firs. Their waters, retained for want of drains, form numerous ponds, and throw themselves by various streams into the Morawa, or March, and by the Morawa and the Danube.

All these characters are found together in the position between Brunn and Austerlitz, which Napoleon has rendered forever celebrated. The high road of Moravia, running from Vienna to Brunn, rises in a direct line to the northward, then, in passing from Brunn to Olmutz, descends abruptly to the right, that is to the east, thus forming a right angle with its first direction. In the angle is situated the position in question. It commences on the left towards the Olmutz road, with heights studded with firs; it then runs to the right in an oblique direction towards the Vienna road, and after subsiding gradually, terminates in ponds full of deep water in winter. Along this position, and in front of it, runs a rivulet, which has no name known in geography, but which, in part of its course, is called Goldbach by the people of the country. It runs through the little villages of Girzikowitz, Puntowitz, Kobelnitz, Sokolnitz, and Telnitz, and, sometimes forming marshes, sometimes confined in channels, terminates in the ponds above mentioned, which are called the ponds of Satschau and Menitz.

Concentrated with all his forces on this ground, defended on the one hand upon the wooded hills of Moravia, and particularly upon a rounded knoll to which the soldiers of Egypt gave the name of the Centon, defended on the other, upon the ponds of Satschau and Menitz—thus covering by his left the Olmutz road, by his right the Vienna road—Napoleon was in a condition to accept with advantage a decisive battle. He meant not, however, to confine his operations to self-defence, for he was accustomed to reckon upon greater results; he had divined, as though he had read them, the plans framed at great length by General Weirother. The Austro-Russians, having no chance of wresting from him the *point d'appui* which he found for his left in the high wooded hills, would be tempted to turn his right, which was not close to the ponds, and to take the Vienna road from him. There was sufficient inducement for this step; for Napoleon, if he lost that road, would have no other resource but to retire into Bohemia. The rest of his forces, hazarded towards Vienna, would be obliged to ascend separately the valley of the Danube. The French army, thus divided, would find itself doomed to a retreat, eccentric, perilous, nay, even disastrous, if it should fall in with the Prussians by the way.

Napoleon was perfectly aware that such must be the plan of the enemy. Accordingly, after concentrating his army towards his left and the heights, he left towards his right, that is towards Sokolnitz, Telnitz, and the ponds, a space almost unguarded. He thus invited the Russians to persevere in their plans. But it was not precisely there that he prepared the mortal stroke for them. The ground facing him presented a feature from which he hoped to derive a decisive result.

Beyond the stream that ran in front of the position, the ground spread at first, opposite to the left, into a slightly undulated plain, through which passed the Olmutz road; then, opposite to the centre, it rose successively, and at last formed facing the right a plateau, called the plateau of Pratzen, after the name of a village situated half-way up, in the hollow of a ravine. This plateau terminated on the right in rapid declivities towards the ponds, and at the back in a gentle slope towards Austerlitz, the chateau of which appeared at some distance.

There were to be seen considerable forces; there a multitude of fires blazed at night, and a great movement of men and horses was observable by day. On these appearances, Napoleon had no longer any doubt of the designs of the Austro-Russians. They intended evidently to descend from the position which they occupied, and, crossing the Goldbach rivulet, between the ponds and the French right, to cut them off from the Vienna road. But, for this reason, it was resolved to take the offensive in turn, to cross the rivulet at the villages of Girzikowitz and Puntowitz, to ascend to the plateau of Pratzen while the Russians were leaving it, and to take possession of it. In case of success, the enemy's army would be cut in two; one part would be thrown to the left into the plain crossed by the Olmutz road; the other to the right into the ponds. Thenceforward the battle could not fail to be disastrous for the Austro-Russians. But, for this effect, it was requisite that they should not blunder by halves. The prudent, nay even timid attitude of Napoleon, exciting their silly confidence, would induce them to commit the entire blunder.

Agreeably to these ideas, Napoleon made his dispositions. Expecting for two days past to be attacked, he had ordered Bernadotte to quit Iglau on the frontier of Bohemia, to leave there the Bavarian division which he had brought with him, and to hasten by forced marches to Brunn. He had ordered Marshal Davoust to march Friant's and if possible Gudin's division towards the abbey of Gross Raigern, situated on the road from Vienna to Brunn, opposite to the ponds. In consequence of these orders, Bernadotte marched, and had arrived on the 1st of December. General Friant, being alone apprised in time, because General Gudin was at a greater distance towards Presburg, had set out immediately, and travelled in forty-eight hours the thirty-six leagues which separate Vienna from Gross Raigern. The soldiers sometimes dropped on the road, exhausted with fatigue; but at the least sound, imagining that they heard the cannon, they rose with ardor to hasten to the assistance of their comrades, engaged, they said, in a bloody battle. On the night of the 1st of December, which was extremely cold, they bivouacked at Gross Raigern, a league and a half from the field of battle. Never did troops on foot perform so astonishing a march; for it is a march of eighteen leagues a day for two successive days.

On the 1st of December, Napoleon, reinforced by Bernadotte's corps and Friant's division, could number sixty-five or seventy thousand men, present under arms, against ninety thousand men, Russians and Austrians, likewise present under arms.

At his left he placed Lannes, in whose corps Caffarelli's division supplied the place of Gazan's. Lannes, with the two divisions of Suchet and Caffarelli, was to occupy the Olmutz road, and to fight in the undulated plain outspread on either side of that road. Napoleon gave him, moreover, Murat's cavalry, comprising the cuirassiers of Generals d'Hautpoul and Nansouty, the dragoons of General Walther and Beaumont, and the chasseurs of Generals Milhaud and Kellermann. The level surface of the ground led him to expect a prodigious engagement of cavalry on this spot. On the knoll of the Centon, which commands this part of the ground, and is topped by a chapel called the chapel of Bosenitz, he placed the 17th light artillery, commanded by General Claparede, with eighteen pieces of cannon, and made him take an oath to defend this position to the death.

At the centre, behind the Goldbach rivulet, he ranged Vandamme's and St. Hilaire's divisions, which belong to the corps of Marshal Soult. He destined them to cross that stream at the villages of Girzikowitz and Puntowitz, and to gain possession of the plateau of Pratzen, when the proper moment should arrive. A little further behind the marsh of Kobelnitz and the chateau of Kobelnitz, he placed Marshal Soult's third division, that of General Legrand. He reinforced it with two battalions of tirailleurs, known by the names of chasseurs of the Po and Corsican chasseurs, and by a detachment of light cavalry, under General Margaron. This division was to have only the third of the line and the Corsican chasseurs at Telnitz, the nearest point to the ponds, and to which Napoleon was desirous of drawing the Russians. Far in rear, at the distance of a league and a half, was posted Friant's division at Gross Raigern.

Having ten divisions of infantry, Napoleon, therefore, presented but six of them in line. Behind Marshals Lannes and Soult, he kept in reserve Oudinot's grenadiers, separated on this occasion from Lannes's corps, the corps of Bernadotte, composed of Drouet's and Rivaud's divisions, and, lastly, the imperial guard. He thus kept at hand a mass of twenty-five thousand men, to move to any point where they might be needed, and particularly to the heights of Pratzen, in order to take those heights at any cost, if the Russians should not have cleared them sufficiently.

Such were the skilful dispositions of the Emperor, and having completed what may be called the foundation of victory, he issued a confident proclamation to his soldiers, as follows:

"Soldiers—The Russian army appears before you to avenge the Austrian army of Ulm. They are the same battalions that you beat at Hollabrunn, and that you have since been constantly pursuing to this spot.

"The positions which we occupy are formidable; and while they are marching to turn my right, they will present their flank to me.

"Soldiers, I shall myself direct your battalions. I shall keep out of the fire, if, with your usual bravery, you throw disorder and confusion into the enemy's ranks. But, if the victory should be for a moment uncertain, you will see your Emperor the foremost to expose himself to danger. For victory must not hang doubtful on this day, most particularly, when the honor of the French infantry, which so deeply concerns the honor of the whole nation, is at stake.

"Let not the ranks be thinned upon pretence of carrying away the wounded, and let every one be thoroughly impressed with this thought, that it behoves us to conquer these hirelings of England, who are animated with such bitter hatred against our nation.

"This victory will put an end to the campaign, and we shall then be able to return to our winter-quarters, where we shall be joined by the new armies which are forming in France, and then the peace which I shall make will be worthy of my people, of you, and of myself.

NAPOLEON."

Napoleon had passed the whole day on horseback, and had himself placed every division in position, inspecting every position. All his marshals dined with him, and received his careful and precise orders for the operations of the next day. He then once more glanced at the position of the Russian and Austrian armies, and a smile illumined his features as he said to his marshals,

"Before to-morrow night that army will be in my power. Since the Czar refuses to negotiate for a peace, we must drub him into it."

He then entered a rude hut, which his soldiers had constructed for him, and stretched himself upon some straw to repose. A hard couch for an emperor! Yet there Napoleon fell into so deep a sleep that his aid-de-camp, Savary, was obliged to shake him, in order to wake him up, to listen to a report which he had ordered to be brought to him. Rousing himself, he left the hut, accompanied by his aid, and proceeded to visit the bivouacs of the army. The night was cold and dark; and the Emperor had reason to believe that he could go among the soldiers without being noticed. But he had only proceeded a few steps before he was discovered, and in a few moments, the whole line was illuminated with torches of straw, while the air was filled with acclamations of "Vive l'Empereur!" It was a glorious sight, and the glare of the torches must have astonished the enemy. That tremendous shout must have told Kutusoff, the Prussian general, that he would be compelled to fight an enemy, full of spirit and confidence.

As Napoleon passed along, one of the old grenadiers,

a veteran of Italy, stepped forward, and accosted him with an air of republican familiarity and kindly patronage.

"Sire," said this old soldier, "you will have no need to expose yourself to danger; I promise you, in the name of the grenadiers of the army, that you will only have to fight with your eyes, and that we will bring you all the flags and cannon of the Russian army, to celebrate the anniversary of your coronation."

The Emperor was delighted at the spirit displayed by the troops, and, in accordance with their general request, he promised to keep beyond the reach of the enemy's guns.

Sir Walter Scott finely remarks upon this: "Napoleon," says he, "promises that he will keep his person out of the reach of the fire: thus showing the full confidence that the assurance of his personal safety would be considered as great an encouragement to the troops as the usual protestations of sovereigns and leaders, that they will be in the front, and share the dangers of the day. This is, perhaps, the strongest proof possible of the complete and confidential understanding which subsisted between Napoleon and his soldiers. Yet there have not been wanting those who have thrown the imputation of cowardice on the victor of a hundred battles, and whose reputation was so well established amongst those troops, who must have been the best judges, that his attention to the safety of his person was requested by them, and granted by him, as a favor to his army."

The Emperor was on the field by one o'clock in the

morning, to get an army under arms in silence. A thick fog, through which the light of the torches could not penetrate to the distance of ten paces, enveloped all the bivouacs; but he knew the ground as well as the environs of Paris. His army, amounting in all to about seventy thousand men, was arranged as follows. The two divisions of Marshal Soult, placed on a vast plateau, formed the right; the division of united grenadiers, drawn up in line behind, constituting the reserve of the right. The two divisions of Marshal Bernadotte, in line with the united grenadiers, formed the centre of the army. The left wing was composed of the two divisions of Marshal Lannes; the infantry of the guard forming the reserve of the left. In advance of the centre, and between the right and left wings, was posted the whole of the cavalry, under the command of Murat. The divisions of hussars and chasseurs were entrusted to Kellermann; the dragoons, to Valther and Beaumont. The cuirassiers and eighty pieces of light artillery formed the reserve of the cavalry. The right of the army rested on some long and narrow defiles formed by ponds; the left, on the strongly fortified position of the Centon. The two divisions of Marshal Davoust were posted on the extreme right, beyond the ponds, to face the left wing of the Russians, which had been extended, as we have said, to a dangerous distance from their centre, and intended, as the Emperor perceived, to commence the battle with an attempt to turn his right. The Emperor himself, with Berthier, Junot, and the whole of his staff, occupied a commanding position, as the reserve of the army, with ten battalions of the imperial guard, and ten battalions of grenadiers, commanded by Oudinot and Duroc. This reserve was ranged in two lines, in columns, by battalions, having in their intervals forty pieces of cannon served by the artillery of the guard. With this reserve, equal to turning the fate of almost any battle, he held himself ready to act wherever occasion should require.

As the day dawned, the mist which had overhung all the dreadful show, began slowly to ascend, like a vast curtain, from the broad plain below. The sun rose in unclouded and majestic brilliancy; and dissipating all remains of the vapors, disclosed to view the great Russian army, commanded by Field-Marshal Kutusoff, to the number of eighty thousand men, ranged in six divisions, on the opposite heights of Pratzen. The magnificence of the sunrise of this eventful morning, enhanced at the time by the previous dense mist, and by the national memories ever since, has caused the "sun of Austerlitz" to become proverbial with the people of France. The two emperors of Russia and Austria were witnesses of the fierce contest; being stationed on horseback on the heights of Austerlitz. As the first rays of the sun were flung from the horizon, the Emperor Napoleon appeared in front of his army, surrounded by his marshals, and formed every division, both of infantry and cavalry, into columns. A brisk fire had just commenced on the extreme right, where Davoust was already at his post; and the Russians began to put themselves in motion to descend from the heights upon the plain. The marshals who surrounded the Emperor importuned him to begin. "How long will it take you," said he to Soult, "to crown those opposite heights which the Russians are now abandoning?" "One hour," answered the marshal. "In that case, we will wait yet a quarter of an hour," replied the Emperor. The cannonade increased, denoting that the attack had become serious. The extreme of the Russian left had commenced its movement to turn the right flank of the French army, but had encountered the formidable resistance of Davoust's two divisions, with whom they were just engaged. Napoleon now dismissed all the marshals to their posts, and ordered them to begin.

The whole of the right and left wings at once moved forward, in columns, to the foot of the Russian position. They marched as if to exercise, halting at times to rectify their distances and directions; while the words of command of the individual officers were distinctly heard. The two divisions of Marshal Soult came first within reach of the enemy's fire. The division commanded by General Vandamme overthrew the opposing column, and was master of its position and artillery in an instant; the other, commanded by General St Hilaire, had to sustain a tremendous fire, which lasted for two hours, and brought every one of its battalions into action. The Emperor now dispatched the united grenadiers, and one of Marshal Bernadotte's division, to support those of Soult, while Lannes had engaged the right of the Russians, and effectually prevented them frem moving to the assistance of their left, which was wholly engaged by the tremendous attack we have described, and entirely cut off from their centre. The extreme left of the Russians, which had begun the battle, perceiving the fatal mistake which had been made, attempted to re-ascend the Pratzer, but were so desperately pressed by Davoust, that they were compelled to fight where they stood, without daring either to advance or retire.

Marshal Soult now ordered his division, under Vandamme, supported by one of Bernadotte's divisions, to make a change of direction by the right flank, for the purpose of turning all the Russian troops which still resisted St. Hilaire's division. The movement was completely successful; and Soult's two divisions crowned the heights to which the Emperor had pointed before the battle began.

The right wing of the Russian army was meanwhile sustaining the tremendous onset of Lannes with both his divisions. The fight raged in that quarter throughout the whole of the operations we have detailed; but at this point, Bernadotte's division being no longer required to support those of Soult, the Emperor ordered the centre of the army to support the left. The Russian right was now entirely broken; the French cavalry by desperate and repeated charges completed the rout, and pursued the fugitives, who took the road to Austerlitz, till nightfall. Bernadotte, after pursuing the Russian infantry a full league, returned to his former position; nobody knew why. Had he, on the contrary, continued marching another half hour, he would have entirely intercepted the retreat, and taken or destroyed the whole of the Russian right. As it was, their flight was disastrous in the extreme: they were forced into a hollow, where numbers attempted to escape across a frozen lake; but the ice proving too weak for them, gave way, and the horrible scene which ensued—the crashing of the broken fragments, the thundering of the artillery, and the groans and shrieks of wounded and drowning men—baffles the imagination.

Marshal Soult, now changing his position again by the right flank, descended the heights, having traversed a complete semi-circle, and took the Russian extreme left in the rear. The Emperor of Russia, who perceived the imminent danger of his whole army, dispatched his fine regiment of Russian guards, supported by a strong force of artillery, to attack Soult. Their desperate charge broke one of the French regiments. It was at this crisis that Napoleon brought his reserve into action. Bessieres, at the head of the imperial guard, rushed with irresistible fury into the fight. The Russians were entirely broken; their army, surprised in a flank movement, had been cut into as many separate masses as there were columns brought up to attack it. They fled in disorder, and the victory of Austerlitz was decided.

It was with the utmost difficulty that the two emperors of Russia and Austria effected their personal escape. The Emperor Alexander lost all his artillery, baggage, and standards; twenty thousand prisoners, and upwards of twenty thousand killed and wounded. In the precipitate flight, the wounded were abandoned to their fate. Kutusoff, however, with laudable humanity, left placards in the French language, on the doors of the churches and the barns towards which they had crept, inscribed with these words:—"I recommend these unfortunate men to the generosity of the Emperor Napoleon, and the humanity of his brave soldiers."

In attempting to escape across some frozen ponds, the Russians broke through, and a large number of them were drowned. An eye-witness, General Langeron, says, "I have previously seen some lost battles, but I had no conception of such a defeat."

Napoleon, who had participated in the pursuit, returned about night-fall. He was received with shouts by his triumphant troops, and they could scarcely be prevented from taking him in their arms. He soon commanded silence, and set about relieving the wounded, who actually covered the field. He administered brandy with his own hand to some suffering Russians, who could only repay him with a blessing, and gave orders that all the wounded should be attended to as speedily as possible. The troops had already given a name to the battle, that of the "Three Emperors." But Napoleon himself gave this great conflict the name of the village near which it was fought. He issued the following proclamation, immediately after victory had been achieved.

"Soldiers—I am satisfied with you: in the battle of Austerlitz you have justified all that I expected from your intrepidity. You have decorated your eagles with immortal glory. An army of one hundred thousand men, commanded by the Emperors of Russia and Austria, has been in less than four hours either cut in pieces or dispersed. Those who escaped your weapons are drowned in the lakes.

"Forty colors, the standards of the imperial guard of Russia, one hundred and twenty pieces of cannon, more than thirty thousand prisoners, are the result of this ever-celebrated battle. That infantry, so highly vaunted and superior in number, could not withstand your shocks, and thenceforward you have no rivals to fear. Thus, in two months, this third coalition has been vanquished and dissolved. Peace cannot now be far distant, but, as I promised my people, before I passed the Rhine, I will make only such a peace as gives us guarantees and insures rewards to our allies.

"Soldiers, when all that is necessary to secure the welfare and the prosperity of our country is accomplished, I will lead you back to France: there you will be the object of my tenderest concern. My people will see you again with joy, and it will be sufficient to say, I was at the battle of Austerlitz, for them to reply, there is a brave man.

"NAPOLEON."

THE CAMP-FIRE AT PALENY.

THE disaster at Austerlitz affected the Emperors Francis and Alexander very differently. Alexander was deeply dejected; but Francis was tranquil. Under the common misfortune, he had at least the consolation, that the Russians could no longer allege that the cowardice of the Austrians constituted all the glory of Napoleon. The two emperors retreated precipitately over the plain of Moravia, amidst profound darkness, separated from their household, and liable to be insulted through the barbarity of their own soldiers. Francis took it upon himself to send their gallant Prince John of Litchtenstein to Napoleon, to solicit an armistice, with a promise to sign a peace in a few days. He commissioned him, also, to express to Napoleon, his wish to have an interview with him at the advanced posts of the army. The French Emperor, having returned to his head-quarters at Posoritz, there received Prince John. He treated him as a conqueror full of courtesy, and agreed to an interview with the Emperor of Austria. But an armistice was not to be granted until the Emperors had met and explained themselves.

Napoleon hastened to recall his columns to Nasiedlowitz and Goding. Marshal Davoust, reinforced by the junction of Friant's whole division, and by the arrival in line of Gudin's division, had lost no time, thanks to his nearer position to the Hungary road. He set out in pursuit of the Russians, and pressed them closely. He intended to overtake them before the passage of the Morava, and to cut off perhaps a part of their army. After marching on the 3d, he was, on the morning of the 4th, in sight of Goding and nearly up with them. The greatest confusion prevailed in Goding. Beyond that place there was a mansion belonging to the Emperor of Germany, that of Holitsch, where the two allied sovereigns had taken refuge. The perturbation there was as great as at Goding. The Russian officers continued to hold the most unbecoming language respecting the Austrians. They laid the blame of the common defeat on them, as if they ought not to have attributed it to their own presumption, to the incapacity of their generals, and to the levity of their government. The Austrians, moreover, had behaved quite as well as the Russians on the field of battle.

The two vanquished monarchs were very cool towards each other. The Emperor Francis wished to confer with the Emperor Alexander, before he went to the interview agreed upon with Napoleon. Both thought that they ought to solicit an armistice and peace, for it was impossible to continue the struggle. Alexander was desirous, though he did not acknowledge it, that himself and his army should be saved as soon as possible from the consequences of an impetuous pursuit, such as might be apprehended from Napoleon. As for the conditions, he left his ally to settle them as he pleased. The Emperor Francis alone having to defray the expenses of the war, the conditions on which peace should be signed concerned him exclusively. Some time before, the Emperor Alexander, setting himself up for the arbiter of Europe, would have insisted that those conditions concerned him also. His pride was less exigent since the battle of the 2d of December.

The Emperor Francis accordingly set out for Nasiedlowitz, a village and there,near the mill of Paleny, between Nasiedlowitz and Urschitz, amidst the French and the Austrian advanced posts, he found Napoleon waiting for him, before a bivouac fire kindled by his soldiers. Napoleon had had the politeness to arrive first. He went to meet the Emperor Francis, received him as he alighted from his carriage and embraced him. The Austrian monarch, encouraged by the welcome of his all-powerful foe, had a long conversation with him. The principal officers of the two armies, standing aside, beheld with great curiosity the extraordinary spectacle of the successor of the Cæsars vanquished and soliciting peace of the crowned soldier, whom the French Revolution had raised to the pinnacle of human greatness.

Francis wore the brilliant costume of an Austrian field-marshal, and was a monarch of dignified aspect.

Napoleon apologized to the Emperor Francis for receiving him in such a place. "Such are the palaces," said he, "which your majesty has obliged me to inhabit for these three months."—"The abode in them," replied the Austrian monarch, "makes you so thriving, that you have no right to be angry with me for it." The conversation then turned upon the general state of affairs, Napoleon insisting that he had been forced into the war against his will at a moment when he least expected it, and when he was exclusively engaged with England; the Emperor of Austria affirming that he had been urged to take arms solely by the designs of France in regard to Italy. Napoleon declared that, on the conditions already specified to M. de Giulay, and which he had no need to repeat, he was ready to sign a peace. The Emperor Francis, without explaining himself on this subject, wished to know how Napoleon was disposed in regard to the Russian army. Napoleon first required that the Emperor Francis should separate his cause from that of the Emperor Alexander, and that the Russian army should retire by regulated marches from the Austrian territories, and promised to grant him an armistice on this condition. As for peace with Russia, he added, that would be settled afterwards, for this peace concerned him alone. "Take my advice," said Napoleon to the Emperor Francis, "do not mix up your cause with that of the Emperor Alexander. Russia alone can now wage only a *fancy war* in Europe. Vanquished, she retires to her deserts, and you, you pay with your provinces the costs of the war." The forcible language of Napoleon expressed but too well the state of things in Europe between that great empire and the rest of the continent. The Emperor Francis pledged his word as a man and a sovereign not to renew the war, and above all to listen no more to the suggestions of powers which had nothing to lose in the struggle. He agreed to an armistice for himself—and for the Emperor Alexander, an armistice, the condition of which was that the Russians should retire by regulated marches—and that the Austrian cabinet should immediately send negotiators empowered to sign a separate peace with France.

The two emperors parted with reiterated demonstrations of cordiality. Napoleon handed into his carriage that monarch whom he had just called his brother, and remounted his horse to return to Austerlitz.

General Savary was sent to suspend the march of Davoust's corps. He first proceeded to Holitsch, with the suite of the Emperor Francis, to learn whether the Emperor Alexander acceded to the proposed conditions. He saw the latter, around whom every thing was much changed since the mission on which he was sent to him a few days before. "Your master," said Alexander to him, "has shown himself very great. I acknowledge all the power of his genius, and, as for myself, I shall retire, since my ally is satisfied." General Savary conversed for some time with the young czar on the late battle, explained to him how the French army, inferior in number to the Russian army, had nevertheless appeared superior on all points, owing to the art of manœuvring which Napoleon possessed in so eminent a degree. He courteously added that with experience Alexander, in his turn, would become a warrior, but that so difficult an art was not to be learned in a day. After these flatteries to the vanquished monarch, he set out for Goding to stop Marshal Davoust, who had rejected all the proposals for a suspension of arms, and was ready to attack the relics of the Russian army. To no purpose he had been assured in the name of the Emperor of Russia himself that an armistice was negotiating between Napoleon and the Emperor of Austria. He would not on any account abandon his prey. But General Savary stopped him with a formal order from Napoleon. These were the last musket-shots fired during that unexampled campaign. The troops of the several nations separated to go into winter-quarters, awaiting what should be decided by the negotiators of the belligerent powers.

THE CAMP-FIRE AT JENA.

ENA was one of Napoleon's most decisive fields. There, in the conflict of a day, Prussia, who had dared to defy a power which had brought Austria and Russia to the dust, was completely annihilated. There the descendants of the great Frederick reaped the bitter consequences of his weak presumption. At Jena, the valley of the Saale begins to widen.

The right bank is low, damp and covered with meadows. The left bank presents steep heights, whose peaked tops overlook the town of Jena, and are ascended by narrow, winding ravines, overhung with wood. On the left of Jena, a gorge more open, less abrupt, called the Muhlthal, has become the passage through which the high road from Jena to Weimar has been carried. This road first keeps along the bottom of the Mulhthal, then rises in form of a spiral staircase, and opens upon the plateaux in rear. It would have required a fierce assault to force this pass.

The principal of the heights that overlook the town of Jena is called Landgrafenberg, and, since the memorable events of which it has been the theatre, it has received from the inhabitants the name of Napoleonsberg. It is the highest in these parts. Napoleon and Lannes, surveying from that height the surrounding country, with their backs turned to Jena, beheld on their right the Saale running in a deep, winding, wooded gorge, to Naumberg, which is six or seven leagues from Jena. Before them they saw undulated plateaux, extending to a distance, and subsiding by a gentle slope to the little valley of the Ilm, at the extremity of which is situated the town of Weimar. They perceived on their left the high road from Jena to Weimar, rising by a series of slopes from the gorge of the Muhlthal to these plateaux, and running in a straight line to Weimar. These slopes, somewhat resembling a sort of snail's shell, have thence received in German the appellation of the *Schneeke* (snail.)

It was in September, 1806, that Napoleon, having

set all his divisions in motion, left Paris and put himself at the head of his grand army. The Prussians were superior in numbers, well disciplined, and full of spirit. They numbered between one hundred and thirty thousand and one hundred and forty thousand men. The cavalry especially, bore a high reputation, which, however, as we shall see, it could not sustain. The French Emperor had an army of one hundred and seventy thousand men in the field, with a power of concentrating one hundred thousand of them within a few hours.

On learning that the Prussian army was changing its position and advancing from Erfurt upon Weimar, with a view to approach the banks of the Saale, Napoleon manœuvred to meet the changes of the enemy.

They might be coming thither with one of the two following intentions : either to occupy the bridge over the Saale at Naumburg, over which passes the great central road of Germany, in order to retire upon the Elbe, while covering Leipzig and Dresden ; or to approach the course of the Saale, for the purpose of defending its banks against the French. To meet this double contingency, Napoleon took a first precaution, which was to dispatch Marshal Davoust immediately to Naumburg, with orders to bar the passage of the bridge there with the twenty-six thousand men of the third corps. He sent Murat, with the cavalry, along the banks of the Saale, to watch its course, and to push reconnoisances as far as Leipzig. He directed Marshal Bernadotte upon Naumburg, with instructions to support Marshal Davoust in case of need. He sent Marshals Lannes and Augereau to Jena itself. His object was to make himself master immediately of the two principal passages of the Saale, those at Naumburg and Jena, either to stop the Prussian army there, if it should design to cross and to retire to the Elbe, or to go and seek it on the heights bordering that river, if it purposed to remain there on the defensive. As for himself, he continued with Marshals Ney and Soult, within reach of Naumburg and Jena, ready to march for either point according to circumstances.

On the morning of the 13th, he learned by more circumstantial accounts that the enemy was definitively approaching the Saale, with the yet uncertain resolution of fighting a defensive battle on its banks, or of crossing and pushing on to the Elbe. It was in the direction from Weimar to Jena that the largest assemblage appeared. Without losing a moment, Napoleon mounted his horse to proceed to Jena. He gave himself his instructions to Marshals Soult and Ney, and enjoined them to be at Jena in the evening, or at latest in the night. He directed Murat to bring his cavalry towards Jena, and Marshal Bernadotte to take at Dornburg an intermediate position between Jena and Naumburg. He set out immediately, sending officers to stop all troops on march to Gera, and to make them turn back for Jena.

In the evening of the preceding day, Marshal Davoust had entered Naumburg, occupied the bridge of the Saale, and taken considerable magazines, with a fine bridge equipage. Marshal Bernadotte had joined him. Murat had sent his light cavalry as far as Leipzig, and surprised the gates of that great commercial city. Lannes had proceeded towards Jena, a small university town, seated on the very banks of the Saale, and had driven back pell-mell the enemy's troops left beyond the river, as well as the baggage, which encumbered the road. He had taken possession of Jena, and immediately pushed his advanced posts upon the heights which command it. From these heights he had perceived the army of the Prince of Hohenlohe, which, after recrossing the Saale, encamped between Jena and Weimar, and he had reason to suspect that a great assemblage was collecting in that place.

Napoleon had arrived at Jena on the afternoon of the 13th of October. Marshal Lannes, who had outstripped him, was waiting for him with impatience, like that of a war-horse, snuffing the battle. Both mounted their horses to reconnoitre the localities. We have described the ground upon which the battle was fought. The Prussians were posted on the heights which overlook the town of Jena. The French were coming up on the low ground on the opposite side of the river. The chief difficulty was to reach the Prussians. There was but one method that appeared practicable. The bold tirailleurs of Lannes, entering the ravines which are met with on going out of Jena, had succeeded in ascending the principal eminence, and all at once perceived the Prussian army encamped on the plateaux of the left bank. Followed presently by some detachments of Suchet's division, they had made room for themselves by driving in General Tauenzien's advanced posts. Thus by force of daring, the heights which commanded the left bank of the Saale were gained; but by a route which was scarcely practicable to artillery. Thither, Lannes conducted the emperor, amidst an incessant fire of tirailleurs which rendered reconnoisance extremely dangerous.

Napoleon, having before him a mass of troops, the force of which could scarcely be estimated, supposed that the Prussian army had chosen this ground for a field of battle, and immediately made his dispositions, so as to debouch with his army on the Landgrafenberg, before the enemy should hasten up, *en masse*, to hurl him into the precipices of the Saale. He was obliged to make the best use of his time, and to take advantage of the space gained by the tirailleurs to establish himself on the height. He had, it is true, no more of it than the summit, for, only a few paces off, there was the corps of General Tauenzien, separated from the French only by a slight ridge of ground. This corps was stationed near two villages, one on the right, that of Closewitz, surrounded by a small wood, the other on the left, that of Cospoda, likewise surrounded by a wood of some extent. Napoleon purposed to leave the Prussians quiet in this position till the next day, and meanwhile to lead part of his army up the Landgrafenberg. The space which it occupied was capable of containing the corps of Lannes and the guard. He ordered them to be led up immediately through the steep ravines which serve to ascend from Jena to the Landgrafenberg. On the left, he placed Gazan's division. On the right, Suchet's division; in the centre, and a little in rear, the foot-guard. He made the latter encamp in a square of four thousand men, and in the centre of this square he established his own bivouac.

But it was not enough to bring infantry upon the

Landgrafenberg—it was necessary to mount artillery too upon it. Napoleon, riding about in all directions, discovered a passage less steep than the others, and by which the artillery might be dragged up with great exertion. Unluckily, the way was too narrow. Napoleon sent forthwith for a detachment of the engineers, and had it widened by cutting the rock; he himself, in his impatience, directed the works, torch in hand. He did not retire till the night was far advanced, when he had seen the first pieces of cannon rolled up. It required twelve horses to drag each gun-carriage to the top of the Landgrafenberg. Napoleon purposed to attack General Tauenzien at day-break, and, by pushing him briskly, to conquer the space necessary for deploying his army. Fearful, however, of debouching by a single outlet, wishing also to divide the attention of the enemy, he directed Augereau towards the left, to enter the gorge of the Muhlthal, to march one of his two divisions upon the Weimar road, and to gain with the other the back of the Landgrafenberg, in order to fall upon the rear of General Tauenzien. On the right, he ordered Marshal Soult, whose corps, breaking up from Gera, was to arrive in the night, to ascend the other ravines, which, running from Lobstedt and Dornburg, debouch upon Closewitz, likewise for the purpose of falling upon the rear of General Tauenzien. With this double diversion, on the right and on the left, Napoleon had no doubt of forcing the Prussians in their position, and gaining for himself the space needed by his army for deploying. Marshals Ney and Murat were to ascend the Landgrafenberg by the route Lannes and the guard had followed.

The day of the 13th had closed; profound darkness enveloped the field of battle. Napoleon had placed his tent in the centre of the square formed by his guard, and had suffered only a few fires to be lighted; but all those of the Prussian army were kindled. The fires of the Prince of Hohenlohe were to be seen over the whole extent of the plateaux, and at the horizon on the right, topped by the old castle of Eckartsberg, those of the army of the Duke of Brunswick, which had all at once become visible for Napoleon. He conceived that, so far from retiring, the whole of the Prussian forces had come to take part in the battle. He sent immediately fresh orders to Marshals Davoust and Bernadotte. He enjoined Marshal Davoust to guard strictly the bridge of Naumberg, even to cross it, if possible, and to fall upon the rear of the Prussians, while they were engaged in front. He ordered Marshal Bernadotte, placed immediately, to concur in the projected movement, either by joining Marshal Davoust, if he was near the latter, or by throwing himself directly on the flank of the Prussians, if he had already taken at Dornburg a position nearer to Jena. Lastly, he desired Murat to arrive as speedily as possible with his cavalry.

While Napoleon was making these dispositions, the Prince of Hohenlohe was in complete ignorance of the lot which awaited him. Still persuaded that the bulk of the French army, instead of halting before Jena, was hurrying to Leipzig and Dresden, he supposed that he should at most have to deal with the corps of Marshals Lannes and Augereau, which, having passed the Saale, would, he imagined, make their appearance between

Jena and Weimar, as if they had descended from the heights of the forest of Thuringia. Under this idea, not thinking of making front towards Jena, he had on that side opposed only the corps of General Tauenzien, and ranged his army along the road from Jena to Weimar. His left, composed of Saxons, guarded the summit of the Schnecke; his right extended to Weimar, and connected itself with General Ruchel's corps. However, a fire of tirailleurs, which was heard on the Landgrafenberg, having excited a sort of alarm, and General Tauenzien applying for succor, the Prince of Hohenlohe ordered the Saxon brigade of Cerini, the Prussian brigade of Sanitz, and several squadrons of cavalry, to get under arms, and dispatched these forces to the Landgrafenberg, to dislodge from it the French, whom he conceived to be scarcely established on that point. At the moment when he was about to execute this resolution, Colonel de Massenbach brought him from the Duke of Brunswick a reiterated order not to involve himself in any serious action, to guard well the passages of the Saale, and particularly that of Dornburg, which excited uneasiness because some light troops had been perceived there. The Prince of Hohenlohe, who had become one of the most obedient of lieutenants when he ought not to have been so, desisted at once, in compliance with these injunctions from the head-quarters. It was singular, nevertheless, that in obeying the order not to fight, he should abandon the *debouche* by which, on the morrow, a disastrous battle was to be forced upon him. Be this as it may, relinquishing the idea of retaking the Landgrafenberg, he contented himself with sending the Saxon brigade of Cerini to General Tauenzien, and with placing at Nerkwitz, facing Dornburg, the Prussian brigade of Schemmelpfennig, lastly several detachments of cavalry and artillery, under the command of General Holzendorf. He sent some light horse to Dornburg itself, to learn what was passing there. The Prince of Hohenlohe confined himself to these dispositions: he returned to his head-quarters at Capellendorf.

Napoleon, stirring before daylight, gave his last instructions to his lieutenants, and orders for his soldiers to get under arms. The night was cold, the country covered to a distance with a thick fog, like that which for some hours enveloped the field of Austerlitz. Escorted by men carrying torches, Napoleon went along the front of the troops, talking to the officers and soldiers. He explained the position of the two armies, demonstrated to them that the Prussians were as deeply compromised as the Austrians in the preceding year; that, if vanquished in that engagement, they would be cut off from the Elbe and the Oder, separated from the Russians, and forced to abandon to the French the whole Prussian monarchy; that, in such a situation, the French corps which should suffer itself to be beaten would frustrate the grandest designs, and disgrace itself for ever. He exhorted them to keep on their guard against the Prussian cavalry, and to receive it in square with their usual firmness. His words everywhere drew forth shouts of "Forward! *vive l'Empereur!*" Though the fog was thick, yet through its veil the enemy's advanced posts perceived the glare of the torches, heard the acclamations of the French, and went to give the alarm to General Tauenzien. At that moment, the corps of Lannes set itself in motion, on a signal from Napoleon. Suchet's division, formed into three brigades, advanced first. Claparede's brigade, composed of the 17th light infantry, and a battalion of *elite*, marched at the head, deployed in a single line. On the wings of this line, and to preserve it from attacks of cavalry, the 34th and 40th regiments, forming the second brigade, were disposed in close column. Vedel's brigade, deployed, closed this sort of square. On the left of Suchet's division, but a little in rear, came Gazan's division, ranged in two lines and preceded by its artillery. Thus they advanced, groping their way through the fog. Suchet's division directed its course towards the village of Closewitz, which was on the right, Gazan's division towards the village of Cospoda, which was on the left. The Saxon battalions of Frederick Augustus and Rechten, and the Prussian battalion of Zweifel, perceiving through the fog a mass in motion, fired all together. The 17th light infantry sustained that fire, and immediately returned it. This fire of musketry was kept up for a few minutes, the parties seeing the flash and hearing the report, but not discerning one another. The French, on approaching, at length discovered the little wood which surrounded the village of Closewitz. General Claparede briskly threw himself into it, and, after a fight hand to hand, had soon carried it, as well as the village of Closewitz itself. Having deprived General Tauenzien's line of this support, the French continued their march amidst the balls that issued from that thick fog. Gazan's division, on its part. took the village of Cospoda, and established itself there. Between these two villages, but a little farther off, was a small hamlet, that of Lutzenrode, occupied by Erichsen's fusiliers. Gazan's division carried that also, and was then able to deploy more at its ease.

At this moment the two divisions of Lannes were assailed by fresh discharges of artillery and musketry. These were from the Saxon grenadiers of the Cerini brigade, who, after taking up the advanced posts of General Tauenzien, continued to move forward, firing battalion volleys with as much precision as if they had been at a review. The 17th light infantry, which formed the head of Suchet's division, having exhausted its cartridges, was sent to the rear. The 34th took its place, kept up the fire for some time, then encountered the Saxon grenadiers with the bayonet, and broke them. The route having soon extended to the whole corps of General Tauenzien. Gazan's and Suchet's divisions picked up about twenty pieces of cannon and many fugitives. From the Landgrafenberg, the undulated plateaux, on which the French had just deployed, gradually subsided to the little valley of the Ilm. Hence they marched rapidly upon sloping ground, to the heels of a fleeing enemy. In this quick movement they encountered two battalions of Cerini, and also Pelet's fusiliers, which had been left in the environs of Closewitz. These troops were flung back for the rest of the day towards General Holzendorf, commissioned on the preceding day to guard the *debouche* of Dornburg.

This action had not lasted two hours. It was nine

o'clock, and Napoleon had thus early realized the first part of his plan, which consisted in gaining the space necessary for deploying his army. At the same moment his instructions were executed at all points with remarkable punctuality. Towards the left, Marshal Augereau, having sent off Heudelet's division, and likewise his artillery and cavalry, to the extremity of the Muhlthal, on the high road from Weimar, was climbing with Desjardin's divisions, the back of the Landgrafenberg, and coming to form on the plateaux to the left of Gazan's division. Marshal Soult, only one of whose divisions, that of General St. Hilaire, had arrived, was ascending from Lobstedt, in the rear of Closewitz, facing the positions of Nerkwitz and Alten-Krone, occupied by the relics of Tauenzien's corps and by the detachment of General Holzendorf. Marshal Ney, impatient to share in the battle, had detached from his corps a battalion of voltigeurs, a battalion of grenadiers, the 25th light infantry, two regiments of cavalry, and had gone on before with this body of *elite.* He entered Jena at the very hour when the first act of the engagement was over. Lastly, Murat, returning at a gallop, with the dragoons and cuirassiers, from reconnoisances executed on the Lower Saale, was mounting in breathless haste towards Jena. Napoleon resolved, therefore, to halt for a few moments on the conquered ground, to afford his troops time to get into line.

Meanwhile, the fugitives belonging to General Tauenzien's force had given the alarm to the whole camp of the Prussians. At the sound of the cannon, the Prince of Hohenlohe had hastened to the Weimar road, where the Prussian infantry was encamped, not yet believing the action to be general, and complaining that the troops were harassed by being obliged needlessly to get under arms. Being soon undeceived, he took his measures for giving battle. Knowing that the French had passed the Saale at Saalfeld, he had expected to see them make their appearance between Jena and Weimar, and had drawn up his army along the road running from one to the other of these towns. As this conjuncture was not realized, he was obliged to change his dispositions, and he did it with promptness and resolution. He sent the bulk of the Prussian infantry, under the command of General Grawert, to occupy the positions abandoned by General Tauenzien. Towards the Schnecke, which was to form his right, he left the Niesemuchel division, composed of the two Saxon brigades of Burgsdorf and Nehroff, of the Prussian Boguslawski battalion, and of a numerous artillery, with orders to defend to the last extremity the winding slopes by which the Weimar road rises to the plateaux. To aid them, he gave them the Cerini brigade, rallied and reinforced by four Saxon battalions. In rear of his centre, he placed a reserve of five battalions under General Dyherrn, to support General Grawert. He had the wrecks of Tauenzien's corps rallied at some distance from the field of battle, and supplied with ammunition. As for his left, he directed General Holzendorf to push forward, if he could, and to fall upon the right of the French, while he would himself endeavor to stop them in front. He sent General Ruchel information of what was passing, and begged him to hasten his march. Lastly, he hurried off himself with the Prussian cavalry and the artillery horses, to meet the French, for the purpose of keeping them in check and covering the formation of General Grawert's infantry.

It was about ten o'clock, and the action of the morning, interrupted for an hour, was about to begin again with greater violence, while, on the right, Marshal Soult, debouching from Lobstedt, was climbing the heights with St. Hilaire's division; while in the centre Marshal Lannes, with Suchet's and Gazan's divisions, was deploying on the plateaux won in the morning; and while, on the left, Marshal Augereau, ascending from the bottom of the Muhlthal, had reached the village of Iserstedt, Marshal Ney, in his ardour for fighting, had advanced with his three thousand men of the *elite*, concealed by the fog, and had placed himself between Lannes and Augereau, facing the village of Vierzehn-Heiligen, which occupied the centre of the field of battle. He arrived at the very moment when the Prince of Hohenlohe was hastening up at the head of the Prussian cavalry. Finding himself all at once facing the enemy, he engaged before the Emperor had given orders for renewing the action. The horse artillery of the Prince of Hohenlohe having already placed itself in battery, Ney pushed the 10th chasseurs upon this artillery. This regiment, taking advantage of a clump of trees to form, dashed forward on the gallop, ascended by its right upon the flank of the Russian artillery, cut down the gunners, and took seven pieces of cannon, under the fire of the whole line of the enemy. But a mass of Prussian cuirassiers rushed upon it, and he was obliged

MARSHAL LANNES.

to retire with precipitation. Ney then dispatched the 3d hussars. This regiment, manœuvring as the 10th chasseurs had done, took advantage of the clump of trees to form, ascended upon the flank of the cuirassiers, then fell upon them suddenly, threw them into disorder, and forced them to retire. Two regiments of light cavalry, however, were not enough to make head against thirty squadrons of dragoons and cuirassiers. The chasseurs and hussars were soon obliged to seek shelter behind the infantry. Marshal Ney then sent forward the battalion of grenadiers and the battalion of voltigeurs which he had brought, formed two squares, then placing himself in one of them, opposed the charges of the Prussian cavalry. He allowed the enemy's cuirassiers to approach within twenty paces of his bayonets, and terrified them by the aspect of a motionless infantry which had reserved its fire. At his signal, a discharge within point-blank range strewed the ground with dead and wounded. Though several times assailed, these two squares remained unbroken.

Napoleon, on the top of the Landgrafenberg, had been highly astonished to hear the firing recommence without his order. He learned with still more astonishment that Marshal Ney, whom he had supposed to be in the rear, was engaged with the Prussians. He hastened up greatly displeased, and on approaching Vierzehn-Heiligen, perceived from the height Marshal Ney defending himself, in the middle of two weak squares, against the whole of the Prussian cavalry. This heroic demonstration was enough to dispel all displeasure. Napoleon sent General Bertrand with two regiments of light cavalry, all that he had at hand, in the absence of Murat, to assist in extricating Ney, and ordered Lannes to advance with his infantry. During the time that elapsed before relief arrived, the intrepid Ney was not disconcerted. While, with four regiments of horse, he renewed his charges of cavalry, he moved the 25th infantry to his left, in order to station himself on the wood of Iserstedt, which Augereau, on his part, was striving to reach; he made the battalion of grenadiers advance as far as the little wood which had protected his chasseurs, and dispatched the battalion of voltigeurs to gain possession of the village of Vierzhn-Heiligen. But, at the same instant, Lannes, coming to his assistance, threw the 21st regiment of light infantry into the village of Vierzehn-Heiligen, and, putting himself at the head of the 100th, 103d, 34th, 64th, and 88th of the line, debouched in the face of the Prussian infantry of General Grawert. The latter deployed before the village of Vierzehn-Heiligen, with a regularity of movement due to long exercises. It drew up in order of battle, and opened a regular and terrible fire of small arms. Ney's three little detachments suffered severely; but Lannes, ascending on the right of General Grawert's infantry, endeavored to turn it in spite of repeated charges of the Prince of Hohenlohe's cavalry, which came to attack him in his march.

The Prince of Hohenlohe bravely supported his troops amidst the danger. The regiment of Sanitz was completely broken; he formed it anew under the fire. He then purposed that the Zastrow regiment should retake the village of Vierzhen-Heiligen at the point of the bayonet, hoping thereby to decide the victory. Meanwhile he was informed that more hostile columns began to appear; that General Holzendorf, engaged with superior forces, was incapable of seconding him; that General Ruchel, however, was on the point of joining him with his corps. He then judged it expedient to wait for this powerful succor, and poured a shower of shells into the village of Vierzehn-Heiligen, resolved to try the effect of flames before he attacked it with his bayonets. He sent at the same time officers to General Ruchel, to urge him to hasten up, and to promise him the victory if he arrived in time; for, according to him, the French were on the point of giving way. At that very hour fortune was deciding otherwise. Augereau debouching at last from the wood of Iserstedt with Desjardin's division, disengaged Ney's left, and began to exchange a fire of musketry with the Saxons who were defending the Schnecke, while General Heudelet attacked them in column on the high road from Jena to Weimar. On the other side of the field of battle, the corps of Marshal Soult, after driving the remains of the Cerini brigade, as well as the Pelet fusiliers, out of the wood of Closewitz, and flinging back Holzendorf's detachment to a distance, opened its guns on the flank of the Prussians. Napoleon, seeing the progress of his two wings, and learning the arrival of the troops which had been left in rear, was no longer afraid to bring into action all the forces present on the ground, the guard included, and gave orders for advancing. An irresistible impulse was communicated to the whole line. The Prussians were driven back, broken, and hurled down the sloping ground which descends from Landgrafenberg to the valley of the Ilm. The regiments of Hohenlohe and the Hahn grenadiers, of Grawert's division, were almost entirely destroyed by the fire or by the bayonet. The Cerini brigade, assailed with grape, fell back upon the Dyherrn reserve, which in vain opposed its five battalions to the movement of the French. That reserve, being soon left uncovered, found itself attacked, surrounded on all sides, and forced to disperse. Tauenzien's corps, rallied for a moment, and brought back into the fire by the Prince of Hohenlohe, was hurried away, like the others, in the general rout. The Prussian cavalry, taking advantage of the absence of the heavy French cavalry, made charges to cover its broken infantry; but the chasseurs and hussars kept it in check; and though driven back several times, returned incessantly to the charge. A terrible carnage followed this disorderly retreat. At every step prisoners were made; artillery was taken by whole batteries.

In this great danger, General Ruchel at length made his appearance, but too late. He marched in two lines of infantry, having on the left the cavalry belonging to his corps, and on the right the Saxon cavalry, commanded by the brave General Zeschwitz, who had come of his own accord and taken that position. He ascended at a foot-pace those plateaux, sloping from the Landgrafenberg to the Ilm. While mounting, Prussian and French poured down around him like a torrent, the one pursued by the other. He was thus met by a sort of tempest, at the moment of his appearance on the field of battle. While he was advancing, his heart rent with grief at this disaster, the French rushed upon him with the impetuosity of victory. The cavalry which covered his left flank was first dispersed. That unfortunate general, an unwise but ardent friend of his country, was the first to oppose the shock in person. A ball entered his chest, and he was borne off dying in the arms of his soldiers. His infantry, deprived of the cavalry which covered it, found itself attacked in flank by the troops of Marshal Soult, and threatened in front by those of Marshals Lannes and Ney. The battalions placed at the left extremity of the line, seized with terror, dispersed, and hurried along the rest of the corps in their flight. To aggravate the disaster, the French dragoons and cuirassiers came up at a gallop, under the conduct of Murat, impatient to take a share in the battle. They surrounded those hapless and dispersed battalions, cut in pieces all who attempted to resist, and pursued the others to the banks of the Ilm, where they made a great number of prisoners.

On the field of battle were left only the two Saxon brigades of Burgsdorf and Nehroff, which, after honorably defending the Schnecke against Heudelet's and Desjardin's division of Augereau's corps, had been forced in their position by the address of the French tirailleurs, and effected their retreat, formed into two squares. These squares presented three sides of infantry and one of artillery, the latter being the rear side. The two Saxon brigades retired, halting alternately, firing their guns, and then resuming their march. Augereau's artillery followed, sending balls after them; a swarm of French tirailleurs ran after them, harassing them with their small arms. Murat, who had just overthrown the relics of Ruchel's corps, fell upon the two Saxon brigades, and ordered them to be charged to the utmost extremity by his dragoons and cuirassiers. The dragoons attacked first without forcing an entrance; but they returned to the charge, penetrated and broke the square. General d'Hatpoul, with the cuirassiers, attacked the second, broke it, and made that havoc which a victorious cavalry inflicts on a broken infantry. Those unfortunate men had no other resource but to surrender. The Prussian battalion of Boguslawski was forced in its turn, and treated like the others. The brave General Zeschwitz, who had hastened with the Saxon cavalry to the assistance of its infantry, made vain efforts to support it, and was driven back, and forced to give way to the general rout.

Murat rallied his squadrons, and hastened to Weimar, to collect fresh trophies. At some distance from that town were crowded together, pell-mell, detachments of infantry, cavalry, artillery, at the top of a long and steep slopé, formed by the high road leading down to the bottom of the valley of the Ilm. These troops, confusedly huddled together, were supported upon a small wood, called the wood of Webicht. All at once, the bright helmets of the French cavalry made their appearance. A few musket-shots were instinctively fired by this affrighted crowd. At this signal, the mass, seized with terror, rushed down the hill, at the foot of which Weimar is situated: foot, horse, artillerymen, all tumbled over one another into this gulf—a new and tremendous disaster. Murat now sent after them a part of his dragoons, who goaded on this mob with the points of their swords, and pursued it into the streets of Weimar. With the others he made a circuit to the other side of Weimar, and cut off the retreat of the fugitives, who surrendered by thousands.

Out of the seventy thousand Prussians who had appeared on the field of battle, not a single corps remained entire, not one retreated in order. Out of one hundred thousand French troops, composed of the corps of Marshals Soult, Lannes, Augereau, Ney, Murat, and the guard, not more than fifty thousand had fought, and they had been sufficient to overthrow the Prussian army. The greater part of that army, seized with a sort of vertigo, throwing away its arms, ceasing to know either its colors or its officers, covered all the roads of Thuringin. About twelve thousand Prussians and Saxons, killed and wounded, about four thousand French killed and wounded also, strewed the ground from Jena to Weimar. On the ground were seen stretched a great number—a greater number, indeed, than usual—of Prussian officers, who had nobly paid for their silly passions with their lives. Fifteen thousand prisoners, two hundred pieces of cannon, were in the hands of the French, intoxicated with joy. The shells of the Prussians had set fire to the town of Jena, and from the plateaux where the battle was fought, columns of flame were seen bursting from the dark bosom of night. French shells ploughed up the city of Weimar, and threatened it with a similar fate. The shrieks of fugitives while ruuning through the streets, the tramp of Murat's cavalry, dashing through them at a gallop, slaughtering without mercy all who were not quick enough in flinging down their arms, had filled with horror that charming city—the noble asylum of letters.

At Weimar, as at Jena, part of the inhabitants had fled. The conquerors, disposing like masters of their almost deserted towns, established their magazines and their hospitals in the churches and public buildings. Napoleon, on returning from Jena, directed his attention, according to his custom, to the collecting of the wounded, and heard shouts of *Vive l'Empereur!* mingled with the moans of the dying.

But Napoleon knew not yet the full measure of his victory. In the course of the day, he had heard the distant thundering of the cannon in the direction of Naumberg, where he had posted Marshal Davoust. He had the greatest confidence in the wisdom, valor, and inflexible resolution of that great general, but he did not know of the immensely superior forces the Marshal had to fight, to maintain his position. The facts were soon learned. Marshal Davoust, with only twenty-six thousand men, had not only sustained his position for many hours against the impetuous attack of seventy thousand Prussians, commanded by the Duke of Brunswick, and cheered by the presence of Frederick William himself, but had routed his enemy, and thus achieved the victory of Auerstadt. Never had there been a grander display of heroic firmness by general and soldiers. The Prussians had lost three thousand prisoners, nine or ten thousand men, killed or wounded, besides the Duke of Brunswick, Marshal Mollendorf and General Schwettan mortally wounded, together with a prodigious number of their gallant officers. Davoust had suffered a loss of seven thousand men, killed or wounded, and half the generals of brigade and colonels were placed *hors de combat*. The king was denied the consolation of his army retreating in good order. Nearly every corps was broken and disbanded, being seized with a panic. The roads were crowded with fear-stricken fugitives.

During the terrible night, which followed the bloody day of Jena and Auerstadt, the victors suffered not less than the vanquished. The night was intensely cold, and they were obliged to bivouac on the ground, having scarcely any thing to eat. Many of them wounded, more or less severely, were stretched on the cold earth beside wounded enemies, mingling their groans. Napoleon made every effort in his power to relieve their sufferings, and many a poor soldier, almost fainting from loss of blood, exerted his feeble strength to shout "*Vive l'Empereur!*"

But the Prussian army was annihilated. The road to Berlin was open, and thither the French Emperor hastened, in following up his decisive victory. A few small actions were fought and the French made thousands of prisoners almost every day. Frederick William solicited an armistice, but the Emperor refused to grant it for wise military reasons. He was destined to enter the Prussian capital in triumph. Never did Europe dread the name of Napoleon so notably as when that Prussian army, upon which the last hope was founded, vanished before his resistless arms.

THE CAMP-FIRE ON THE NAREW.

NAPOLEON, having vanquished the Prussians, once more turned his arms against the Russians, who, under the command of Kamenski and Bennigsen, numbered about one hundred and fifteen thousand men. They were posted upon the Vistula; but as Napoleon easily passed that great river, they retired behind the

Narew. The passage of this stream was one of the remarkable achievements of the French, during this portion of the Emperor's splendid career.

Having arrived in the night, between the 18th and 19th of December, 1806, Napoleon reconnoitred the position of Marshal Davoust on the Narew, but a thick fog prevented him from attaining much accurate intelli gence. He made his dispositions for attacking the enemy on the 22d or 23d of December. It is high time, he wrote to Marshal Davoust, to take our winter quarters; but this cannot be done till we have driven back the Russians.

The four divisions of General Bennigsen first presented themselves. Count Tolstoy's division, posted at Czarnowo, occupied the apex of the angle formed by the junction of the Ukra and the Narew. That of General Sacken, also placed in rear towards Lopaczym, guarded the banks of the Ukra. The division of Prince Gallitzin was in reserve at Pultusk. The four divisions of General Buxhovden were at a great distance from those of General Bennigsen, and not calculated to render support to him.

It is easy to perceive that the distribution of the Russian corps was not judiciously combined in the angle of the Ukra and the Narew, and that they had not sufficiently concentrated their forces. If, instead of having a single division at the point of the angle, and one on each side at too great a distance from the first, lastly, five out of reach, they had distributed themselves with intelligence over ground so favourable for the defensive; if they had strongly occupied, first the conflux, then the two rivers, the Narew from Czarnowo to Pultusk, the Ukra from Pomichowo to Kolozomb; if they had placed in reserve in a central position, at Nasielsk, for example, a principal mass, ready to run to any threatened point, they might have disputed the ground with advantage. But Generals Bennigsen and Buxhovden were on bad terms; they disliked to be near each other; and old Kamenski, who had arrived only on the preceding day, had neither the necessary intelligence nor spirit for prescribing other dispositions than they had adopted in following each of them his whim.

Napoleon, who saw the position of the Russians from without only, certainly concluded that they were intrenched behind the Narew and the Ukra, for the purpose of guarding the banks, but without knowing how they were established and distributed there. He thought that it would be advisable to take, in the first place, the conflux, where it was probable, they would defend themselves with energy, and having carried that point, to proceed to the execution of his plan, which consisted in throwing the Russians, by a wheel from right to left, into the marshy and woody country in the interior of Poland. In consequence, having repeated the order to Marshals Ney, Bernadotte and Bessieres, forming his left, to proceed rapidly from Thorn to Biezun on the upper course of the Ukra; to Marshals Soult and Augereau, forming in his centre, to set out from Plock and Modlin, and form a junction at Plonsk on the Ukra; he put himself at the head of his right, composed of Davoust's corps, Lannes's corps, of the guard, and the reserves, resolved to force immediately the position of the Russians at the conflux of the Ukra and the Narew. He left in the works of Praga the Poles of the new levy, with a division of dragoons, a force sufficient to ward off all accidents, as the army was not to remove far from Warsaw.

Having arrived on the morning of the 23d of December at Okunin on the Narew, in wet weather, by muddy and almost impassable roads, Napoleon alighted, to superintend in person the dispositions of attack. This general, who, according to some critics, while directing armies of three hundred thousand men, knew not how to lead a brigade into fire, went himself to reconnoitre the enemy's positions, and to place his forces on the ground, down to the very companies of the voltigeurs.

The Narew had been already crossed at Okunin, below the conflux of the Ukra and the Narew. To penetrate into the angle formed by those two rivers, it was necessary to pass either the Narew or the Ukra above their point of junction. The Ukra, being the narrower of the two, was deemed preferable for attempting a passage. Advantage had been taken of an island which divided it into two arms, near its mouth, in order to diminish the difficulty. On this island the French had established themselves, and they had yet to pass the second arm to reach the point of land occupied by the Russians between the Ukra and the Narew. This point of land, covered with woods, coppices, marshes, &c., looked like one very dense thicket. Further off, the ground became somewhat clearer, then rose and formed a steep declivity, which extended from the Narew to the Ukra. To the right of this natural intrenchment appeared the village of Czarnowo on the Narew, to the left of the village of Pomichowo on the Ukra. The Russians had advanced guards of tirailleurs in the thicket, several battalions and a numerous artillery on the elevated part of the ground, two battalions in reserve, and all their cavalry in the rear. Napoleon repaired to the island, mounted the roof of a barn by means of a ladder, studied the position of the Russians with a telescope, and immediately made the following dispositions. He scattered a great quantity of tirailleurs all along the Ukra, and to a considerable distance above the point of passage. He ordered them to keep up a brisk firing, and to kindle large fires with damp straw, so as to cover the bed of the river with a cloud of smoke, and to cause the Russians to apprehend an attack above the conflux, towards Pomichowo. He even directed to that quarter Gauthier's brigade, belonging to Davoust's corps, in order the more effectually to draw the enemy's attention thither. During the execution of these orders, he collected at dusk all the companies of voltigeurs of Morand's division, on the intended point of passage, and ordered them to fire from one bank to the other, through the clumps of wood, to drive off the enemy's posts, while the seamen of the guard were equipping the craft collected on the Narew. The 17th of the line and the 13th light infantry were in column, ready to embark by detachments, and the rest of Morand's division was assembled in the rear, in order to pass as soon as the bridge was established. The other divisions of Davoust's corps were at the bridge of Okunin, awaiting the moment for acting. Lannes was advancing from Warsaw to Okunin.

The seamen of the guard soon brought some boats, by means of which several detachments of voltigeurs were conveyed from one bank to the other. These penetrated into the thicket, while the officers of the pontoniers and the seamen of the guard were occupied in forming a bridge of boats with the utmost expedition. At seven in the evening, the bridge being passable, Morand's division crossed in close column, and marched forward, preceded by the 17th of the line and the 13th light infantry, and by a swarm of tirailleurs. They advanced under cover of the darkness and the wood. The sappers of the regiment cleared a passage through the thicket for the infantry. No sooner had they overcome these first obstacles, than they found themselves unsheltered, opposite to the elevated plateau which runs from the Narew to the Ukra, and which was defended either by abattis or by a numerous artillery. The Russians, amidst the darkness of the night, opened upon the French columns a continuous fire of grape and musketry, which did some mischief. While the voltigeurs of Morand's division and the 13th light infantry approached as tirailleurs, Colonel Lanusse, at the head of the 17th of the line, formed in column of attack on the right, to storm the Russian batteries. He had already carried one of them, when the Russians advancing in mass upon his left flank, obliged him to fall back. The rest of Morand's division came up to the support of the two first regiments. The 13th light. infantry having exhausted its cartridges, was replaced by the 30th, and again they marched by the right to attack the village of Czarnowo, while on the left, General Petit proceeded with four hundred picked men to the attack of the Russian intrenchments facing the Ukra, opposite to Pomichowo. In spite of the darkness, they monœuvred with the utmost order. Two battalions of the 30th and one of the 17th attacked Czarnowo, one by going along the bank of the Narew, the two others by directly climbing the plateau on which the village is seated. These three battalions carried Czarnowo, and, followed by the 51st and the 61st regiments, debouched on the plateau, driving back the Russians into the plain beyond it. At the same moment General Petit had assaulted the extremity of the enemy's intrenchments towards the Ukra, and, seconded by the fire of artillery, kept up by Gauthier's brigade from the other side of the river, had carried them. At midnight, the assailants were masters of the position of the Russians from the Narew to the Ukra, but, from the tardiness of their retreat, which could be discerned in the dark, it was to be inferred that they would return to the charge, and, for this reason, Marshal Davoust sent the second brigade of General Gudin's division to the assistance of General Petit who was most exposed. During the night, the Russians, as it had been foreseen, returned three times to the charge, with the intention of retaking the position which they had lost, and hurling down the French from the plateau towards that point of woody and marshy ground on which they had landed. Thrice were they suffered to approach within thirty paces, and each time the French replying to their attack by a point-blank fire, brought them to a dead stand, and then, meeting them with the bayonet, repulsed them. At length, the night being far advanced, they betook themselves in full retreat, towards Nasielsk. Never was night action fought with greater order, precision, and hardihood. The Russians left, killed, wounded and prisoners, about eighteen hundred men, and a great quantity of artillery. The French had six hundred wounded, and about one hundred killed.

Napoleon, at his evening camp-fire on the Narew, congratulated General Morand and Marshal Davoust upon their gallant conduct, and hastened to reap the benefits of the victory. Then followed a series of actions in terrible weather, and in a country now hardened with frost, and then slushed with rain. In all these, the lieutenants of the Emperor, and especially the indomitable Lannes, gained unfading glory.

THE CAMP-FIRE AT EYLAU.

THE Russians, under General Bennigsen, were pursued and harassed by the French Marshals after the passage of the Narew, until the evening of the 7th of February, 1807, when they halted beyond the village of Eylau, and evinced a determination to give battle on the following day. The French army was worn with fatigue, reduced in number by rapid marches and rear-guard actions, pinched with hunger and suffering from cold. But they were now to fight a great battle against a superior number of brave and disciplined troops.

Napoleon, losing no time, dispatched the same evening several officers to Marshals Davoust and Ney, to bring them back, the one to his right, the other to his left. Marshal Davoust had continued to follow the Alle to Bartenstein, and he was not more than three or four leagues off. He replied that he should arrive at daybreak upon the right of Eylau (the right of the French army) ready to fall upon the flank of the Russians. Marshal Ney, who had been directed upon the left, so as to keep the Prussians at a distance, and to be able to rush upon Konigsberg, in case the Russians should throw themselves behind the Pregel—Marshal Ney was marching for Krentzburg. Messengers were dispatched after him, though it was not so sure that he could be brought back in time to the field of battle, as it was that Marshal Davoust would make his appearance there.

Deprived of Ney's corps, the French army amounted at most to fifty and some thousand men. If Marshal Ney were to arrive in time, it would be possible to oppose sixty-three thousand men to the enemy, all present under fire. No expectation could be entertained of the arrival of Bernadotte's corps, which was thirty leagues off.

Napoleon, who slept that night but three or four hours in a chair in the house of the postmaster, placed the corps of Marshal Soult at Eylau itself, partly within the town, partly on the right and left of it, Augereau's corps and the imperial guard a little in rear, and all the cavalry upon the wings, till daylight should enable him to make his dispositions.

General Bennigsen had at last determined to give battle. He was on level ground, or nearly so, excellent ground for his infantry, not much versed in manœuvres, but solid, and for his cavalry, which was numerous. His heavy artillery, which he had directed to make a circuit, that it might not cramp his movements, had just rejoined him.

His army, amounting to seventy-eight or eighty thousand men, and to ninety thousand with the Prussians, had sustained considerable losses in the late battles, but scarcely any in marches, for an army in retreat, without being in disorder, is rallied by the enemy that pursues it, whereas the pursuing army, not having the same motives for keeping close together, always leaves part of its effective force behind. Deducting the losses sustained at Mohrungen, Bergfried, Waltersdorf, Hoff, Heilsberg, and at Eylau itself, one may say that General Bennigsen's army was reduced to about eighty thousand men, seventy-two thousand of whom were Russians, and eight thousand Prussians. Thus, in case General Lestocq and Marshal Ney should not arrive, fifty-four thousand French would have to fight seventy-two thousand Russians. The Russians had, moreover, a formidable artillery, computed at four or five hundred pieces. That of the French amounted to two hundred at most, including the guard. It is true that it was superior to all the artilleries of Europe, even to that of the Austrians. General Bennigsen, therefore, determined to attack at daybreak. The character of his soldiers was energetic, like that of the French soldiers, but governed by other motives. The Russians had neither that confidence of success nor that love of glory which the French exhibited, but a certain fanaticism of obedience, which induced them to brave death blindly.

Since debouching upon Eylau, the country appeared level and open. The little town of Eylau, situated on a slight eminence, and topped by a Gothic spire, was the only conspicuous point. The ground gently sloping, on the right of the church, presented a cemetery. In front it rose perceptibly, and on this rise, marked by some hillocks, appeared the Russians in a deep mass. Several lakes, full of water in spring, frozen in winter, at this time covered with snow, were not distinguishable in any way from the rest of the plain. Scarcely did a few barns united into hamlets, and lines of barriers for folding cattle, form a *point d'appui*, or an obstacle on this dreary field of battle. A gray sky, dissolving at times into thick snow, added its dreariness to that of the country, a dreariness which seized upon both the eye and heart.

During the greater part of the night Napoleon was employed in learning the force and position of the enemy, and drawing a plan of the battle, as he reclined on the snow by his dreary camp-fire. The four hours of sleep in a chair was quite sufficient to refresh his energies, and prepare him for the great struggle of the next day. The troops who bivouacked in the vicinity of Eylau, suffered severely from the cold. They had but few fires, as fuel was scarce. Most of these gallant soldiers, who had been marching and fighting for several days, dared not trust themselves to slumber on the ground for fear of freezing to death.

At break of the day, the position of the Russians was discovered. They were drawn up in two lines, very near to each other, their front being covered by three hundred pieces of cannon, planted on the salient points of the ground. In the rear, two close columns, appuying, like two flying buttresses, this double line of battle seemed designed to support it, and to prevent its breaking under the shock of a charge from the impetuous French. A strong reserve of artillery was placed at some distance. The cavalry was partly in the rear, and partly on the wings. The Cossacks kept with the body of the army.

Napoleon, on horseback, at daybreak, stationed himself in the cemetery to the right of Eylau, where, scarcely protected by a few trees from the cannonade which the Russians had already commenced, he surveyed the positions of the enemy. He could foresee that victory would cost him dearly, from the solid and obstinate mass which the Russian general had formed.

Owing to the position of Eylau, which stretched itself out facing the Russians, Napoleon could give the less depth to his line of battle, and consequently the less scope to the balls of the artillery. Two of Marshal Soult's divisions were placed at Eylau, Legrand's division in advance and a little to the left, Leval's division, partly on the left of the town, upon an eminence topped by a mill, partly on the right, at the cemetery itself. The third division of Marshal Soult's, St. Hilaire's division, was established still further to the right, at a considerable distance from the cemetery, in the village of Rothenen, which formed the prolongation of the position of Eylau. In the interval between the village of Rothenen, and the town of Eylau, an interval left vacant for the purpose of making the rest of the army debouch there, was posted a little in rear, Augereau's corps, drawn up in two lines, and formed of Desjardins's and Heudelet's divisions. Augereau, tormented with fever, his eyes red and swollen, but forgetting his complaints at the sound of the cannon, had mounted his horse to put himself at the head of his troops. Further in rear of that same *debouche* came the infantry and cavalry of the imperial guard, the divisions of cuirassiers and dragoons, both ready to present themselves to the enemy by the same outlet, and meanwhile somewhat sheltered from the cannon by a hollow of the ground. Lastly, at the extreme right of this field of battle, beyond and in advance of Rothenen, at the hamlet of Serpallen, the corps of Marshal Davoust was to enter into action in such a manner as to fall upon the flank of the Russians.

Thus Napoleon was in open order, and his line having the advantage of being covered on the left by the buildings of Eylau, on the right by those of Rothenen, the combat of artillery, by which he designed to demolish the kind of wall opposed to him by the Russians, would be much less formidable for him than for them. He had caused all the cannon of the army to be removed from the corps, and placed in order of battle. To these he had ordered the forty pieces belonging to the guard, and he was thus about to reply to the formidable artillery of the Russians by an artillery far inferior in number, but much superior in skill.

The Russians had commenced the firing. The French had answered it immediately by a violent cannonade at half cannon-shot. The earth shook under the tremendous detonation. The French artillerymen, not only more expert, but firing at a living mass, which served them for a butt, made dreadful havoc. The balls swept down whole files. Those of the Russians, on the contrary, directed with less precision, and striking against buildings, inflicted less mischief. The town of Eylau and the village of Rothenen were soon set on fire. The glare of the conflagration added its terrors to the horrors of the carnage. Though there fell far fewer French than Russians, still there fell a great many, especially in the ranks of the imperial guard, motionless in the cemetery. The projectiles, passing over the head of Napoleon, and sometimes very close to him, penetrated the walls of the church, or broke branches from the trees at the foot of which he had placed himself to direct the battle.

This cannonade lasted for a long time, and both armies bore it with heroic tranquillity, never stirring, and merely closing their ranks as fast as the cannon made breaches in them. The Russians seemed first to feel a sort of impatience. Desirous of accelerating the result by the taking of Eylau, they moved off to carry the position of the mill, situated on the left of the town.

Part of their right formed in column, and came to the attack. Leval's division gallantly repulsed it, and by their firmness left the Russians no hope of success.

As for Napoleon, he attempted nothing decisive, for he would not endanger, by sending it forward, the corps of Marshal Soult, which had done so well to keep Eylau under such a tremendous cannonade. He waited for acting till the presence of Marshal Davoust's corps, which was coming on the right, should begin to be felt on the flank of the Russians.

This lieutenant, punctual as he was intrepid, had actually arrived at the village of Serpallen. Friant's division marched at the head. It debouched the first, encountered the Cossacks, whom it had soon driven back, and occupied the village of Serpallen with some companies of light infantry. No sooner was it established in the village and in the grounds on the right, than one of the masses of cavalry posted on the wings of the Russian army detached itself, and advanced towards. General Friant, availing himself with intelligence and coolness of the advantages afforded by the accidents of the locality, drew up the three regiments of which his division was then composed behind the long and solid wooden barrier, which served for folding cattle. Sheltered behind this natural intrenchment, he kept up a fire within point-blank range upon the Russian squadrons, and forced them to retire. They fell back, but soon returned, accompanied by a column of nine or ten thousand infantry. It was one of the two close columns, which served for flying buttresses to the Russian line of battle, and which now bore to the left of that line, to retake Serpallen. General Friant had but five hundred men to oppose to it. Still, sheltered behind the wooden barrier with which he had covered himself, and able to deploy without apprehension of being charged by the cavalry, he saluted the Russians with a fire so continuous and so well directed, as to occasion them considerable loss. Their squadrons having shown an intention to turn him, he formed the 33d into square on his right, and stopped them by the imperturbable bearing of his foot-soldiers. As he could not make use of his cavalry, which consisted of some horse chasseurs, he made amends for it by a swarm of tirailleurs, who kept up such a fire upon the flanks of the Russians, as to oblige them to retire towards the heights in rear of Serpallen, between Serpallen and Klein-Sausgarten. On retiring to these heights, the Russians covered themselves by a numerous artillery, the downward fire of which was very destructive. Morand's division had arrived in its turn on the field of battle. Marshal Davoust, taking the first brigade, that of General Ricard, went and placed it beyond and on the left of Serpallen; he then posted the second, composed of the 51st and the 61st, on the right of the villages, so as to support either Ricard's brigade or Friant's division. The latter had proceeded to the right of Serpallen, towards Klein-Sausgarten. At this very moment, Gudin's division was accelerating its speed to get into line. Thus the Russians had been obliged by the movement of the French right to draw back their left from Serpallen towards Klein-Sausgarten.

The expected effect on the flank of the enemy's army was therefore produced. Napoleon, from the position which he occupied, had distinctly seen the Russian reserves directed towards the corps of Marshal Davoust.

The hour for acting had arrived; for, unless he interfered, the Russians might fall in mass upon Marshal Davoust and crush him. Napoleon immediately gave his orders. He directed St. Hilaire's division, which was at Rothenen, to push forward and to give a hand to Morand's division about Serpallen. He commanded the two divisions of Augereau's corps, to debouch by the interval between Rothenen and Eylau, to connect themselves with St. Hilaire's division, and to form all together an oblong line from the cemetery of Eylau to Serpallen. The result expected from this movement was to overturn the Russians, by throwing their right upon their centre, and thus break down, beginning at its extremity, the long wall which he had before him.

It was ten in the morning. General St. Hilaire moved off, left Rothenen, and deployed obliquely in the plain, under a terrible fire of artillery, his right at Serpallen, his left towards the cemetery. Augereau moved nearly at the same time, not without a melancholy foreboding of the fate reserved for his *corps d'armee,* which he saw exposed to the danger of being dashed to pieces against the centre of the Russians, solidly appuyed upon several hillocks. While General Corbineau was delivering the orders of the Emperor to him, a ball pierced the side of that gallant officer. Marshal Augereau marched immediately. The two divisions of Desjardins and Heudelet debouched between Rothenen and the cemetery, in close columns; then, having cleared the defile, formed in order of battle, the first brigade of each division deployed, the second in square. While they were advancing, a squall of wind and snow, beating all at once into the faces of the soldiers, prevented them from seeing the field of battle. The two divisions, enveloped in this kind of cloud, mistook their direction, and bore a little to the left, leaving on their right a considerable space between them and St. Hilaire's division. The Russians, but little incommoded by the snow, which they had at their backs, seeing Augereau's two divisions advancing towards the hillocks on which they appuyed their centre, suddenly unmasked a battery of seventy-two pieces, which they kept in reserve. So thick was the grape poured forth by this formidable battery, that in a quarter of an hour half of Augereau's corps was swept down. General Desjardins, commanding the first division, was killed; General Heudelet, commanding the second, received a wound that was nearly mortal. The staff of the two divisions was soon *hors de combat*. While they were sustaining this tremendous fire, being obliged to re-form while marching, so much were their ranks thinned, the Russian cavalry, throwing itself into the space which separated it from Morand's division, rushed upon them *en masse*. Those brave divisions, however, resisted—but they were obliged to fall back towards the cemetery of Eylau, giving ground without breaking, under the repeated assaults of numerous squadrons. The snow having suddenly ceased, they could then perceive the melancholy spectacle. Out of six or seven thousand combatants, about four thousand killed or wounded strewed the ground. Augereau, wounded, himself, but more affected by the disaster of his *corps d'armee* than by his personal danger, was carried into the cemetery of Eylau to the feet of Napoleon, to whom he complained, not without bitterness, of not having been timely succored. Silent grief pervaded every face in the imperial staff. Napoleon, calm and firm, imposing on others the impassibility which he imposed on himself, addressed a few soothing words to Augereau, then sent him to the rear, and took his measures for repairing the mischief. Dispatching, in the first place, the chasseurs of his guard and some squadrons of dragoons which were at hand, to drive back the enemy's cavalry, he sent for Murat, and ordered him to make a decisive effort on the line of infantry which formed the centre of the Russian army, and which, taking advantage of Augereau's disaster, began to press forward. At the first summons, Murat came up at a gallop. "Well," said Napoleon, "*are you going to let those fellows eat us up?*" He then ordered that heroic chief of his cavalry to collect the chasseurs, the dragoons, the cuirassiers, and to fall upon the Russians with eighty squadrons, to try what effect the shock of such a mass of horse, charging furiously, would have on an infantry reported not to be shaken. The cavalry of the guard was brought forward, ready to add its shock to the cavalry of the army. The moment was critical, for, if the Russian infantry were not stopped, it would go and attack the cemetery, the centre of the position, and Napoleon had only six foot battalions of the imperial guard to defend it.

Murat galloped off, collected his squadrons, made them pass between the cemetery and Rothenen, through the same debouch by which Augereau's corps had already marched to almost certain destruction. General

Grouchy's dragoons charged first, to sweep the ground, and clear it of the enemy's cavalry. That brave officer, whose horse fell with him, put himself, on rising, at the head of a second brigade, and effected his purpose of dispersing the groups of cavalry which preceded the Russian infantry. But, for overturning the latter, nothing short of the heavy iron-clad squadrons of General d'Hautpoul was required. That officer, who distinguished himself by consummate skill in the art of managing a numerous cavalry, came forward with twenty-four squadrons of cuirassiers, followed by the whole mass of dragoons. These cuirassiers, ranged in several lines, started off and threw themselves upon the Russian bayonets. The first lines, arrested by the fire, could not penetrate, and falling back to right and left, went to form afresh behind those who followed them, in order to charge anew. At length, one of them, rushing on with more violence, broke the enemy's infantry at one point, and opened a breach, through which cuirassiers and dragoons strove which should penetrate first. As a river, which has begun to break down a dike, soon carries it away entirely, so the masses of the squadrons, having once penetrated the infantry of the Russians, finished in a few moments the overthrow of their first line. The horse then dispersed to slaughter. A most horrible fray ensued between them and the Russian foot soldiers. They went, and came, and struck on all sides those obstinate antagonists. While the first line of infantry was thus overturned and cut in pieces, the second fell back to a wood that bounded the field of battle. A last reserve of artillery had been left there.

The Russians placed it in battery, and fired confusedly at their own soldiers and at the French, not caring whether they slaughtered friends or foes, if they only got rid of the formidable horse. General d'Hautpoul was mortally wounded by a rifle ball. While the cavalry was thus engaged with the second line of the Russian infantry, some parties of the first rallied and renewed their fire. At this sight the horse grenadiers of the guard, headed by General Lepic, one of the heroes of the army, came forward in their turn to second Murat's efforts. Dashing off at a gallop, they charged the groups of infantry which they perceived to be still on their legs, and crossing the ground in all directions, completed the destruction of the centre of the Russian army, the wrecks of which at last fled for refuge to the patches of wood which had served them for an asylum.

During this scene of confusion, a fragment of that vast line of infantry had advanced to that same cemetery. Three or four thousand Russian grenadiers, marching straight forward with the blind courage of braver and more intelligent troops, came to throw themselves on the church of Eylau, and threatened the cemetery occupied by the imperial staff. The foot guard, motionless till then, had endured the cannonade without firing a piece. With joy it beheld an occasion for fighting arrive. A battalion was called for; two disputed the honor of marching. The first in order, led by General Dorsenne, obtained the advantage of measuring its strength with the Russian grenadiers, went up to them without firing a shot, attacked them with the bayonet, and threw one upon another, while

Murat dispatched against them two battalions of chasseurs under General Bruyere. The Russian grenadiers, hemmed in between the bayonets of the grenadiers of the guard and the swords of the chasseurs, were almost all taken or killed, before the face of Napoleon, and only a few paces from him.

This cavalry action, the most extraordinary perhaps of any in the great wars, had for its result to overthrow the centre of the Russians, and to drive it back to a considerable distance. It would have been requisite to have at hand a reserve of infantry, in order to complete the defeat of troops which, after being laid on the ground, rose again to fire. But Napoleon durst not venture to dispose of Marshal Soult's corps, reduced to half of its effective, and necessary for keeping Eylau. Augereau's corps was almost destroyed.

Napoleon, in the cemetery, in which were heaped the bodies of a great number of his officers among the time-browned tombstones, was graver than usual; but his countenance was inflexible as ever, and no thought of retreat crossed his resolute soul. Crowds of his bravest veterans were lying mangled around him; and the prospect of the field must have been gloomy, indeed. But his iron will did not bend; he had confidence that the star of his fortune had not yet begun to descend.

Marshal Davoust and General St. Hilaire justified the confidence of their chief, and not only maintained their own position against the enemy, but had even pushed detachments upon their rear. But the event which Napoleon dreaded had occurred.

General Lestocq, perseveringly pursued by Marshal

Ney, appeared on that field of carnage, with seven or eight thousand Prussians, eager to revenge themselves for the disdain of the Russians. General Lestocq, only an hour or two ahead of Marshal Ney's corps, had merely time to strike one blow before he was struck himself. He debouched upon the field of battle at Schmoditten, passed behind the double line of the Russians, now broken by the fire of the artillery, by the swords of the horse, and presented himself at Kuschitten, in front of Friant's division, which, passing beyond Klein-Sausgarten; had already driven back the left of the enemy upon its centre. The village of Kuschitten was occupied by four companies of the 108th, and by the 51st, which had been detached from Morand's division for the support of Friant's division. The Prussians, rallying the Russians around them, dashed impetuously on the 51st, and on the four companies of the 108th, without being able to break them, though they obliged them to fall back to a considerable distance, in rear of Kuschitten. The Prussians, after this first advantage, pushed on beyond Kuschitten, in order to recover the positions of the morning. They marched, deployed in two lines. The Russian reserves, being rallied, formed two close columns on their wings. A numerous artillery preceded them. In this manner they advanced across the rear of the field of battle, to regain the lost ground, and to beat back Marshal Davoust upon Klein-Sausgarten, and from Klein-Sausgarten to Serpallen. But Generals Friant and Gudin, having Marshal Davoust at their head, hastened up. Friant's entire division, and the 12th, 21st and 25th regiments, belonging to Gudin's division, placed themselves foremost, covered by the whole of the artillery of the third corps. To no purpose did the Russians and Prussians exert themselves to overcome the formidable obstacle; they were unsuccessful. The French, appuyed on woods, marshes and hillocks, here deployed in line, there dispersed as tirailleurs, opposed an invincible obstinacy to this last effort of the allies. Marshal Davoust, passing through the ranks till dark, kept up the firmness of his soldiers, saying, "Cowards will be sent to die in Siberia; the brave will die here like men of honor." The Prussians and the rallied Russians desisted from the attack. Marshal Davoust remained firm in that position of Klein-Sausgarten, where he threatened the rear of the enemy.

The two armies were exhausted. That day, so sombre, was every moment becoming more sombre still, and about to terminate in a tremendous night. More than thirty thousand Russians, struck by the balls and the swords of the French, strewed the ground, some dead, others wounded more or less severely. Many of the soldiers began to abandon their colors. General Bennigsen, surrounded by his lieutenants, was deliberating whether to resume the offensive, and try the effect of one more effort. But, out of an army of eighty thousand men, not more than forty thousand were left in a state to fight, the Prussians included. If he were worsted in this desperate engagement, he would not have wherewithal to cover his retreat. However, he was still hesitating, when intelligence was brought him of a last and important incident. Marshal Ney, who had closely followed the Prussians, arriving in the evening on the left, as Marshal Davoust had arrived in the morning on the right, debouched at length near Althof.

Thus Napoleon's combinations, retarded by time, had, nevertheless, brought upon the two flanks of the Russian army the forces that were to decide the victory. The order for retreat could no longer be deferred; for Marshal Davoust, having maintained himself at Klein-Sausgarten, would not have much to do to meet Marshal Ney, who had advanced to Schmoditten; and the junction of these two Marshals would have exposed the Russians to the risk of being enveloped. The order for retreating was instantly given by General Bennigsen; but, to insure the retreat, he purposed to curb Marshal Ney, by attempting to take from him the village of Schmoditten. The Russians marched upon that village, under favor of the night, and in profound silence, in hopes of surprising the troops of Marshal Ney, who had arrived late on the field of battle, when it was difficult to recognise one another. But the latter were on their guard. General Marchand, with the 6th light infantry, and the 39th of the line, allowing the Russians to approach, then receiving them with a point-blank fire, stopped them short. He then rushed upon them with the bayonet, and obliged them to renounce all serious attack. From that moment they definitely commenced their retreat.

Napoleon knew that he was master of the field of battle. He occupied the slightly rising plain beyond Eylau, having his cavalry and his guard before him and at the centre, and his other corps in possession of the positions which the Russians had occupied in the morning.

Certain of being victorious, but grieved to the bottom of his heart, the Emperor had remained amidst his troops, and ordered them to kindle fires, and not leave the ranks, even to go in quest of provisions. A small quantity of bread and brandy was distributed among the soldiers, and, though there was not enough for all, yet no complaints were heard. Less joyous than at Austerlitz and at Jena, they were full of confidence, proud of themselves, ready to renew that dreadful struggle, if the Russians had the courage and the strength to do so. Whoever had given them, at this moment, bread and brandy, which they were in want of, would have found them in as high spirits as usual. Two artillerymen of Marshal Davoust's corps having been absent from their company during this engagement, and arrived too late to be present at the battle, their comrades assembled in the evening at the bivouac, tried them, and not liking their reasons, inflicted upon them, on that frozen and blood-stained ground, the burlesque punishment which the soldiers call the *savate*.

There was no great abundance of any thing but ammunition. The service of the artillery, performed with extraordinary activity, had already replaced the ammunition consumed. With not less zeal was the service of the medical and surgical department performed. A great number of wounded had been picked up; to the others relief was administered on the spot, till they could be removed in their turn. Napoleon, overwhelmed with fatigue, was still afoot, and superintending the attentions that were paid to his soldiers.

In the rear of the army, so firm a countenance was not every where presented. Many stragglers, excluded from the effective in the morning, in consequence of the marches, had heard the din of that tremendous battle, had caught some hourras of the Cossacks, and fallen back, circulating bad news along the roads. The brave collected to range themselves beside their comrades, the others dispersed in the various routes which the army had traversed.

Daybreak next morning threw a light upon that frightful field of battle, and Napoleon himself was moved to such a degree as to betray his feelings in the bulletin which he published. On that icy plain, thousands of dead and dying, cruelly mangled, thousands of prostrate horses, an infinite quantity of dismounted cannon, broken carriages, scattered projectiles, burning hamlets, *all this standing out from a ground of snow*, exhibited a thrilling and terrible spectacle. "This spectacle," exclaimed Napoleon, "is fit to excite in princes a love of peace and a horror of war!"

This singularity struck all eyes. From a propensity for returning to the things of past times, and also from economy, an attempt had been made to introduce the white uniform again into the army. The experiment had been made with some regiments, but the sight of blood on the white dress decided the question. Napoleon, filled with disgust and horror, declared that he would have none but blue uniforms, whatever might be the cost.

The Russians had left upon the field, about seven thousand dead, and five thousand wounded, and they took with them fifteen thousand more wounded. They had consequently twenty-seven thousand men placed *hors de combat*. Besides this loss, four thousand prisoners were made by the French, who also captured twenty-four pieces of cannon and sixteen colors. The loss of the French was about three thousand killed and four thousand wounded. Several eagles had been carried away by Bennigsen. It was a terrible, but indecisive battle. The victor was too much grieved to listen to the pæans of triumph, although his valor and skill had been nobly displayed in defeating a superior enemy.

THE CAMP-FIRE AT FRIEDLAND.

AFTER the bloody struggle of Eylau, in which thirty thousand men were placed *hors de combat*, the Russians seemed desirous of avoiding a conflict until they had received large reinforcements. In the mean time, Napoleon collected about two hundred thousand men between the Vistula and the Memel, besieged and captured Dantzic, and was again in a condition to strike a tremendous blow at the inferior forces of the enemy. Early in June, 1807, the Russian general, Bennigsen, made the first offensive movement. The division of Marshal Ney, stationed at Gustadt, was attacked by a superior force, and that intrepid officer retreated, fighting, as far as Deppen. But on the 8th of June, Napoleon moved forward to extricate his lieutenant, and the Russians then fell back upon Heilsberg. There a desperate action occurred, in which both armies suffered terribly. The Russians were compelled to retreat, but they retired unmolested. On the 13th, Bennigsen approached the town of Friedland, situated on the west bank of the Alle, communicating with the eastern bank by long wooden bridges. Here the decisive battle of the next day was fought.

The course of the Alle, near the spot where the two armies were about to meet, exhibits numerous windings. The French came up by the woody hills, beyond which the ground gradually sinks to the banks of the Alle. The ground at this season was covered with rye of great height. To the right of the French, the river was seen pursuing its way through the plain, then turning round Friedland, coming to the left, thus forming an elbow. At daybreak on the morning of the 14th, Lannes, who commanded the advanced division of the French army, reached Posthenen, whence he could see the Russians marching across the bridges to deploy into the plain, and drawing up in a line of battle facing the heights. A rivulet, called the Mill Stream, there formed a small pond, after dividing the plain into two unequal halves. Bennigsen imagined that he had to contend with but one division of the French army, and, for the time, he had this advantage. But the whole force under

Napoleon's immediate command was coming up to support the gallant Lannes, and by crossing the bridges, the Russian general fairly placed himself in the power of the Emperor. For this Napoleon had manœuvred several days, and he now saw that the victory would be one of that complete, decisive kind he loved.

Marshal Lannes, in his haste to march, had brought with him only Oudinot's voltigeurs and grenadiers, the 9th hussars, Grouchy's dragoons, and two regiments of Saxon cavalry. He could not oppose more than ten thousand men to the enemy's advanced guard, which, successively reinforced, was treble that number, and was soon to be followed by the whole Russian army. Fortunately for the French, the soil afforded numerous resources to the skill and courage of their illustrious marshal. In the centre of the position which it was necessary to occupy, in order to bar the way against the Russians, was a village, that of Posthenen, through which ran the Mill Stream to pursue its course to Friedland. Somewhat in rear rose a plateau, from which the plain of the Alle might be battered. Lannes placed his artillery there, and several battalions of grenadiers to protect it. On the right, a thick wood, that of Sortlack, protruded in a salient, and divided into two the space comprised between the village of Posthenen and the banks of the Alle. There Lannes posted two battalions of voltigeurs, which, dispersed as tirailleurs, would be able to stop for a long time troops not numerous and not very resolute. The 9th hussars, Grouchy's dragoons, the Saxon cavalry, amounted to three thousand horse, ready to fall upon any column which should attempt to penetrate that curtain of tirailleurs. On the left of Posthenen, the line of woody heights extended, gradually lowering in the village of Heinrichsdorf, through which ran the high road from Friedland to Konigsberg. This point was of great importance, for the Russians, desirous to reach Konigsberg, would, of course, obstinately dispute the road thither. Besides, this part of the field of battle being more open, was naturally more difficult to defend. Lannes, who had not yet troops sufficient to establish himself there, had placed on his left, taking advantage of the woods and heights, the rest of his battalions, thus approaching the houses of Heinrichsdorf without being able to occupy them.

The fire, commenced at three in the morning, became all at once extremely brisk. The artillery, placed on the plateau of Posthenen, under the protection of Oudinot's grenadiers, kept the Russians at a distance, and made considerable havoc among them. On the right, the voltigeurs, scattered on the skirt of the wood of Sortlack, stopped their infantry by an incessant tirailleur fire, and the Saxon horse, directed by General Grouchy, had made several unsuccessful charges against their cavalry. The Russians having become threatening towards Heinrichsdorf, General Grouchy, moving from the right to the left, galloped thither, to dispute with them the Konigsberg road, the important point for the possession of which torrents of blood were about to be spilt.

Though, in these first moments, Marshal Lannes had but ten thousand men to oppose twenty-five or thirty thousand, he maintained his ground, thanks to great skill and energy, and also to the able concurrence of General Oudinot, commanding the grenadiers, and of General Grouchy, commanding the cavalry. But the enemy reinforced himself from hour to hour, and General Bennigsen, on arriving at Friedland, had suddenly formed the resolution to give battle—a very rash resolution, for it would have been much wiser for him to have continued to descend the Alle to the junction of that river with the Pregel, and to take a position behind the latter, with his left to Wehlau, his right to Konigsburg. It would have taken him, it is true, another day to reach Konigsberg; but he would not have risked a battle against an army superior in number, in quality, better officered, and in a very unfavorable situation for him, since he had a river at his back, and he was very likely to be pushed into the elbow of the Alle, with all that vigor of impulsion of which the French army was capable.

He lost no time in having three bridges thrown over the Alle, one above and two below Friedland, in order to accelerate the passage of his troops, and also to furnish them with means of retreat. He lined with artillery the right bank, by which he arrived, and which commanded the left bank. Then, nearly his whole army having debouched, he disposed it in the following manner:—In the plain around Heinrichsdorf, on the right for him, on the left for the French, he placed four divisions of infantry, under Lieutenant-General Gortschakoff, and the better part of the cavalry under General Ouwarroff. The infantry was formed in two lines. In the first were two battalions of each regiment deployed, and a third drawn up in close column behind the two others, closing the interval which separated them. In the second, the field of battle gradually narrowing the further it extended into the angle of the Alle, a single battalion was deployed and two were formed in close column. The cavalry, ranged on the side and a little in advance, flanked the infantry. On the left (the right of the French,) two Russian divisions, of which the imperial guard formed part, increased by all the detachments of chasseurs, occupied the portion of the ground comprised between the Mill Stream and the Alle. They were drawn up in two lines, but very near each other, on account of the want of room. Prince Bagration commanded them. The cavalry of the guard was there, under General Kollogribow. Four flying bridges had been thrown across the Mill Stream, that it might interrupt the communications between the two wings as little as possible. The fourth Russian division had been left on the other side of the Alle, on the ground commanding the left bank, to collect the army in case of disaster or to come and decide the victory, if it obtained any commencement of success. The Russians had more than two hundred pieces of cannon upon their front, besides those which were either in reserve or in battery on the right bank. Their army, reduced to eighty or eighty-two thousand men after Heilsberg, separated at this time from Kamenski's corps and from some detachments sent to Wehlau to guard the bridges of the Alle, still amounted to seventy-two or seventy-five thousand men. General

Bennigsen caused the mass of the Russian army to be moved forward in the order just described, so that, on getting out of the elbow of the Alle, it might deploy, extend its fires, and avail itself of the advantages of number which it possessed at the beginning of the battle.

The situation of Lannes was perilous, for he had the whole Russian army upon his hands. Fortunately, the time which had elapsed had procured him some reinforcements. General Nansouty's division of heavy cavalry, composed of three thousand five hundred cuirassiers and carbineers, Dupas's division, which was the first of Mortier's corps, and numbered six thousand foot soldiers, lastly, Verdier's division, which contained seven thousand, and was the second of Lannes's corps, marched off successively, had come with all possible expedition. It was a force of twenty-six or twenty-seven thousand men, to fight seventy-five thousand. It was seven in the morning, and the Russians, preceded by a swarm of Cossacks, advanced towards Heinrichsdorf, where they already had infantry and cannon. Lannes, appreciating the importance of that post, sent thither the brigade of Albert's grenadiers, and ordered General Grouchy to secure possession of it at any cost. General Grouchy, who had been reinforced by the cuirassiers, proceeded immediately to the village. Without stopping to consider the difficulty, he dispatched the brigade of Milet's dragoons to attack Heinrichsdorf, while Carrie's brigade turned the village, and the cuirassiers marched to support this movement. Milet's brigade passed through Heinrichsdorf at a gallop, drove out the Russian foot-soldiers at the point of the sword, while Carrie's brigade, going round it, took or dispersed those who had saved themselves by flight. Four pieces of cannon were taken. At this moment, the enemy's cavalry, coming to the assistance of the infantry, expelled from Heinrichsdorf, rushed upon the dragoons and drove them back. But Nansouty's cuirassiers charged it in their turn, and threw it upon the Russian infantry, which in this fray was obliged to withhold its fire.

During these occurrences, Dupas's division entered into line. Marshal Mortier, whose horse was killed by a cannon-ball, the moment he appeared on the field of battle, placed that division between Heinrichsdorf and Posthenen, and opened on the Russians a fire of artillery which, poured upon deep masses, made prodigious havoc in their ranks. The arrival of Dupas's division rendered disposable those battalions of grenadiers which had at first been drawn up to the left of Posthenen. Lannes drew them nearer to him, and could oppose their closer ranks to the attacks of the Russians, either before Posthenen or before the wood of Sortlack. General Oudinot, who commanded them, taking advantage of all the accidents of ground, sometimes from clumps of wood scattered here and there, sometimes from pools of water, produced by the rains of the preceding days, sometimes from above the corn, disputed the ground with equal skill and energy. By turns he hid or exhibited his soldiers, dispersed them as tirailleurs, or exposed them in a mass, bristling with bayonets, to all the efforts of the Russians. Those brave grenadiers, notwithstanding their inferiority in number, kept up the fight, supported by their general, when, luckily for them, Verdier's division arrived. Marshal Lannes divided it into two movable columns, to be sent alternately to the right, to the centre, to the left, wherever the danger was most pressing. It was the skirt of the wood of Sortlack and the village of the same name, situated on the Alle, that were the most furiously disputed. In the end, the French remained masters of the village, the Russians of the skirts of the wood.

Lannes was enabled to prolong till noon this conflict of twenty-six thousand men against seventy-five thousand. But it was high time for Napoleon to arrive with the rest of his army. Lannes, anxious to apprize him of what was passing, had sent to him almost all his aides-de-camp, one after another, ordering them to get back to him without loss of time, if they killed their horses. They found him coming at a gallop to Friedland, and full of a joy that was expressed in his countenance. "This is the 14th of June," he repeated to those whom he met; "it is the anniversary of Marengo; it is a lucky day for us!" Napoleon, outstripping his troops through the speed of his horse, had successively passed the long files of the guard, of Ney's corps, of Bernadotte's corps, all marching for Posthenen. He had saluted in passing, Dupont's fine division, which from Ulm to Braunsberg, had never ceased to distinguish itself, though never in his presence, and he had declared that it would give him great pleasure to see it fight for once.

The presence of Napoleon at Posthenen fired his soldiers and his generals with fresh ardor. Lannes,

Mortier, Oudinot, who had been there since morning, and Ney, who had just arrived, surrounded him with the most lively joy. The brave Oudinot hastening up with his coat perforated by balls, and his horse covered with blood, exclaimed to the Emperor: "Make haste, Sire, my grenadiers are knocked up; but, give me a reinforcement, and I will drive all the Russians into the water." Napoleon, surveying with his glass the plain, where the Russians, backed in the elbow of the Alle, were endeavoring in vain to deploy, soon appreciated their perilous situation and the unique occasion offered him by Fortune, swayed, it must be confessed, by his genius; for the fault which the Russian army were committing had been inspired, as it were, by him, when he pushed them from the other side of the Alle, and thus forced them to pass in before him, in going to the relief of Konigsberg. The day was far advanced, and it would take several hours to collect all the French troops. Some of Napoleon's lieutenants were, therefore, of opinion that they ought to defer fighting a decisive battle till the morrow. "No, no," replied Napoleon, "one does not catch an enemy twice in such a scrape." He immediately made his dispositions for the attack. They were worthy of his marvellous perspicacity.

To drive the Russians into the Alle was the aim which every individual, down to the meanest soldier, assigned to the battle. But how to set about it, how to ensure that result, and how to render it as great as possible, was the question. At the farthest extremity of the elbow of the Alle, in which the Russian army was engulphed, there was a decisive point to occupy, namely, the little point of Friedland itself, situated on the right, between the Mill Stream and the Alle. There were the four bridges, the sole retreat of the Russian army, and Napoleon purposed to direct his utmost efforts against that point. He destined for Ney's corps the difficult and glorious task of plunging into that gulf, of carrying Friedland at any cost, in spite of the desperate resistance which it would not fail to make, of wresting the bridges from them, and thus barring against them the only way of safety. But at the same time he resolved, while acting vigorously on his right, to suspend all efforts on his left, to amuse the Russian army on that side with a feigned fight, and not to push it briskly on the left till, the bridges being taken on the right, he should be sure, by pushing it, to fling it into a receptacle without an outlet.

Surrounded by his lieutenants, he explained to them, with that energy and that precision of language which were usual with him, the part which each of them had to act in that battle. Grasping the arm of Marshal Ney, and pointing to Friedland, the bridges, the Russians crowded together in front, "Yonder is the goal," said he; "march to it without looking about you: break into that thick mass whatever it costs you; enter Friedland, take the bridges, and give yourself no concern about what may happen on your right, on your left, or on your rear. The army and I shall be there to attend to that." Ney, boiling with ardor, proud of the formidable task assigned to him, set out at a gallop to arrange his troops before the wood of Sortlack

Struck with his martial attitude, Napoleon, addressing Marshal Mortier, said, "That man is a lion!"

On the same ground, Napoleon had his dispositions writtten down from his dictation, that each of his generals might have them bodily present to his mind, and not be liable to deviate from them. He ranged, then, Marshal Ney's corps on the right, so that Lannes, bringing back Verdier's division upon Posthenen, could present two strong lines with that and the grenadiers. He placed Bernadotte's corps (temporarily Victor's) between Ney and Lannes, a little in advance of Posthenen, and partly hidden by the inequalities of the ground. Dupont's fine division formed the head of this corps. On the plateau, behind Posthenen, Napoleon established the imperial guard, the infantry in three close columns, the cavalry in two lines. Between Posthenen and Henrichsdorf was the corps of Marshal Mortier, posted as in the morning, but more concentrated and augmented by the young fusiliers of the imperial guard. A battalion of the 4th light infantry, and the regiment of the municipal guard of Paris, had taken the place of the grenadiers of the Albert brigade in Heinrichsdorf. Dumbrowski's Polish division had joined Dupas's division, and guarded the artillery. Napoleon left to General Grouchy the duty of which he had already so ably acquitted himself, that of defending the plain of Heinrichsdorf. To the dragoons and the cuirassiers commanded by that general he added the light cavalry of Generals Beaumont and Colbert, to assist him to rid himself of the Cossacks. Lastly, having two more divisions of dragoons to dispose of, he placed that of General Latour Maubourg, reinforced by the Dutch cuirassiers, behind the corps of Marshal Ney, and that of General La Houssaye, reinforced by the Saxon cuirassiers, behind Victor's corps. The French in this imposing order amounted to no fewer than eighty thousand men. The order was repeated to the left not to advance, but merely to keep back the Russians till the success of the right was decided. Napoleon required that before the troops recommenced firing, they should wait for the signal from a battery of twenty pieces of cannon placed above Posthenen.

The Russian general, struck by this deployment, discovered the mistake which he had committed in supposing that he had to do with but the single corps of Marshal Lannes; he was surprised, and naturally hesitated. His hesitation had produced a sort of slackening in the action. Scarcely did occasional discharges of artillery indicate the continuance of the battle. Napoleon, who desired that all his troops should have got into line, rested for at least an hour, and being abundantly supplied with ammunition, was in no hurry to begin, and resisted the impatience of his generals, well knowing that, at this season, in this country, it was light till ten in the evening, he should have time to subject the Russian army to the disaster that he was preparing for it. At length, the fit moment appeared to him to have arrived, he gave the signal. The twenty pieces of cannon of the battery of Posthenen fired at once; the artillery of the army answered them along the whole line; and at this impatiently awaited signal, Marshal Ney moved off his *corps d'armee*.

From the wood of Sortlack issued Marchand's division, advancing the first to the right, Bisson's division the second to the left. Both were preceded by a storm of tirailleurs, who, as they approached the enemy, fell back and returned into the ranks. These troops marched resolutely up to the Russians, and took from them the village of Sortlack, so long disputed. Their cavalry, in order to stop the offensive movement, made a charge on Marchand's division. But Latour Maubourg's dragoons and the Dutch cuirassiers, passing through the intervals of the battalions, charged that cavalry in their turn, drove it back upon its infantry, and, pushing the Russians against the Alle, precipitated a great number into the deeply embanked bed of that river. Some saved themselves by swimming; many were drowned. His right once appuyed on the Alle, Marshal Ney slackened his march, and pushed forward his left, formed by Bisson's division, in such a manner as to thrust back the Russians into the narrow space comprised between the Mill Stream and the Alle. When arrived at this point, the fire of the enemy's artillery redoubled. The French had to sustain not only the fire of the batteries in front, but also the fire of those on the right bank of the Alle; and it was impossible to get rid of the latter by taking them, as they were separated from them by the deep bed of the river. The columns, battered at once in front and flank by the balls, endured with admirable coolness this terrible convergence of fires. Marshal Ney, galloping from one end of the line to the other, kept up the courage of his soldiers by his heroic bearing.

Meanwhile, whole files were swept away, and the fire became so severe that the very bravest of the troops could no longer endure it. At this sight, the cavalry of the Russian guard, commanded by General Kollogribow, dashed off at a gallop, to try to throw into disorder the infantry of Bisson's division, which appeared to waver. Staggered for the first time, that valiant infantry gave ground, and two or three battalions threw themselves in rear. General Bisson, who, from his stature, overlooked the lines of his soldiers, strove in vain to detain them. They retired, grouping themselves around their officers. The situation soon became most critical. Luckily, General Dupont, placed at some distance on the left of Ney's corps, perceived this commencement of disorder, and without waiting for directions to march, moved off his division, passing in front of it, reminding it of Ulm, Dirnstein and Halle, and taking it to encounter the Russians. It advanced, in the finest attitude, under the fire of that tremendous artillery, while Latour Maubourg's dragoons, returning to the charge, fell upon the Russian cavalry which had scattered in pursuit of the foot soldiers, and succeeded in the attempt to drive it back. Dupont's division, continuing its movement on that open ground, and, supporting its left on the Mill Stream, brought the Russian infantry at a stand. By its presence it filled Ney's soldiers with confidence and joy. Bisson's battalions formed anew, and the whole line, re-invigorated, began to march forward again. It was necessary to reply to the formidable artillery of the enemy, and Ney's artillery was so very inferior in number, that it could scarcely stand in battery before that of the Russians. Napoleon ordered General Victor to collect all the guns of his division, and to range them in mass on the front of Ney. The skilful and intrepid General Senarmont commanded that artillery. He moved it off at full trot, joined it to that of Marshal Ney, took it some hundred paces ahead of the infantry, and, daringly placing himself in front of the Russians, opened upon them a fire, terrible from the number of the pieces and the accuracy of aim. Directing one of his batteries against the right bank, he soon silenced those which the enemy had on that side. Then, pushing forward his line of artillery, he gradually approached to within grape-shot range, and, firing upon the deep masses, crowding together as they fell back into the elbow of the Alle, he made frightful havoc among them. The line of infantry followed this movement, and advanced under the protection of General Senarmont's numerous guns. The Russians, thrust further and further back into this gulf, felt a sort of despair, and made an effort to extricate themselves. Their imperial guard, placed upon the Mill Stream, issued from that retreat, and marched, with bayonet fixed, upon Dupont's division, also placed along the rivulet. The latter, without waiting for the imperial guard, went to meet it, repulsed it with the bayonet, and forced it back to the ravine. Thus driven, some of the Russians threw themselves beyond the ravine, the others upon the suburbs of Friedland. General Dupont, with part of his division, crossed the Mill Stream, drove before him all that he met, found himself on the rear of the right wing of the Russians engaged with the left in the plain of Heinrichsdorf, turned Friedland, and attacked it by the Konigsberg road; while Ney, continuing to march straight forward, entered by the Eylau road. A terrible conflict ensued at the gates of the town. The assailants pressed the Russians in all quarters; they forced their way into the street in pursuit of them; they drove them upon the bridges of the Alle, which General Senarmont's artlllery, left outside, enfiladed with its shot. The Russians crowded upon the bridges to seek refuge in the ranks of the fourteenth division, left, in reserve, on the other side of the Alle, by General Bennigsen. That unfortunate general, full of grief, had hurried to this division, with the intention of taking it to the bank of the river to the assistance of his endangered army. Scarcely had some wrecks of his left wing passed the bridges, when those bridges were destroyed—set on fire by the French, and, by the Russians themselves, in their anxiety to stop pursuit. Ney and Dupont, having performed their task, met in the heart of Friedland in flames, and congratulated one another on this glorious success.

Napoleon, placed in the centre of the divisions which he kept in reserve, had never ceased to watch this grand sight. While he was contemplating it attentively, a ball passed at the height of the bayonets, and a soldier, from an instinctive movement, stooped his head. "If that ball was intended for you," said Napoleon, smiling, "though you were to burrow a hundred feet under ground, it would be sure to find you there." Thus he wished to give currency to that useful belief that Fate strikes the brave and the coward without distinction, and that the coward who seeks a hiding-place disgraces himself to no purpose.

On seeing that Friedland was occupied and the bridges of the Alle destroyed, Napoleon at length pushed forward his left upon the right wing of the Russian army, deprived of all means of retreat, and having behind it a river without bridges. General Gortschakoff, who commanded that wing, perceived the danger with which he was threatened, and, thinking to dispel the storm, made an attack on the French line, extending from Posthenen to Heinrichsdorf, formed by the corps of Marshal Lannes, by that of Mortier, and by General Grouchy's cavalry. But Lannes, with his grenadiers, made head against the Russians. Marshal Mortier, with the 15th and the fusiliers of the guard, opposed to them an iron barrier. Mortier's artillery, in particular, directed by Colonel Balbois and an excellent Dutch officer, M. Vanbriennen, made incalculable havoc among them. At length, Napoleon, anxious to take advantage of the rest of the day, carried forward his whole line. Infantry, cavalry, artillery, started all at once. General Gortschakoff, while he found himself thus pressed, was informed that Friedland was in the possession of the French. In hopes of retaking it, he dispatched a column of infantry to the gates of the town. That column penetrated into it, and for a moment drove back Dupont's and Ney's soldiers; but these repulsed in their turn the Russian column. A new fight took place in that unfortunate town, and the possession of it was disputed by the light of the flames that were consuming it. The French finally remained masters, and drove Gortschakoff's corps into that plain without thoroughfare which had served it for field of battle. Gortschakoff's infantry defended itself with intrepidity, and threw itself into the Alle rather than surrender. Part of the Russian soldiers were fortunate enough to find fordable passages, and contrived to escape. Another drowned itself in the river. The whole of the artillery was captured. A column, the furthest on the right (right of the Russians) fled and descended the Alle, under General Lambert, with a portion of the cavalry. The darkness of the night and the disorder of victory facilitated its retreat, and enabled it to escape.

It was half-past ten at night. The victory was complete on the right and on the left. Napoleon, in his vast career, had not gained a more splendid one. He had for trophies eighty pieces of cannon, few prisoners, it is true, for the Russians chose rather to drown themselves, than to surrender, but twenty-five thousand men, killed, wounded, or drowned, covered with their bodies both banks of the Alle. The right bank, to which great numbers of them had dragged themselves, exhibited almost as frightful a scene of carnage as the left bank. Several columns of fire, rising from Friedland and the neighboring villages, threw a sinister light over that place, a theatre of anguish for some, of joy for others. The French had to regret upwards of eight thousand men, killed or wounded. The Russian army, deprived of twenty-five thousand combatants, weakened, moreover, by a great number of men who had lost their way, was thenceforward incapable of keeping the field.

The French Emperor slept near the camp-fire, surrounded by his soldiers, who continued to shout "*Vive l'Empereur!*" They had eaten nothing but a ration of bread, which they had carried in their knapsacks, during their hurried march. But their souls had drunk deeply of the intoxicating nectar of glory, and they felt not the pang of hunger. The night was clear and beautiful. The Russians were not pursued. If Napoleon had had his entire cavalry, with Murat at their head, he could have captured the whole force which, under command of General Lambert, descended the Alle. But only half the cavalry were with the army, and the Russians were left to escape as speedily as possible.

Friedland was a decisive field. Konigsberg surrendered soon afterwards; and the Russians were pursued till they took refuge beyond the Niemen. Here ended that daring march of the French Emperor—the new Alexander—from Boulogne to the Niemen, to crush the only power which could offer any effectual resistance to his arms. In the transport of triumph, the Emperor issued the following noble proclamation to his soldiers:

Soldiers—On the 5th of June we were attacked in our cantonments by the Russian army. The enemy had mistaken the causes of our inactivity. He perceived too late that our repose was that of the lion: he repents of having disturbed it.

"In the battles of Guttstadt and Heilsberg, and in that ever memorable one of Friedland, in a campaign of ten days; in short, we have taken one hundred and twenty pieces of cannon, seven colors, killed, wounded, or made prisoners, sixty thousand Russians, taken from the enemy's army all its magazines, its hospitals, its *ambulances*, the fortress of Konigsberg, the three hundred vessels which were in that port, laden with all kinds of military stores, one hundred and sixty thousand muskets which England was sending to arm our enemies.

"From the banks of the Vistula, we have come with the speed of the eagle to those of the Niemen. You celebrated at Austerlitz the anniversary of the coronation; this year you have worthily celebrated that of the battle of Marengo, which put an end to the war of the second coalition.

"Frenchmen, you have been worthy of yourselves and of me. You will return to France covered with laurels, and, after obtaining a glorious peace, which carries with it the guarantee of its duration. It is high time for our country to live in quiet, screened from the malignant influence of England. My bounties shall prove to you my gratitude, and the full extent of the 'ove I feel for you."

Then followed the interview of Napoleon and Alexander upon the Niemen, and the treaty of Tilsit, by which the two emperors parcelled out Europe as if it were their own. The star of Napoleon had reached its zenith, and truly its lustre dazzled the eyes of the world.

THE CAMP-FIRE AT MADRID.

THE war of the Peninsula and the invasion of Russia were the great sources of Napoleon's overthrow. Having summarily dethroned Ferdinand VII. of Spain, he placed the crown of that kingdom upon the head of his elder brother Joseph. But the Spaniards resisted this transfer from Bourbon to Bonaparte, and having taken the field, with enthusiasm, they defeated and captured a French army, commanded by General Dupont, and drove King Joseph beyond the Ebro. Napoleon then left Paris, (October, 1808,) and placed himself at the head of two hundred thousand men, to crush all opposition in Spain.

In the meantime, the Spaniards had vested the management of their affairs in a central or supreme junta, stationed at their recovered capital of Madrid. The determined spirit of opposition to French interference continued as strong as ever; but the power to act in concert, or maintain well directed efforts in a common cause, already appeared doubtful. The Supreme Junta found it difficult, sometimes impossible, to enforce obedience on their generals; and the provincial juntas were too apt to act independently, and assert their own right to separate command. The English government, at the same time, though promising aid, and making large preparations to afford it, yet continually procrastinated; and when Napoleon invaded the country, the native forces alone were in the field. Three armies had been formed, all intended to co-operate, and amounting to about one hundred thousand men, but, unfortunately, all under independent generals. Blake commanded the army on the western frontier, which extended from Burgos to Bilbao. General Romana, who commanded one of the auxiliary divisions of Spanish soldiers in the French service, had dexterously contrived to escape from the Island of Funen, and had been landed in Spain, with ten thousand men, by British ships. His corps was attached to that of General Blake. The head-quarters of the central army under Castanos, were at Soria; those on the eastern side, under Palafox, extended between Saragossa and Sanguesa. The Spanish armies were therefore arranged in the form of a long and weak crescent, the horns of which advanced towards France. The fortresses in the north of Spain were all in the possession of the French, and strongly garrisoned.

Napoleon was at Bayonne on the 3d of November, and by the 8th, he had directed the movements of the last columns of his advancing army across the frontier: on the same evening, he arrived at Vittoria, where Joseph held his court. The civil and military authorities met him at the gates, and prepared to conduct him with pomp to the house prepared for his reception; but he leaped off his horse, entered the first inn he observed, and called for maps and detailed reports of the position of the armies. In two hours, he had arranged the plan of the campaign; and by daybreak on the 9th, Soult took the command of Bessieres's corps, and began to push forward his columns upon the plains of Burgos, against an auxiliary corps, under the Count de Belvidere, designed to support the right flank of Blake's army. Belvidere was completely defeated at Gomenal; one of his battalions, composed entirely of students from Salamanca and Leon, refused to fly, and fell in their ranks. Blake was then routed at Espinosa, by General Victor, and again at Reynosa, by Soult, whence the wreck of his army fled in disorder, and took refuge in Santander. Nearly the whole of Romana's corps perished in the cliffs of Espinosa, after the batttle. Palafox and Castanos had, mean time, united their forces, and waited the attack of the French under Lannes, at Tudela, on the 22d of November. The Spaniards were on this occasion, also, utterly defeated, with the loss of four thousand killed, and three thousand prisoners. Castanos fled, after the action, in the direction of Calatayud; and Palafox once more threw himself and the remains of his troops into Saragossa, where he was immediately invested closely by Lannes.

The road to Madrid was now open to Napoleon. He advanced at the head of his guards and the first division of the army, and reached the strong pass of the Somosierra Chain, about ten miles distant from the city, on the 30th of November. The way lies through a very steep and narrow defile, and twelve thousand men, with sixteen pieces of cannon, which completely swept the road, were strongly posted to dispute his passage. On the 1st of December, the French began the attack at daybreak, with an attempt to turn the flanks of the Spaniards. Napoleon rode into the mouth of the pass, and surveyed the scene. His infantry were straggling along the sides of the defiles, and making no efficient progress; but the smoke of the sharp skirmishing fire, mingling with the morning fog, was curling up the rocks, and almost hid the combatants from view. Under this veil, he ordered the Polish lancers of the guard to charge up the road in face of the artillery. They obeyed with impetuous courage. The Spanish infantry, panic struck, fired, threw down their arms, and fled: the Poles dashing onward, seized the cannon in an instant. The whole of the Spanish force fled.

On the 2d of December, the French soldiers celebrated the anniversary of the coronation of King Joseph under the walls of Madrid. The city had been prepared for defence. A strong, but irregular force were in array within the gates. The pavement had been taken up to form barricades; the houses on the out-skirts loop-holed; and a spirit of desperate resolution, similar to that which had immortalized the people of Saragossa, was displayed. The French officer sent to summon the town, narrowly escaped being torn to pieces by the mob. The Emperor then made his dispositions for attack, and long after the camp-fires of his troops had encircled Madrid with flame, and scared the darkness of the night, the work of investure proceeded. The French were in high spirits. Their invincible Emperor was with them, and they had the greatest contempt for the Spaniards. About midnight, Napoleon again summoned the city to surrender; but an answer of defiance was returned; and then, dispositions were made for storming. There was but little sleep that night among besieged or besiegers. The clangor of arms, "the dreadful note of preparation," resounded on the air until the dawn, when the Emperor was on horseback to direct operations. The Retiro and the palace of the Duke of Medina Celi were stormed, and as terror began to fill the breasts of the citizens, Napoleon again summoned the authorities to surrender. The governor came out to the French, and said he desired a suspension of arms, but was afraid of openly talking of surrender. Napoleon, wishing to avert the horrors of assault, gave a little longer time to the distracted city, whence there issued, throughout the night, "a sound," says Napier, with vivid force, "as if some mighty beast was struggling and howling in the toils." At eight or nine in the morning of the 4th of December, the gates were opened to the conqueror, and the French took possession of Madrid.

Joseph was now restored to his authority in the capital. Corunna followed, and the English were driven out of Spain. Napoleon then returned to Paris. But the subjection of the Spaniards was not complete, and was destined never to be completed by his arms. His ablest lieutenants, although successful for a time, were at length overthrown by the British and Spaniards, under Wellington, and the contest proved but an exhausting struggle, in which were developed the influences which brought the imperial throne to the dust.

THE CAMP-FIRE AT RATISBON.

NAPOLEON could never trust his allies. Completely beaten, they submitted to the conqueror; and yet they hated as deeply as they feared him, and therefore took advantage of every opportunity to rupture the peace of Europe, and attack his power. No wonder that he lost patience, and treated their representations, when humbled, with contempt. These old legitimates proved themselves as false as they were imbecile, and they deserved the contempt of a man who was an Emperor by nature. After the peace of Tilset, Napoleon turned his attention to Spanish affairs, and placed his brother Joseph upon the throne of Spain. The Spaniards immediately took up arms to restore Ferdinand VII. to the crown of his ancestors, although they had long suffered from the misrule of the Bourbons. They resisted the armies of France, and being aided by the English, threatened the invaders with a terrible overthrow. This spectacle caused the faithless house of Austria to break all its engagements. Once more the Austrian Emperor resolved to make an effort to destroy the dominion of Napoleon. He collected an army of one hundred and fifty thousand men, which was placed under the command of the brave and skilful Archduke Charles.

Napoleon collected an army much inferior in number to that of the enemy, and with his usual rapidity advanced to the attack. The Empress Josephine accompanied him as far as Strasburg, and there watched the event of the campaign, although its termination was destined to be so melancholy for herself.

The Archduke Charles's plan was to act upon the offensive. His talents were undoubted, his army greatly superior in numbers to the French, and favorably disposed, whether for attack or defence; yet, by a series of combinations, the most beautiful and striking, perhaps, which occur in the life of one so famed for his power of forming such, Buonaparte was enabled, in the short space of five days, totally to defeat the formidable masses which were opposed to him. Napoleon found his own force unfavorably disposed, on a long line, extending between the towns of Augsburg and Ratisbon, and presenting, through the incapacity, it is said, of Berthier, an alarming vacancy in the centre, by operating on which the enemy might have separated the French army into two parts, and exposed each to a flank attack. Sensible of the full, and perhaps fatal consequences, which might attend this error, Napoleon determined on the daring attempt to concentrate his army by a lateral march, to be accomplished by the two wings simultaneously. With this view he posted himself in the centre, where the danger was principally apprehended, commanding Massena to advance by a flank movement from Augsburg to Pfaffenhoffen, and Davoust to approach the centre by a similar manœuvre from Ratisbon to Neustadt. These marches must necessarily be forced, that of Davoust, being eight, that of Massena between twelve and thirteen leagues. The order for this daring operation was sent to Massena on the night of the 17th, and concluded with an earnest recommendation of speed and intelligence. When the time for executing these movements had been allowed, Bonaparte, at the head of the centre of his forces, made a sudden and desperate assault upon two Austrian divisions, commanded by the Archduke Louis and General Hiller. So judiciously was this timed, that the appearance of Davoust on the one flank kept in check those other Austrian corps *d'armee*, by whom the divisions attacked ought to have been supported; while the yet more formidable operations of Massena, in the rear of the Archduke Louis, achieved the defeat of the enemy. The victory, gained at Abens-

berg, upon the 20th of April, broke the line of the Austrians, and exposed them to farther misfortunes. The Emperor attacked the fugitives the next day at Landshut, where the Austrians lost thirty pieces of cannon, nine thousand prisoners, and much ammunition and baggage.

On the 22d of April, Napoleon manœuvred so as to bring his entire force, by different routes upon Eckmuhl, where tho Archduke had collected full one hundred thousand men. Here, perhaps, was one of the most splendid triumphs of military combination ever displayed. The Austrians were attacked on all sides about two o'clock in the afternoon. They fought with stubborn courage, and the Archduke displayed great bravery. But nothing could avail against the overwhelming attack of a scientific adversary, and about dusk the Austrians were completely defeated. All the Austrian wounded, a great part of their artillery, and twenty thousand prisoners, remained in the hands of the French, and many more prisoners were taken during the pursuit. Davoust, whose services were conspicuous on this occasion, was created Prince of Eckmuhl.

On the 23d, the Austrians made an attempt to cover the retreat of their army, by defending Ratisbon. Six regiments occupied the town, and seemed determined upon a vigorous defence. The Emperor himself came up to order the attack. Ratisbon is situated on the Upper Danube, across which it communicates with its suburb Stadt-an-Hop, by a bridge a thousand German feet in length. It is one of the oldest towns in Germany, and has an antique aspect. Its streets are narrow and irregular, and its houses, although lofty, are old fashioned and inconvenient. Many have tall battlemented towers, loop-holed for musketry, etc. Among the most striking public buildings are the cathedral, an old Roman tower, and the bishop's palace. The ramparts are dilapidated, and scarcely useful for defence.

The French soon effected a breach in the ancient walls, but again and again were they repulsed by a tremendous fire of musketry. At length there was difficulty to find volunteers to renew the attack. Such a storm of death appalled even brave men. But nothing could daunt the impetuous Lannes. His courage was of the kind that rose with the danger. He rushed to the front, seized a ladder, and fixed it against the wall. "I will show you!" he shouted, "that your general is still a grenadier!" In spite of the tremendous fire, the troops followed the example of their glorious leader, for whom there were never laurels enough—scaled the walls, and continued the fight in the streets of the town, which was set on fire.

A detachment of French, rushing to charge a body of Austrians, which still occupied one end of a burning street, were interrupted by some wagons belonging to the enemy's train. "They are tumbrils of powder," cried the Austrian commanding, to the French. "If the flames reach them, both sides perish." The combat ceased, and the two parties joined in averting a calamity which must have been fatal to both, and finally, saved the ammunition from the flames. At length the Austrians were driven out of Ratisbon, leaving much cannon, baggage, and prisoners, in the hands of the French.

In the middle of this last *melee*, Bonaparte, who was speaking with his adjutant, Duroc, observing the affair at some distance, was struck on the foot by a spent musket-ball, which occasioned a severe contusion. "That must have been a Tyrolese," said the Emperor, coolly, "who has aimed at me from such a distance. These fellows fire with wonderful precision." Those around remonstrated with him for exposing his person; to which he answered, "What can I do? I must needs see how matters go on." The soldiers crowded about him in alarm at the report of his wound; but he would hardly allow it to be dressed, so eager was he to get on horseback, and show himself publicly among the troops.

That night the Emperor fixed his quarters in Ratisbon, and the watch-fires of his victorious troops illumined the air for miles around. There was much revelry that night. A glorious, decisive campaign of five days had prostrated the foes of the Emperor, and why should not the soldiers rejoice? The following proclamation was issued by the Emperor:

"Soldiers—You have justified my expectations; you have made up for numbers by your courage; you have gloriously marked the difference which exists between the soldiers of Cæsar and the armies of Xerxes.

"In a few days, we have triumphed in the three battles of Tann, Abensberg and Eckmuhl, and the affairs of Peissing, Landshut and Ratisbon. One hundred pieces of cannon, fifty thousand prisoners, three equipages, three thousand baggage wagons, all the funds of the regiments, are the result of the rapidity of your your courage.

"The enemy intoxicated by a perjured cabinet, appeared to have lost all recollection of us; they have been promptly awakened; you have appeared to them more terrible than ever. But lately, they had crossed the Inn, and invaded the territory of our allies; but lately they had promised themselves to carry the war into the bosom of our country. Now, defeated, dismayed they fly in disorder; already my advance-guard has passed the Inn; before a month we shall be at Vienna."

As Sir Walter Scott says: "It was no wonder that others, nay, that he himself, should have annexed to his person the degree of superstitious influence claimed for the chosen instruments of Destiny, whose path must not be crossed, and whose arms cannot be arrested." When before had Europe witnessed such a campaign? So much glory was enough to intoxicate even Napoleon, and we have yet to see that his deep draught of the nectar was fatal.

BATTLE OF ESSLING.

CAMP-FIRES AT ASPERN AND ESSLING.

AFTER the taking of Ratisbon, Napoleon advanced upon Vienna, which offered but a feeble resistance, and was easily occupied. But the Austrian army, in abandoning the capital of the empire, had not given up the struggle.

Sheltered by the Danube, the bridges over which they had destroyed at Vienna, and the surrounding places, they awaited a favorable opportunity of taking the offensive. The bridge of Lintz was the first object of their attacks; but Vandamme opposed to them a vigorous resistance, and Bernadotte, arriving, completely routed them. On his side, Napoleon was also impatient to force the passage of the river, in order to finish this glorious campaign. The reconstruction of the bridge, was, therefore, his first care. Massena had thrown several over the arms of the Danube, which bathe the island of Lobau; Napoleon resolved to make use of it for the passage of the whole army. In three days, the corps of Lannes, Bessieres, and Massena had taken up a position on the island. The communication with the right bank, was by a bridge of boats, five hundred yards in length, and extending over three arms of the river. Another bridge, which was not more than sixty-one yards in length, connected the island with the left bank. It was here, that on the 21st of May, thirty-five thousand men crossed without opposition, to give battle between Aspern and Essling.

The reports brought to the French during the night were contradictory. Many lights were seen on the heights of Bisamberg; but nearer to the French and in their front, the horizon exhibited a pale streak of about a league in length, the reflected light of numerous watch-fires, which a rising ground between prevented from being themselves visible. From such indications as could be collected, Lannes was of opinion that they were in presence of the whole Austrian army. Napoleon was on horseback by break of day on the 21st, to judge for himself; but clouds of light troops prevented his getting near enough to reconnoitre accurately. Presently the skirmishers were withdrawn, and the Austrians were seen advancing with their whole force, double in number to the French, and with two hundred and twenty pieces of artillery. Yet with this vast disproportion of odds, they were strangely astonished at the stand which they made on this occasion, as the French were mortified and reproached with having suffered a repulse or made only a drawn battle of it instead of a complete victory. The conflict commenced about four in the afternoon with a furious attack on the village of Aspern, which was taken and retaken several times, and at the close of the day remained (except the church and church-yard) in the possession of Massena, though on fire with the bombs and choked up with the slain. Essling was the object of three general attacks, against all which the French stood their ground. Lannes was at one time on the point of being overpowered, had not Napoleon by a sudden charge of cavalry come to his relief. Night separated the combatants.

The hundred thousand Austrians of the Archduke had not been able to gain an inch of ground from the thirty-five thousand French of Massena, Lannes and Bessieres. After the camp-fires were kindled among the dead of Aspern and Essling, both armies received reinforcements. The grenadiers of Oudinot, the division of St. Hilaire, two brigades of light cavalry, and the train of artillery passed the bridges, and took up a position on the line of battle. Napoleon confidently expected to achieve a decisive victory on the following day.

At four o'clock in the morning, the signal for battle was again given by the enemy against the village of

Aspern; but Massena was there to defend it. This illustrious warrior, whose intrepidity, coolness and military talents, never appeared to better advantage than in difficult positions, did not content himself with repulsing the Austrians each time they attacked; he soon took upon himself the defensive, and completely overthrew the columns which were opposed to him. At the same moment, Lannes and the young guard fell impetuously on the centre of the Austrian army, in order to cut off the communication with the two wings. Every thing gave way before the heroic marshal, and the victory became certain and decisive, when, about seven o'clock in the morning, it was announced to the Emperor, that a sudden increase of the Danube, which had carried away trees, vessels and even houses, had also borne away the great bridge which joined the island of Lobau with the right bank, and which formed the only method of communication between the troops engaged on the left bank, and the rest of the French army. At this news, Napoleon, who had scarcely fifty thousand men with him, to make head against a hundred thousand, suspended the movement in advance, and ordered his marshals merely to retain their position, in order, afterwards to effect their retreat in good order to the island of Lobau. This order was executed. Generals and soldiers valorously upheld the honor of the French flag. The enemy informed of the destruction of the bridges, which had kept back the park of reserve of the French army, and which thus deprived the cannon and infantry of cartridges, became so emboldened as to resume the offensive on all points. They attacked Aspern and Essling, three times at the same moment, and were three times repulsed. General Mouton distinguished himself at the head of the fusileers of the guard. Marshal Lannes, whom the Emperor had charged to maintain the field of battle, valiantly fulfilled his task; he powerfully contributed to save this fine portion of the French army, the existence of which a stroke of fate had nearly compromised. But this striking service was the last which this illustrious soldier was to render to his country and to the great captain who was rather his friend than his master. A bullet struck him in the thigh towards the close of the day. Amputation was immediately performed, and with such success as caused hopes to be conceived which were not to be realized.

Lannes was borne on a litter before the Emperor, who wept at the sight of the companion of all his victories mortally wounded.

"Was it requisite," said he in a tone of anguish, "that my heart on this day should have been struck so severe a blow, to force me to give way to other cares than those of my army!"

Lannes was conveyed to the island of Lobau. He had fainted. But he recovered his senses in the presence of Napoleon, the god of his idolatry: he clung around his neck, and said—

"In an hour you will have lost him who dies with the glory and conviction of having been your best friend!"

But Lannes lingered in agony for ten days. He did not want to die. He had not drank deep enough of glory. He said the man who could not cure a Marshal and a Duke of Montebello ought to be hanged!

"It is at the moment of quitting life," said Napoleon, later, "that one clings to it with all one's strength Lannes, the bravest of all men, Lannes, deprived of both legs, wished not to die. Every moment, the unfortunate man asked for the Emperor; he clung to me for the rest of his life; he wished but for me, thought of me only. A species of instinct! Assuredly he loved his wife and children better than me; and yet he spoke not of them; it was because he expected nought from them; it was he who protected them, whilst, on the contrary, I was his protector. I was for him something vague, superior; I was his providence; he prayed to me! It was impossible," added Napoleon, "impossible to be more brave than Lannes and Murat. Murat remained brave only. The mind of Lannes would have increased with his courage; he would have become a giant. If he had lived in these times, I do not think it would have been possible to have seen him fail either in honor or duty. He was of that class of men who change the face of affairs by their own weight and influence."

The illustrious marshal expired at Viluna on the 31st of May. He was lamented as the Roland of the army, and one of the greatest generals France had produced. General St. Hilaire, also, an excellent officer, was mortally wounded in this bloody struggle. He was highly esteemed by the Emperor, and if he had lived would doubtless have risen to the rank of marshal.

Napoleon was now cooped up in the island of Lobau. He had fought two indecisive battles. But that they were indecisive, when he contended with an army double his own in number, was a triumph, of which any other commander would not have ceased to boast. However, the Emperor prepared himself to strike a blow as decisive as was Friedland after Eylau.

In the meantime, Napoleon ordered the funeral obsequies of the illustrious Lannes to be celebrated in a style which astonished all Europe, and showed how a man should be honored who had risen from the ranks by force of talent, to be a marshal and a Duke of Montebello. It was a funeral procession of an army of thirty thousand men, detailed for this service, who escorted the remains of the illustrious warrior from Germany to France. They remind us of Alexander honoring the remains of his friend Hœphestion. Paris had never witnessed a grander procession than that which conveyed the remains of Lannes from the Invalides to the Pantheon. It was not a cortege; it was a whole army marching in mourning for a hero, with arms lowered and flags bound with crape, and bearing a magnificent cenotaph. The funeral march was composed by the greatest composer of Germany, the peerless Beethoven, and it was performed by a band, the like of which had never been heard in Paris. Occasionally, the mournful strains were interrupted by the solemn roll of three hundred drums, and the firing of many guns reminded those who listened, of those tremendous storms of battle, in which the lion-hearted Lannes had so often bled for France. The whole funeral ceremony was eminently worthy of the Emperor and his illustrious friend.

THE CAMP-FIRE AT WAGRAM.

AFTER the bloody conflicts of Essling and Aspern, Napoleon remained stationary for a considerable time. The Archduke, uneasy at the movements of Marshal Davoust before Presburg, dared not assume the offensive, and employed himself in fortifying his position between Aspern and Ebersdorf. Napoleon labored at the reconstruction of the bridges, and the communication between the island and the right bank was re-established. Soon afterwards, the Emperor learned that the army of Italy, under the command of Prince Eugene, had defeated the Austrians, and that the victors had effected a junction with the army of Germany, on the heights of Simmering. On the 14th of June, the Prince gained another victory over the Austrians at Raab. Marmont, after some successes in Dalmatia, came to re-unite himself with the Grand Army, and to place himself within the circle of the Emperor's operations. Napoleon's eagle eye saw that the moment for a decisive stroke had arrived, and he immediately began the advance movement, which led to the famous battle of Wagram.

About ten o'clock at night, on the 4th of July, the French began to cross the Danube. Gunboats, prepared for the purpose, silenced some of the Austrian batteries. Others were avoided by passing the river out of reach of their fire, which the French were enabled to do by their new bridges. At daybreak, on the morning of the 5th, the Archduke Charles was astonished to see the whole French army on the left bank of the Danube, and so posted as to render the fortifications which he had constructed with so much labor utterly useless for defence.

Greatly frightened at the progress of the French army, and at the great results obtained by it, almost without effort, the Archduke ordered all the troops to march, and at six o'clock in the evening, occupied the following position :—the right, from Stradelau to Gerasdorf; the centre, from Gerasdorf to Wagram, and the left, from Wagram to Neusiedel. The French army had their left at Gros-Aspern, their centre at Rachsdorf, and their right at Glinzendorf. In this position, the day had almost closed, and a great battle was expected on the morrow; but this would be avoided, and the position of the enemy destroyed, by preventing them from conceiving any system, if, in the night, possession were taken of Wagram; then their line, already immense, taken by surprise and exposed to the chances of battle, would allow the different bodies of the army to err without order or directions, and they would thus become an easy prey without any serious engagement. The attack on Wagram took place; the French carried this place; but a column of Saxons and another of French mistook each other in the obscurity for hostile troops, and so the operation failed.

When the bloody and indecisive struggle was relinquished for the night, only one house was left standing of the village of Wagram, which had been taken and retaken, and at length destroyed by the furious cannonade.

As the movement designed by the Emperor had failed, it remained to prepare for the struggle of the next day. It appeared that the dispositions of the French and Austrian generals was reversed. The Emperor passed the whole night in strengthening his centre, where he was in person within cannon-shot of Wagram. To effect this, the lion-hearted Massena marched to the left of Aderklau, leaving a single division at Aspern, which had orders to fall back if hard pressed, upon the island of Lobau. The intrepid and inexorable

Davoust received orders to leave the village of Grosshoffen to approach the centre. The Austrian general, on the contrary, committed the time-condemned error of weakening his centre in order to strengthen his wings. All night could be seen the far-extending lines of the blazing fires, which seemed to join each other in the distance; and all night could be heard the heavy tread of the troops, marching to take up positions under the vigilant eye of the Emperor. Brave, confident hearts, how many of them were destined to be swept to earth by the storm of the Austrian artillery!

At length, the day of the 6th dawned upon the plain of Wagram, and exhibited the two vast bodies of men, whose accoutrements glittered in the light, who were about to be hurled together in deadly conflict. At the first peep of day, Bernadotte occupied the left, leaving Massena in the second line. Prince Eugene, with the laurels of Raab freshly enwreathing his brow, connected him with the centre, where the corps of Oudinot, Marmont, those of the imperial guard, and the divisions of the cuirassiers, formed eight lines of battle-scarred veterans, eager for the fray. Davoust marched from the right in order to reach the centre.

The enemy, on the contrary, ordered the corps of Bellegarde to march upon Stradelau. The corps of Colowrath, Lichtenstein, and Hiller, connected this right with the position of Wagram, where the Prince of Hohenzollern was, and to the extremity of the left, at Neusiedel, to which extended the corps of Rosemberg, in order to fall upon Davoust. The corps of Rosemberg and that of Davoust, making an inverse movement, met with the first rays of the sun, and gave the signal for battle. The Emperor made immediately for this point, reinforced Davoust with the divisions of cuirassiers, and took the corps of Rosemberg in flank with a battery of twelve pieces of General Count Nansouty. In less than three quarters of an hour, the fine corps of Davoust had defeated Rosemberg's troop, and driven it beyond Neusiedel, with great loss.

In the meantime the cannonade commenced throughout the line, and the dispositions of the enemy became developed every moment; the whole of their left was studded with artillery; one would have said that the Austrian general was not fighting for the victory, but that the only object he had in view, was how to profit by it. This disposition of the enemy appeared so absurd, that some snare was dreaded, and the Emperor hesitated some time before ordering the easy dispositions which he had to make, in order to annul those of the enemy, and render them fatal to him. He ordered Massena to make an attack on a village occupied by the foe, and which somewhat pressed the extremity of the centre of the army. He ordered Davoust to turn the position of Neusiedel, and to push from thence upon Wagram; and bade Massena and General Macdonald form in column, in order to carry Wagram the moment Davoust should march upon it.

While this was going forward, word was brought that the enemy was furiously attacking the village which Massena had carried; that the left had advanced about three thousand yards; that a heavy cannonade was already heard at Gross-Aspern, and that the interval from Gros-Aspern to Wagram appeared covered by an immense line of artillery. It could no longer be doubted: the enemy had committed an enormous fault, and it only remained to profit by it. The Emperor immediately ordered General Macdonald to dispose the divisions of Broussier and Lamarque in attacking columns; they were supported by the division of General Nansouty, by the horse guards, and by a battery of sixty pieces of the guard and forty pieces of different corps. General Count de Lauriston, at the head of this battery of a hundred pieces of artillery, galloped towards the enemy, advanced without firing to within half cannon-shot, and then commenced a prodigious cannonade which soon silenced that of the enemy, and carried death into their ranks. General Macdonald marched forward to the charge. And such a charge had never before been witnessed upon the field of battle. Macdonald advanced, as it were, in the face of a volcano pouring forth a red tide of death. Whole squadrons were swept to the earth, but, led by a man without fear, the guards never even faltered; but on, on—still on—they advanced, like a decree of fate, which nothing could check. To sustain them, Bessieres charged with the cavalry of the old guard, but was hurled from his horse by a cannon-shot, which damped the enthusiasm of his troops, and rendered their onset weak. Napoleon, who, riding on a splendid white charger, was a conspicuous mark for the balls of the enemy, seeing his faithful Bessieres fall, turned away, saying, "Let us avoid another scene!" alluding to the incidents attending the death of the illustrious Lannes. But Macdonald continued his rapid advance, attacked and broke the centre of the Austrians, and captured their guns. But here he was compelled to halt; the column which he had led to the charge had been reduced to between two and three thousand effective men. Its path was piled with the slain. But the centre of the enemy was broken. Their right, seized with a panic, fell back in haste, and Massena then attacked in front, while Davoust, who had carried Neusiedel and Wagram, attacked and penetrated the left. It was but ten o'clock, and yet the victory already clung to the eagles of the French. From that time until noon, the Archduke only fought for a safe retreat. The French continued to gain ground; until, when the sun had reached the meridian, the dispirited Austrian general gave the order for retreat. The French pursued. But Murat, to Napoleon's regret, was not at the head of the cavalry, and many of the advantages of such a glorious victory were lost. Long before night's shadows descended, the Austrians were out of sight, and the French encamped upon the field of their victory, although the cavalry had posts advanced as far as Soukirchen.

At dark, the Emperor could sum up the results of this terrible battle, in which between three and four hundred thousand men, with from twelve to fifteen hundred pieces of artillery, did the work of death. Ten flags, forty pieces of cannon, twenty thousand prisoners, of whom three or four hundred were officers, were the trophies. Besides these, the Austrians left upon the field about nine thousand men wounded, and an immense number of slain. The Archduke himself was wounded in this bloody struggle. The French had suffered a severe loss. Besides a great number of brave men who had been swept into the sea of death by the storm of the Austrian artillery, there were six thousand wounded, among whom were Marshal Bessieres, and the Generals Sahuc, Seras, Defranc, Grenier, Vignoble and Frere.

It was a fitting time to do honor to the unrivalled commanders of the army. Macdonald had been in a kind of disgrace. But the Emperor now forgot all but his unequalled charge. He advanced to that intrepid general, and said, "Shake hands, Macdonald; no more animosity between us: let us henceforth be friends!" That night, by the camp-fire of Wagram, three new marshals of the empire were created, viz.:—Macdonald, Oudinot and Marmont.

The troops were excessively fatigued, and were glad when they received orders from the Emperor to cease the pursuit, and bivouac on the plain of Wagram. The Emperor then entered his tent to seek repose. But he had not tasted its sweets more than half an hour, when an aid-de-camp came in hurriedly, crying, "Up! up! to arms!" This cry was caught up and repeated throughout the whole army, startling the quiet night. "In five minutes," says the author of Travels in Moravia, "the troops were in position and ready for action, and the Emperor was on horseback, with all his generals around him. This rapid and regular movement was unparalleled. And certainly it was an astonishing display of perfect discipline and promptitude. The cause of this alarm was the approach of an Austrian corps, numbering three thousand men, under the Archduke

John. But that body, having failed in an attempt at surprise, retreated, and the French returned to their bivouacs, much amused with the incident of the night. In a short time, all was silent again upon the bloody plain of Wagram.

Then followed the treaty of Schœnbrunn, which once more prostrated the coalition, and secured Maria Louisa, a daughter of the proud house of Hapsburg-Lorraine, in the place of the beloved Josephine, as Empress of France. Thus the child of the people had conquered an alliance with the daughter of emperors.

MURAT.

THE CAMP-FIRE ON THE NIEMEN.

THE oppressive continental policy of Napoleon caused the rupture of the peace of Tilsit, and led to the grand, but disastrous invasion of Russia. Alexander gave the first offence by not fulfilling the condition of his treaty with Napoleon. The French Emperor then began to see the error of that treaty. It should have secured the independence of Poland. The czar pressed Napoleon for a declaration that Poland should never be re-established, but the Emperor refused to make this concession. Both rulers then prepared for a struggle on a gigantic scale. Napoleon determined to invade, and Alexander was resolved to make a resolute defence.

Napoleon determined to concentrate an army of four hundred thousand men upon the banks of the Niemen. He was thoroughly informed of the vast resources of France and of the condition of the country through which he would be compelled to march. As far as human calculation could reach, his views were clear and accurate.

It was from the bosom of that France, of which he had made a "citadel," which appeared impregnable, and across that Germany whose sovereigns were at his feet, that Napoleon wended his way towards the frontier of the Russian empire, in order to place himself at the head of the most formidable army which the genius of conquest had ever led. Fouche, Cardinal Fesch, and other noted councillors strove to dissuade Napoleon from the impending war; but the Emperor was confident, and seems to have entertained no doubt of his success. "The war," he said, "is a wise measure, called for by the true interests of France and the general welfare. The great power I have already attained, compels me to assume an universal dictatorship. My views are not ambitious. I desire to obtain no further acquisition; and reserve to myself only the glory of doing good, and the blessings of posterity. There must be but one European code; one court of appeal; one system of money, weights and measures; equal justice and uniform laws throughout the continent. Europe must constitute but one great nation, and Paris must be the capital of the world." Grand but premature conception!

The signal for the advance of the Grand Army was now sounded. It moved forward in thirteen divisions, besides the Imperial Guard, and certain chosen troops. The first division was headed by the stern and intrepid Davoust; the second, by Oudinot; the third, by the indomitable Ney; the fourth, by the skilful Prince Eugene; the fifth, by the devoted Poniatowski; the sixth, by that cool and skilful general, Gouvion St. Cyr; the seventh, by the veteran Regnier; the eighth, by the brave but reckless Jerome Bonaparte; the ninth, by the resolute Victor; the tenth, by the hero of Wagram, Macdonald; the eleventh, by the old veteran of Italy, Augereau; the twelfth, by the bold and brilliant Murat; and the thirteenth by Prince Schwartzenberg. The Old Guard—that solid and impenetrable phalanx—was commanded by Bessieres, Le Febre and Mortier.

Long before daybreak, on the 23d of June, the French army approached the Niemen. It was only two o'clock in the morning, when the Emperor, accompanied only by General Hays, rode forward to reconnoitre. He wore a Polish dress and bonnet, and thus escaped observation. After a close scrutiny, he discovered a spot near the village of Poineven, above Kowno, favorable to the passage of the troops, and gave orders for three bridges to be thrown across, at nightfall. The whole day was occupied in preparing facilities for the passage of the river, the line which separated them from the Russian soil.

The first who crossed the river were a few sappers

in a boat. The day had been very warm, and the night was welcomed by the weary soldiers, who knew they had yet a difficult task to perform. Napoleon, who had been somewhat depressed all day, now seemed to regain his cheerful spirits. He posted himself upon a slight eminence, where he could superintend operations. The sappers found all silent on the Russian soil, and no enemy appeared to oppose them, with the exception of a single Cossack officer on patrole, who asked, with an air of surprise, who they were, and what they wanted. The sappers quickly replied, "Frenchmen!" and one of them briskly added, "Come to make war upon you; to take Wilna, and deliver Poland." The Cossack fled into the wood, and three French soldiers discharged their pieces at him without effect. These three shots were the signals for the opening of this ever-memorable campaign. Their echoes roused Napoleon from the lethargy into which he had fallen, and he immediately planned the most active measures.

Three hundred voltigeurs were sent across to protect the erection of the bridges. At the same time, the dark masses of the French columns began to issue from the valleys and forests, and to approach the river, in order to cross it at dawn of day.

All fires were forbidden, and perfect silence was enjoined. The men slept with their arms in their hands, on the green corn, heavily moistened with dew, which served them for beds, and their horses for provender. Those on watch, passed the hours in reading over the Emperor's proclamation, and speculating on the prospect which the daylight would disclose. The night was keen, and pitch dark. The silence maintained amidst such a prodigious mass of life—felt to be there, whilst nothing could be seen—rendered the hours unspeakably solemn.

Before dawn, the whole array was under arms; but the first beams of the sun shewed no opposing enemy; nothing but dry and desert sand, and dark silent forests. On their own side of the river, men and horses, and glittering arms, covered every spot of ground within the range of the eye, and the Emperor's tent in the midst of them stood on an elevation. At a given signal, the immense mass began to defile in three columns towards the bridges. Two divisions of the advanced guard, in their ardor for the precedence, nearly came to blows. Napoleon crossed among the first, and stationed himself near the bridges to encourage the men by his presence. They saluted him with their usual acclamations. He seemed depressed, for a time, partly owing to his previous exertions and want of rest, partly from the excessive heat of the day, but no doubt still more from the passive desolation which met his forces, when he had expected a mortal enemy to contend with him in arms. This latter feeling was presently manifested in its reaction, and with a fierce impatience he set spurs to his horse, dashed into the country, and penetrated the forest which bordered the river; "as if," says Segur, "he were on fire to come in contact with the enemy alone." He rode more than a league in the same direction, surrounded throughout by the same solitude. He then returned to the vicinity of the bridges, and led the army into the country, while a menacing sky hung black and heavy over the moving host. The distant thunder began to roar and swell, and the storm soon descended. The lightning flamed across the whole expanse above their heads; they were drenched with torrents of rain; the roads were all inundated; and the recently oppressive heat of the atmosphere was suddenly changed to a bitter chilliness. Some thousands of horses perished on the march, and in the bivouacs which followed: many equipages were abandoned on the sands; and many men fell sick and died.

The Emperor found shelter in a convent, from the first fury of the tempest, but shortly departed for Kowno, where the greatest disorder prevailed. The passage of Oudinot had been impeded by the bridge across the Vilia having been broken down by the Cossacks. Napoleon treated this circumstance with contempt, and ordered a squadron of the Polish guard to spur into the flood, and swim across. This fine picked troop instantly obeyed. They proceeded at first in good order, and soon reached the centre of the river; but here the current was too strong, and their ranks were broken. They redoubled their exertions, but the horses became frightened and unmanageable. Both men and horses were soon exhausted. They no longer swam, but floated about in scattered groups, rising and sinking, while some among them went down. At length, the men, finding destruction inevitable, ceased their struggles, but as they were sinking, they turned their faces towards Napoleon, and cried out, "Vive l'Empereur!" Three of these noble-spirited patriots uttered this cry, while only a part of their faces were above the waters. The army was struck with a mixture of horror and admiration. Napoleon watched the scene apparently unmoved, but gave every order he could devise for the purpose of saving as many of them as possible, though with little effect. It is probable that his strongest feeling, even at the time, was a presentiment that this disastrous event was but the beginning of others, at once tremendous and extensive.

Marshal Oudinot with the second corps crossed the Vilia, by a bridge at Keydani. Meanwhile the rest of the army was still crossing the Niemen, in which operation three entire days were consumed.

After the first night of the arrival upon the Niemen, camp-fires were permitted, and their vast line illumined the sky to a great distance. The troops suffered severely from the sudden changes of the weather—from oppressive heat to piercing cold. But when we learn their sufferings in the rest of the campaign, we forget this first taste of misery. Before the army had entirely crossed the Niemen, Napoleon reached the plain of Wilna, which he found the Russians had deserted. However, he was received by the inhabitants of Wilna as a deliverer, and the restorer of the nationality of Poland. Still the steady movement of retreat, laying waste the country—the plan which the Russian generals had adopted—caused the Emperor to be gloomy, and it seemed as if the cloud of adversity had already begun to obscure his star.

MASSENA.

THE CAMP-FIRE AT WITEPSK.

THE first combat of importance during the Russian campaign was fought at Ostrowna. On the 18th of July, Napoleon reached Klubokoe. There he was informed that the Russian general, Barclay de Tolly, had abandoned the camp at Drissa, and was marching towards Witepsk. He immediately ordered all his corps upon Beszenkowici; and so admirable and precise were his combinations, that the whole of his immense mass of armies reached the place in one day. Segur has graphically described the apparent chaos of confusion which seemed to result from that very regularity itself. The columns of infantry, cavalry, and artillery, presenting themselves on every side; the rush, the crossing, the jostling; the contention for quarters, and for forage and provisions; the aides-de-camp bearing important orders vainly struggling to open a passage. At length, before mid night, order had taken the place of this apparent anarchy. The vast collection of troops had flowed off towards Ostrowno, or been quartered in the town, and profound silence succeeded the tumult. The Russian army had got the start of Napoleon, and now occupied Witepsk.

The first combat of Ostrowno took place on the 25th of July. The Russian infantry, protected by a wood, fiercely contested the ground, but were beaten back at every point by the repeated charges of Murat, seconded by the eighth regiment of infantry, and the divisions of Bruyeres and St. Germains; and at length the division of Delzons coming up completed the victory of the French. On the 26th, the Russians who had been reinforced, and had occupied a very strong position, seemed disposed to renew the struggle. Barclay had thrown forward this portion of his force to retard the French ad vance, while he daily looked for the junction of Bagration. The French van had also been reinforced; Prince Eugene with the Italian division having joined in the night. The numbers and strong position of the Russians gave them an immense superiority in the beginning of the day. They attacked with fury, issuing in large masses out of their woods with deafening war cries. The French regiments opposed to this onset were mowed down, beaten back, and in danger of an irretrievable rout. At this critical moment, Murat placed himself at the head of a regiment of Polish lancers, and with word and gesture incited them to an unanimous and energetic rush. Roused by his address, and inspired with rage at the sight of their oppressors, they obeyed with impetuosity. His object had been to launch them against the enemy, not to mingle personally in the torrent of the fight, which must disqualify him for the command; but their lances were in their rests, and closely filed behind him; they occupied the whole width of the ground; they hurried him forwards at the full speed of their horses, and he was absolutely compelled to charge at their head, which he did, as the eye-witnesses affirm, "with an admirable grace," his plumed hat and splendid uniform giving him on this occasion, and numberless others in which he displayed a most joyous and reckless courage, the air of some knight of romance. This impetuous onset was seconded by the other French leaders. Eugene, General Girardin, and General Pire attacked at the head of their columns, and finally the wood was gained. The Russians retreated, and disappeared from view in a forest two leagues in depth, into the recesses of which even the impetuosity of Murat hesitated to follow. The forest was the last obstacle which hid Witepsk from their view. At this moment of uncertainty, Napoleon appeared with the main body of the army, and all difficulties and uncertainties soon vanished. After hearing the report of the two princes, he went without delay to the highest point of ground he could reach. There he observed long and carefully the nature of the position, and calculated the movements of his enemies; he then ordered an immediate advance. The whole army rapidly traversed the forest, and began to debouch upon the plain of Witepsk before night-fall. The approaching darkness, the multitude of Russian watch-fires which covered the open ground, and the time requisite to complete the extrication of his several divisions from the defiles of the forest, obliged Napoleon to halt at this point. He believed himself to be in presence of the main Russian army, and on the eve of the great battle he so ardently desired. He left his tent, and repaired to his advanced posts before daybreak on the 27th, and the first rays of the sun shewed him the whole of Barclay's forces encamped on an elevated position, commanding all the avenues of Witepsk. The deep channel of the river Lucszissa marked the foot of this position, and ten thousand cavalry and a body of infantry were stationed in advance of the river to dispute its approaches; the main body of the Russian infantry was in the centre on the high road; its left, on woody eminences; its right, supported by cavalry, resting on the Dwina.

Napoleon took his station on an insulated hill in view of both armies. Here, surrounded by a circle of chasseurs of his guard, he directed the movements of his troops as they successively advanced to form in line of battle. Two hundred Parisian voltigeurs of the ninth regiment of the line, were the first who debouched, and were ranged on the left in front of the Russian cavalry, and resting, like it, on the Dwina; they were followed by the sixteenth chasseurs and some artillery. The Russians looked on with coolness, offering no opposition. This favorable state of inaction was suddenly interrupted by Murat. Intoxicated at the brilliant and imposing assemblage of so many thousands of spectators, he precipitated the French chasseurs upon the whole Russian cavalry. They were met by an overwhelming opposition; broken, put to flight, and the foremost cut to pieces. The King of Naples, stung to the quick at this result, threw himself into the thickest of the rout and confusion, sword in hand. His life had nearly been forfeited to his headstrong valor. A furious and well-directed blow was just descending on his head, aimed from behind by a Russian trooper, and it was only averted by a sudden slash from the sabre of the orderly who attended Murat, which cut off the trooper's arm. The consequences of these rash proceedings did not stop here. The successful resistance of the Russian cavalry impelled them to advance nearly as far as the hill on which Napoleon was posted, and his guard with great difficulty drove them back by repeated discharges of their carbines. The two hundred Parisian voltigeurs, left in an isolated position by the disorder into which the chasseurs had been thrown, were next placed in imminent peril. The Russian cavalry in returning to the main body, attacked and surrounded the voltigeurs. Both armies, spectators of this sudden and unequal conflict, regarded that small band of men as utterly lost. To the amazement of both French and Russians, however, this handful of apparent victims was presently seen to emerge unhurt from the dense cloud of assailants, who continued their original movement upon their own position. The voltigeurs had rapidly thrown themselves into square on a woody and broken space of ground, close to the river. Here the Russian cavalry could not act, while the steady fire of the voltigeurs made such havoc that their assailants were glad to leave them as they found them. Napoleon sent the cross of the Legion of Honor to every one of them on the spot.

The remainder of the day was spent by Napoleon in stationing his army; in waiting for the successive arrivals of different corps,—to be brief, in preparing for a decisive battle on the morrow. The more ardent of his generals wished that he had not waited till "the morrow," and when he took leave of Murat with the words, "To-morrow you will see the sun of Austerlitz," the King of Naples incredulously shook his head, saying, that "Barclay only assumed that posture of defiance, the better to ensure his retreat;" and then, with a temerity verging on the ludicrous, gave vent to his impatient irritation by ordering his tent to be pitched on the banks of the Lucszissa, nearly in the midst of the enemy, that he might be the first to catch the sounds of their retreat.

Murat was right. The Russians retreated while the Emperor was preparing to make Witepsk the scene of a decisive battle. At daybreak, Murat came to inform the Emperor that he was going in pursuit of the Russians who were no longer in sight. Napoleon would not at first credit the report, but their empty camp soon convinced him of the truth. There was not even a trace to indicate the route Barclay had taken. The army then entered Witepsk, and found it deserted. They then followed in pursuit for six leagues, through a deep and burning sand, and during the march the soldiers suffered dreadfully from thirst. At last, night put an end to their progress at Agliaponorchtchina. While the troops were busy in procuring some muddy water to drink, Napoleon held a council, the result of which was, that it was useless to pursue the Russian army any further at present, and that it was advisable to halt where they were, on the borders of Old Russia. As soon as the Emperor had formed this resolution, he returned to Witepsk with his guards. On entering his head-quarters in that city on the 28th, he took off his sword, and laid it down on the maps which covered his table. "Here!" said he, "I halt. I want to reconnoitre, to rally, to rest my army, and to organize Poland. The campaign of 1812 is over; that of 1813 will do the rest." Ah! well for him would it have been, had he been content with the laurels that were heaped upon his head, and fallen back then to devote himself to the restoration of Poland. But his faith in his star had not yet been weakened, and on, on—he would press, till checked by obstacles which no human power could overcome.

THE CAMP-FIRE AT SMOLENSKO.

NAPOLEON halted two weeks at Witepsk. He felt that if he could not find the Russian army, it was necessary to make a conquest that would end the campaign with substantial glory. Now, more than ever the idea of capturing the ancient Moscow entered his head, and he quickly decided to advance. Already full of the plan, which was to crown him with success, he ran to his maps. There he saw nothing but Smolensko and Moscow.

"At the sight of them," says Hazlitt, "he appeared inflamed by the genius of war. His voice became harsh, his glance fiery, and his whole air stern and fierce. His attendants retired from his presence, through fear as well as respect; but at length his mind was fixed, his determination taken, and his line of march traced out. Immediately after, the tempest was calmed, and having given consistency and utterance to his great conceptions, his features resumed their wonted character of placidity and cheerfulness." He did all in his power to gain over his officers to his purposes, and redoubled his attentions to his soldiers. The latter soon displayed a spirit of heroic devotion to his person.

The column of advance consisted of one hundred and eighty-five thousand men; not one half of the complement of the vast army which had entered Russia on the 23d of June.

It must be remembered that the great tract of country already passed was now occupied by his army, and necessarily expended a force, amounting perhaps to nearly eighty thousand men; but it is computed that in addition to this diminution of his army engaged in actual service, he had lost one-third of his original numbers by desertion, wounds, or death, either from fatigue or disease, or in the field of battle. Numbers of his hospital wagons, pontoons, and provision wagons, also, were far in the rear. Still, all these considerations gave way before his ardent desire to hurry the war to a termination, and the exertions he made at Witepsk were all with a view to an advance. Several actions occurred between his generals and the different divisions of the

Russian army during the period in which he held his head-quarters at Witepsk. Schwartzenberg conquered Tormazoff at Gorodeczna; Barclay retreated before Ney at Krasnoi; and Oudinot defeated Witgenstein near Polotsk, in a second combat,—the first in which they encountered was indecisive. It was at this moment that Napoleon received news of the conclusion of peace between Russia and Turkey, an event which much more than counterbalanced these successes.

During the first week of August, intelligence reached Witepsk, that the advanced guard, led by Prince Eugene, had obtained some advantages near Suraij; but that, in the centre, at Tukowo, near the Dnieper, Sebastiani had been surprised, and conquered by superior numbers. This information, together with the march of Barclay upon Rudnia, decided Napoleon. He conjectured that the whole Russian army was united between the Dwina and the Dnieper, and was marching against his cantonments. His conjecture proved to be perfectly correct. The Russian commander-in-chief conceiving that the French army at Witepsk lay considerably more dispersed than his own, had resolved to attempt a surprise. The utmost activity now pervaded head-quarters. On the 10th of August, Napoleon was observed to write eight letters to Davoust, and nearly as many to each of his commanders. "If the enemy defends Smolensko," he said, in one of his letters to Davoust, "as I am tempted to believe he will, we shall have a decisive engagement there, and we cannot have too large a force. Orcha will become the central point of the army. Every thing induces me to believe that there will be a great battle at Smolensko." Barclay having laid a plan for the surprise of Napoleon, the latter by a daring manœuvre avoided it, and almost succeeded in an attempt to turn the very same plan of surprise upon his enemy. Allowing the skirmishing to continue on the advanced posts, he changed his line of operations, and turning the left of the Russians instead of their right, which was expected by Barclay, he gained the rear of their army, and endeavored to occupy Smolensko, and act upon their lines of communication with Moscow. To effect this, he had withdrawn his forces from Witepsk and the line of the Dwina, with equal skill and rapidity, and throwing four bridges across the Dnieper, made a passage for Ney, Eugene Beauharnais, and Davoust, with Murat at the head of two large bodies of cavalry. They were supported by Poniatowski and Junot, who advanced in different routes. The attack was led by Ney and Murat, who bore down all opposition till they reached Krasnoi, where a battle was fought on the 14th of August. He had thus suddenly changed his line of operations from the Dwina to the Dnieper, and the manœuvre has been the subject of much admiration and criticism among French and Russian tacticians.

The Russian general, Newerowskoi, who commanded at Krasnoi, finding himself attacked by a body of infantry stronger than his own, and two large bodies of cavalry besides, retreated upon the road to Smolensko. This road being favorable for the action of cavalry, he was hotly pressed by Murat, who led the pursuit in full splendor of attire, and with all the reckless valor which characterised him. He also dispatched some of his light squadrons to alarm if not attack the front of the retreating corps, while he made furious onsets upon their flank and rear. Newerowskoi, however, effected a skilful and gallantly-conducted retreat, availing himself of a double row of trees on the high road to Smolensko, by which he evaded the charges of the cavalry, and was enabled to pour in a heavy fire. He made good his retreat into Smolensko, with the loss of four hundred men.

The day on which the combat at Krasnoi was fought, happened to be the Emperor's birth-day. There was no intention of keeping it in these immense solitudes, and under the present circumstances of peril and anxiety. There could be no heartfelt festival without a complete victory. Murat and Ney, however, on giving in the report of their recent success, could not refrain from complimenting the Emperor on the anniversary of his nativity. A salute from a hundred pieces of artillery was now heard, fired according to their orders. Napoleon, with a look of displeasure, observed, that in Russia it was important to be economical of French powder. But he was informed in reply, that it was Russian powder, and had been taken the night before. The idea of having his birth-day celebrated at the expense of the Russians made Napoleon smile. Prince Eugene also paid his compliments to the Emperor on this occasion; but was cut short by Napoleon saying, "Every thing is preparing for a battle. I will gain that, and then we will see Moscow."

While Newerowskoi was intrenched in Smolensko, the generals, Barclay and Bagration, who were stationed towards Inkowo, between the Dnieper and Lake Kasplia, hesitated whether to attack the French army, which they believed to be still in their front. But when they heard of the situation of Newerowskoi, the question of forcing the French lines was superseded by the necessity of hurrying to the rescue of Smolensko. Murat had already commenced an attack on the city. Ney had attempted to carry the citadel by a *coup de main*, but was repulsed with the loss of two or three hundred men, and was himself slightly wounded. He withdrew to an eminence on the river's bank, to examine the various positions, when on the other side of the Dnieper he thought he could discern some large masses of troops in motion. He hastened to inform the Emperor. Napoleon was presently on the spot, and distinguished, amidst clouds of dust, long dark columns which seemed electric with the intermittent glancing of innumerable arms. These masses were advancing with rapidity. It was Barclay and Bagration at the head of a hundred and twenty thousand men. At this sight, Napoleon clapped his hands for joy, exclaiming,—"At last I have them!" The moment that was to decide the fate of Russia or the French army, had apparently arrived.

Napoleon passed along the line, and assigned to each commander his station, leaving an extensive plain unoccupied in front, between himself and the Dnieper. This he offered to the enemy as a field of battle. The French army in this position was backed by defiles and precipices; but Napoleon had no anxiety about retreat, so certain felt he of victory.

Instead, however, of accepting the challenge to a decisive battle, Barclay and Bagration were seen next morning in full retreat towards Elnia; a movement which was so bitterly disappointing to Napoleon that he for some time refused to credit the fact. Various plans were contemplated by the Emperor for partially cutting off their retreat, but could not be brought into operation. He instantly ordered the storming of Smolensko, inferring that it should be considered as a mere passage through which he would force his way to Moscow. It appears that Murat was very anxious to dissuade him from this attempt, but finding his efforts in vain, the King of Naples was so exasperated that he rode in front of the most formidable of the Russian batteries while it was in full play upon the French; and having dismounted, remained standing immoveable, while the balls were cutting down men on all sides. The storming proceeded with success, except in the attack made by Ney upon the citadel, which repulsed him with loss. One battalion happening to present itself in flank before the Russian batteries, lost the entire row of a company by a single ball, which thus killed twenty-two men at the same instant. In the mean time, the main army, on an amphitheatre of hills, surveyed in anxiety the struggles of their comrades in arms, and occasionally applauded them with loud clapping hands as in a theatre, while they made good any fresh onset, dashing through a maze of balls and grape-shot which shadowed the air.

The troops were drawn off as night came on, and Napoleon retired to his tent. Count Lobau, having

obtained possession of the ditch, ordered some shells to be thrown into the city, to dislodge the enemy. Almost immediately were seen rising thick and black columns of smoke, with occasional gleams of light; then sparks and burning flakes; and at length pyramids of flame, which ascended from every part. These distinct and distant fires soon became united in one vast conflagration, which rose in whirling and destructive grandeur,—hung over nearly the whole of Smolensko, and consumed it amidst ominous and awful crashes. This disaster, which Count Lobau very naturally attributed to his shells, though it was the work of the Russians, threw him into great consternation. Napoleon, seated in front of his tent, viewed the terrific spectacle in silence. Neither the cause nor the result could as yet be ascertained, and the night was passed under arms. About three in the morning, a subaltern officer, belonging to Davoust, had ventured to the foot of the wall, and scaled it, without giving the least alarm. Emboldened by the silence which reigned around him, he made his way into the city, when suddenly hearing a number of voices speaking with the Sclavonian accent, he gave himself up for lost. But at this instant, the level rays of the sun discovered these supposed enemies to be the Poles of Poniatowski. They had been the first to penetrate the city, which Barclay had just abandoned to the flames. Smolensko having been reconnoitred, the army entered within its walls. The remarks of Segur on this occasion are very fine:—
"They passed over the smoking and bloody ruins in martial order, and with all the pomp of military music

and displayed banners; triumphant over deserted ruins, and the solitary witness of their own glory. A spectacle without spectators; a victory scarcely better than fruitless; a glory steeped in blood; and of which the smoke that surrounded them, and that seemed indeed to be the only conquest, was the best and most characteristic emblem."

Here Napoleon found, as at the Niemen, at Wilna, and at Witepsk, that phantom of victory which had decoyed him onward, had again eluded his grasp; and with mute and gloomy rage he walked along the city over heaps of smoking ruins and the naked bodies of the slain. He sat down in front of the citadel, on a mat at the door of a cottage, and here he held forth for an hour on the cowardice of Barclay, while bullets from the citadel walls were whizzing about his head. He dwelt upon the fine field for action he had offered him, the disgrace it was to have delivered up the keys of Old Russia without a struggle; the advantages he had given him in a strong city to support his efforts or to receive him in case of need. Without taking the slightest notice of the bullets from the Russian riflemen in the citadel, he thus continued to sit and vent his passionate disappointment, uttering the most bitter sarcasms upon the Russian general and army. "He was not yet in the secret," laconically observes Hazlitt, "of the new Scythian tactics of defending a country by burning its capitals." At length, he remounted his horse. One of his marshals remarked, as soon as he was out of hearing, that "if Barclay had been so very wrong in refusing battle, the Emperor would not have taken so much time to convince us of it." The truth was, he had no patience with the Russians for not staying—to be beaten.

The Russians still retained the suburbs of Smolensko, on the right bank of the Dnieper. During the night, Napoleon caused the bridges to be repaired, and a heavy cannonade to be kept up; and by the morning, the suburb had been deserted after being first set on fire. Ney and Junot immediately pressed forward through the burning labyrinth, and halted on the spot at which the roads to Petersburg and Moscow diverge, uncertain in which direction to continue the pursuit. At length, the French scouts brought information that Barclay had retreated in the direction of Moscow, taking at first a circuitous route through marshy and woody defiles. Ney came up with the rear guard at Stubna, where he dislodged them from a strong position, without difficulty; and next at Valoutina, where a desperate conflict took place, in which thirty thousand men were successively engaged on either side. Encumbered as he was by a long line of artillery and baggage, and hard pressed by Ney, Barclay was in extreme danger of losing his whole army, but he was saved by the unaccountable remissness of Junot, who had absolutely got into his rear, yet suspended his attack. Junot was a favorite with Napoleon, but he lost his command for this indecision. It was transferred to Rapp, who had just joined the army. The action had been sanguinary, and among other severe losses, the French general Gudin was mortally wounded. Napoleon visited the field of battle, which would probably have been a decisive one had he been present to direct the manœuvres. The soldiers were ranged round the dead bodies of French and Russians which covered the ground; the ghastly nature of their wounds, and the wrenched and twisted bayonets scattered about, bearing witness to the violence of the conflict. Napoleon felt that the time was come when his men required the support both of praise and rewards. Accordingly, he suppressed his chagrin at the indecisive result of the victory. His looks were never more impressive and affectionate. He declared this battle was the most brilliant exploit in their military history. In his rewards, he was munificent. The division of Gudin alone received eighty-seven decorations and promotions. He watched over and secured the care of the wounded, and left the field amidst the enthusiastic acclamations of his soldiers. He then returned to Smolensko. His carriage jolted over the grisly ruins of the fight, and his eyes were met on every side by all that is odious and horrible in fields of battle. Long lines of wounded were dragging themselves, or being borne along, and retarded his progress; when he entered the ruined city, carts were conveying out of sight the streaming heap of amputated limbs. Smolensko seemed one vast hospital, and its groans of anguish prevailed over and obliterated the glories and acclamations of Valoutina.

The situation of the French army had now become grave and critical. There could no longer be a doubt of the plan which Barclay was pursuing, and disastrous apprehensions crowded upon Napoleon's mind. The burning of Smolensko was evidently one result of a deep laid design; it could not be attributed to accident.

What must have been his reflections on the evening of this disastrous day, when, with a burning city for a camp-fire, he at length discovered the settled policy of his enemy—the policy, namely, by which Robert Bruce, in his last will, directed his countrymen how to conquer the ever-invading English—the policy by which Francis the First baffled his great rival, Charles the Fifth, in his attempt to conquer France—the policy of laying waste the country, burning the cities, retreating without a pitched battle and leaving famine, cold and disease to destroy the invading force?

Whatever misfortune awaited him, the Emperor was resolved to meet it without delay. He really dared fate to do its worst.

THE CAMP-FIRE AT WIAZMA.

VEN after quitting Smolensko, Napoleon did not penetrate the designs of the Russian general, Barclay de Tolly. He called the retreat, flight; their circumspection, pusillanimity.

Barclay had retreated to Dorogobouje, without attempting any resistance; but here he renewed his junction with Bagration, and Murat wishing to reconnoitre a small wood, met with a vigorous resistance, and pressing forwards found himself in front of the whole Russian army. He immediately sent word to Napoleon, who was in the rear. Davoust also, who disapproved of Murat's dispositions, wrote to hasten the Emperor's advance, "if he did not wish Murat to engage without him." Napoleon received the news with transport, and pressed on with his guard twelve leagues without stopping; but on the evening before he arrived, the enemy had disappeared. Barclay persevered in his retreat amidst imputations of treachery from Bagration, and discord and impatience throughout his camp. Rage at the continual falling back before the invaders had produced so many complaints, that Alexander had at last resolved to supersede Barclay by Kutusoff, who was shortly expected. Meantime, the French army advanced, marching three columns abreast; the Emperor, Murat, Davoust, and Ney, in the middle, along the great road to Moscow; Poniatowski on the right, and the army of Italy on the left.

It was not likely that the centre column could obtain any supplies on a road where the advanced guard had found nothing to subsist upon but the leavings of the Russians. They could not in so rapid a march find time to deviate from the direct route; besides which, the right and left columns were collecting and devouring all they could find on each side of the road. It seemed that a second army would have been required to follow them with the requisite necessaries; but as it was, they were obliged to carry everything with them. The existence of the army was a prodigy. With the French and Polish corps, the difficulties were not so great, owing to their excellent arrangements in packing their knapsacks, and by every regiment having attached to it a number of dwarf-horses, carts, and a drove of oxen. Their baggage was conducted by soldiers as drivers. But with the other chiefs in command, the case was very different. They had none of these excellent arrangements among them, and only existed by sending out marauding detachments on every side, who devoured their fill, and then returned to their respective bodies with the remainder—if any remained. Napoleon had not paid sufficient attention to these distinctions, in the arrangements of the various divisions, and the consequences were highly injurious. Very great distress, and very disorderly conduct incessantly occurred in the course of the march, particularly at Slawokowo. But Napoleon seemed only possessed by the idea of Moscow, and victory. He evidently took a great pleasure in frequently dating decrees and dispatches from the middle of Old Russia, which he knew would find their way even into the smallest hamlets throughout France, and make him appear present every where in full power.

Murat and Davoust had frequent misunderstandings at this period, which on one occasion came to an open quarrel. Davoust had been placed under the orders of the King of Naples, but the latter having brought the troops into the greatest peril by his headstrong valor and love of personal display and prowess, Davoust showed an unwillingness to support him. This presently led to a violent altercation in presence of the Emperor. Murat upbraided Davoust with slow and dilatory circumspection, and with a personal hostility towards himself ever since they were in Egypt. He became more vehement as he proceeded, and finally challenged the Prince of Eckmuhl. At this last provocation, the deliberate Davoust gave way to his feelings, and began a long history of the extraordinary pranks played by the King of Naples in pursuing the Russians. He said it was high time that the Emperor should be made acquainted with what passed every day in the management of his advanced guard. He showed that Murat wasted lives by useless attacks upon the Russians, for the sake of gaining a few acres of ground, although it invariably happened that the enemy left the ground of their own accord, whenever a sufficient force came up with them; that Murat was in the constant habit of losing men by slaughterous follies in the front to no purpose, after which he began to think of the propriety of reconnoitering; that he kept the whole of the advanced guard in a state of restless activity during sixteen hours of the twenty-four, with no cause, and finally chose the worst quarters for the night; so that the soldiers, instead of taking their food and rest, were groping about for provisions and forage, and calling to each other in the dark, in order to find their way back to the bivouacs: and that the king did nothing else but storm and rage through the ranks, and then ride close to the enemy's lines in all directions.

Napoleon listened to the whole of this in silence, pushing a Russian bullet backwards and forwards under the sole of his foot. When they were both quite out of breath, he mildly told them that under present circumstances he preferred impetuosity to methodical caution; that each had his merits; it was impossible for one man to combine all descriptions of merit; and enjoining them to be friends for the future, dismissed them to their tents.

On the 28th of August, the army traversed the great plains of Wiazma. They passed hastily onwards, several regiments abreast, over the fields. The high road was given up to the train of artillery, and the hospital wagons. The Emperor appeared among them in all directions. He was occupied in calculating, as he went forward, how many thousands of cannon-balls would be required to destroy the Russian army. He ordered all private carriages to be broken up, as they might tend to impede their progress, and be in the way when a battle occurred. The carriage of his aid-de-camp, General Narbonne, was the first that was demolished. The baggage of all the corps was collected in the rear, comprised of a long train of bat-horses, and of carriages called *kibics*, drawn by rope-traces. These were loaded with provisions, plunder, military stores, sick soldiers, and the arms of these soldiers, and of those who acted as drivers and guards. In this heterogeneous column were seen tall cuirassiers, who had lost their horses, and were mounted on horses not much larger than asses. Among such a confused and disorderly multitude, the Cossacks might have made most harassing attacks; but Barclay seemed cautious to avoid disheartening the French too much. His object was to impede and delay the progress of the invaders, by contests with the advanced guard only, and without inducing them to abandon their design.

This protracted state of affairs, the fatigued condition of the army, the quarrels among the chiefs, and the approach of yet more dangerous circumstances, filled the mind of Napoleon with distrust and apprehension. He had for some time hoped and expected that Alexander would open some negotiation with him, or at least send him a letter. At length, he gave the opportunity himself, by causing Berthier to write to Barclay; and the letter concluded with these words:—" The Emperor commands me to entreat you to present his compliments to the Emperor Alexander, and to say to him that neither the vicissitudes of war, nor any other circumstances, can ever impair the friendship which he feels for him." Napoleon's sincerity in this profession was probably of the same value as the previous good faith of Alexander. No answer was returned. On the very day the letter was sent, the advanced guard of the French drove the Russians into Wiazma. The army was so exhausted by fatigue, heat, and thirst, that the soldiers fought among themselves for precedence in obtaining water from some muddy pools. Napoleon himself was very glad to obtain a little of this thick puddle to allay his thirst. In the course of the night, the Russians destroyed the bridges of the Wiazma; and, after pillaging the town, set fire to it, and decamped. Murat and Davoust, after some opposition, succeeded in making an entrance and extinguishing the flames. Various reports now made to the Emperor left him no longer in the least doubt as to who were the incendiaries, and he clearly perceived the regular plan on which the Russians were acting. Entering Wiazma, he found a few resources had been left in the town, but that his soldiers had wasted them all by pillage. This so exasperated him that he rode in among them, and threw several of them down. Seeing a suttler who had been very busy in this wasteful disorder, he ordered him to be shot. But it is well known of Napoleon, that his fits of passion were of short duration, and always followed by a disposition to clemency. Those, therefore, who heard this order, placed the suttler a few minutes afterwards, in a place which the Emperor would have to pass; and making the man kneel, they got a woman and several children to kneel at his side, who were to appear as his wife and family. Napoleon inquired what they wanted, and granted the offender his pardon.

Belliard, at this time the head of Murat's staff, now rode up to him in a very excited state. He reported that the enemy had shown himself in full force, in an advantageous position, beyond the Wiazma, and ready to engage; that the cavalry on both sides had immediately come to action; and that the infantry becoming necessary, the King of Naples had placed himself at the head of one of Davoust's divisions, and ordered the advance—when Davoust hastened to the spot and commanded them to halt, as he did not approve of the intended manœuvre, and told the king that it was absurd and ruinous. Murat had therefore sent to the Emperor, declaring that he would no longer hold a disputed command. Napoleon was enraged at this renewal of the quarrel at such a moment, and sent off Berthier to place under the command of Murat that division which he had intended to lead. Meantime, the contest was over, and Murat, now reverting to the conduct of Davoust, was boiling with indignation. He asked of what use was his royal rank? It could not obtain him obedience, or even protect him from insult. But as his sword had made him a king, to that alone would he appeal. It was with the greatest difficulty that he was restrained from going to attack Davoust. He then cursed his crown, and shed a torrent of tears. Davoust did not attempt to excuse the insubordination of his conduct, but persisted that Murat had been misled by his own temerity, and that the Emperor had been misinformed as to the whole affair with the Russians.

Napoleon re-entered Wiazma, and here intelligence was brought him from the interior of Russia, that the government deliberately appropriated all his successes to themselves, and that *Te Deum* had been repeatedly celebrated at Petersburg for the Russian "victories" of Witepsk and Smolensko! "*Te Deum!*" ejaculated Napoleon, in amazement—"then they dare to tell lies, not only to man but to God!" He also learned, that while their towns were in flames there was nothing but ringing of bells in Petersburg, hymns of gratitude, and publications of the triumph of the Russian arms.

Yet he did not perceive the plan of the Russian general. For a time, at least, his usual penetration seemed to have been dulled. He remained among the smoking ruins of Wiazma, which might have conveyed to his mind an ominous lesson of the result of a system of tactics to which he was unaccustomed. But now this system, having accomplished its purpose, was to be abandoned. Barclay had persisted in carrying out his plan against all the clamor and imputations of the Russians. He was now superseded by Kutusoff, a general of the school of Suwarrow; but the skilful De Tolly willingly served under that general. This alteration of plan, and change of commanders, Napoleon learned while at Wiazma. He could now expect a battle, and he prepared to render it decisive. He advanced to the bloody field of Borodino.

THE CAMP-FIRE AT BORODINO.

NAPOLEON esteemed the battle of Borodino, or Moskwa, his "greatest feat of arms." But his conduct during the conflict has been the subject of much animadversion, and many critics agree with Segur that he did not display upon that field his usual splendor and power of genius.—But to the incidents of Borodino.

The Russian army halted at Borodino, and intelligence was brought to the Emperor of the French that they were breaking up the whole plain and forming intrenchments in every part. Napoleon then announced to his troops the approaching battle, and allowed them two days rest to prepare their arms and collect their provision.

Napoleon was leading his army onwards farther and farther, through pathless deserts, or over ruined fields, or towns laid in ashes; fatigue, famine, and war, were reducing his numbers, and he was at every step increasing his distance from his resources, while his enemies were in the heart of their own country. Even at Wilna, a deficiency had been discovered in the hospital department; the evil increased at Witepsk. At Smolensko, there was no want of hospitals; fifteen large brick buildings, saved from the flames, had been set apart for this purpose, and there was plenty of wine, brandy, and medicines, but there was a dearth of dressings for the appalling number of wounds. The surgeons had already used all that could be procured—had torn up their own linen, and at length were obliged to substitute the paper found in the city archives. One hospital, containing a hundred wounded men, was forgotten, in the stress of difficulties, for the space of three whole days. The state of its wretched inmates when it was accidentally discovered by Rapp, none of the chroniclers of these events have ever attempted to describe, and the imagination recoils with horror from the attempt to realise it. Napoleon sent them his own stock of wine, and many pecuniary gratuities. The alarming decrease of numbers noticed at Witepsk was still more perceptible now. The army at Smolensko might be computed at about one hundred and fifty-seven thousand men, part of the deficiency being caused by the occupation of additional territory; the rest by desertion, wounds, sickness, or death. With such a force, however, Napoleon had no reason for apprehension, if he could bring his enemies to a battle; but it was evident that Barclay had discovered and resolutely pursued a more efficient plan. It seems certain, therefore, that Napoleon did entertain thoughts of establishing winter-quarters at Smolensko; of intrenching himself strongly, bringing up his reinforcements and supplies, and in this central point commanding the roads to both the capitals of Russia; waiting proposals of peace, or preparing for a fresh campaign in the spring. The danger of so long an absence from France; the difficulty of holding together an army composed of many different nations; the news of fresh successes achieved by his various leaders in different directions; above all, the impetuosity of his own temperament, decided the point. The only doubt which long existed was on which of the two capitals to advance. By the 24th of August, all was decided, and the French army was in full march towards Moscow.

Sixteen thousand recruits, and a vast multitude of peasants, joined the ranks of Kutusoff. On the 4th of September, the French left Gjatz. The heads of their columns were now more than ever annoyed by troops of Cossacks, and the frequent necessity of making his cavalry deploy against so temporary and random an obstacle, provoked Murat to such a degree that he once clapped spurs to his horse, and dashing alone to the front of their line, halted within a few paces, and waving his sabre with the most indignant and menacing authority, signified his command for them to withdraw. The sudden apparition of this splendid figure in front of their ranks, with the air of one who possessed the power of annihilating them with a blow, so took these barbarians by surprise that they instantly withdrew in vague astonishment. They shortly, however, returned, and received the charge of the Italian chasseurs. Platoff has since related that in this affair, a Russian officer, who had brought a sorcerer with him, was wounded; whereupon he ordered the sorcerer to be soundly drubbed, as he had expressly directed him to turn aside all the balls by his conjurations.

Napoleon now surveyed the whole country from an eminence, and displayed marvellous sagacity in the conclusions he drew as to the positions and intentions of the enemy. Vast numbers of troops were posted in front of their left, and he concluded that this must be the point where their ground was most accessible, and that they had there constructed a formidable redoubt. It was, therefore, necessary to carry this. The attack was general, and the Russian rear-guards were driven back upon Borodino. This curtain being removed, the first Russian redoubt was discovered. The division of Compans attacked it, and the 61st regiment took it at the point of the bayonet. Bagration sent reinforcements, and it was retaken. It was again taken by the 61st, and this occurred three times, till finally, with the loss of half the regiment, it remained in possession of the French. But a neighboring wood was swarming with Russian riflemen, and it required the efforts of Morand, Poniatowski, and Murat, to complete the conquest. Firing, nevertheless, continued till nightfall.

Not a single prisoner had been taken. When Napoleon heard this, he asked many questions impatiently. Were the Russians determined to conquer or die? He was answered, that their priests and chiefs had wrought them up to a state of fanaticism in their love for their country and their abhorrence of their invaders. The Emperor at this fell into meditation, and concluded that a battle of artillery would be the only efficient mode to adopt. On that night, a thin, cold rain, began to fall, and autumn proclaimed its approach by violent gusts of wind. The French slept without fires.

On the morning of the 6th of September, the two armies were again visible to each other, in the same position as the preceding day had left them. This excited a general joy among the French. At last, this desultory, vagrant, and irritating war, in which so many brave men had perished, to so little advantage, seemed about to come to a satisfactory issue. The Emperor rode forth at the earliest dawn, and surveyed the whole front of the enemy's army, by passing along a succession of eminences that rose between the two antagonist powers.

The Russians were in possession of all the heights, on a semi-circle of two leagues extent from the Mosqua to the old Moscow road. Their centre, commanded by Barclay, formed the salient part of their line; it was protected by the Kalogha, by a ravine, and by two strong redoubts at its extremities. Their right and left receded. Their right rested on the precipitous and rocky bank of the Kalogha, and was defended by deep and muddy ravines. A strong redoubt also crowned the height, which was lined with eighty pieces of cannon. Bagration commanded the left; it was stationed on a less elevated crest than the centre, and having lost the protection of its great redoubt was the most accessible point of their army. Two small hills crowned with redoubts protected its front. It was flanked by a wood, beyond which, on the extreme left, was a corps commanded by Tutchkoff, but stationed at so great a distance as to permit the possibility of manœuvring on the intervening ground without previously overwhelming this detached corps.

Having concluded his observation, Napoleon made his plan. "Eugene," he said, "should be the pivot; the battle must be begun by the right. As soon as the right, advancing under the protection of the wood, shall have carried the redoubts of the Russian left wing, it must turn to the left, march on the Russian flank, overthrowing and driving back their whole army upon their right wing, and into the Kalogha." Napoleon was still on the heights, taking a last view of the ground, and considering the details of the grand plan he had formed, when Davoust hastily approached him. The marshal had a proposal of his own to make, by which he expected to turn the enemy's left in the night, and by surprise. The Emperor listened to him with great attention, but after silently considering the proposition for a few minutes, rejected it, and persisted in his rejection, notwithstanding the confidence with which it was urged by Davoust. He then re-entered his tent, when Murat pertinaciously strove to persuade him that the Russians would again retreat before he commenced his attack. The Emperor in some agitation returned to the heights of Borodino, where, however, every indication of an intention to remain and fight was observable among the Russians. He had taken very few attendants, to avoid being recognized by the enemy's batteries; but at the moment he was pointing out the signs he had observed to Murat, the discharge of one of their cannon broke the silence of the day;—"for it is frequently the case," observes Segur, "that nothing is so calm as the day which precedes a great battle."

The Emperor now returned to his tent to dictate the order of battle. The two armies were nearly equal,—about a hundred and twenty thousand men, and six hundred pieces of cannon on each side. The Russians had the best position, and the additional advantages of speaking the same language, wearing the same uniform, and fighting for a common cause; and of being near their resources, and in their own country; but they had too many raw recruits in their ranks. The army of Napoleon had just completed a long and harassing march; was made up of many nations, and in the midst of a hostile people; but it was entirely composed of tried soldiers, who had fought their way through many a desperate battle, and held their ranks through every hardship. The proclamation issued by Napoleon was suited to the men and the circumstances. It was grave, simple, and energetic. "Soldiers," said he, "you have now before you the battle which you have so long desired. From this moment, the victory depends upon yourselves. It is necessary for us; it will bring us abundance, good winter quarters, and a speedy return to our country." It happened that the Emperor had that day received the portrait of his son from Paris. He himself exhibited the picture in front of his tent.

Kutusoff, on his part, had worked upon the feelings of the Russians by means suited to their condition. He had induced the chief priests or popes of the Greek church, dressed in their richest robes, to walk in splendid procession before his army. They carried the symbols of their religion, and foremost of all a sacred image of the Virgin, withdrawn from Smolensko by a miracle. He then addressed the soldiers on the subject of heaven, "the only country which slaves have left to them,"—and incited the serfs to defend their master's property in the name of the Great Teacher of universal brotherhood. The whole ceremony worked the effect which he intended, and roused his hearers to the highest pitch of courage and fanaticism.

During the night, the whole French army was stationed in order of battle, and three batteries, of sixty pieces each, were opposed to the Russian redoubts. Poniatowski commanded the right wing, which was destined to commence the attack on the Russian left. The whole of the artillery were to support his attack. Davoust and Ney, supported by Junot, with the Westphalians, and Murat with the cavalry, were in the centre, and ready to precipitate themselves upon the Russians after the opening of the battle by Poniatowski. Prince Eugene, with the army of Italy, and the Bavarian cavalry, formed the left. The Emperor held his guard in reserve. He appeared very unwell, depressed in spirits, and unable to sleep. He was oppressed with fever and excessive thirst, probably the result of over fatigue and anxiety. The news of the defeat of his troops at Salamanca, had just been brought to him by Fabvier, an aid-de-camp of Marmont; but he received the account with great firmness and temper. Present events only seemed to weigh on his mind. He repeatedly called to ascertain the hour, and to inquire whether any sounds indicative of a retreat had been heard in the opposite army. On one occasion his aid-de-camp found him resting his head on his hands, and the few words he said indicated that his thoughts were dwelling on the vanity of human glory. He asked Rapp, whether he thought they should gain the victory? "Undoubtedly," answered Rapp, "but it will be a bloody one!" On which Napoleon replied, "I know it; but I have eighty thousand men. I shall lose twenty thousand of them, and with sixty thousand shall enter Moscow. The stragglers will there rejoin us, and afterwards the battalions of recruits now on their march, and we shall be stronger than before the battle." He seemed neither to comprehend the guard nor the cavalry in this calculation. Before day-break, one of Ney's officers announced the Russians still in view, and asked leave to begin the attack. These words restored the Emperor. He rose; summoned his officers; and leaving his tent exclaimed, "At last we have them! March!—We will to-day open for ourselves the gates of Moscow!"

It was half-past five in the morning, when Napoleon took his station near the great redoubt which had been taken on the 5th. As the sun rose, he pointed to the east, saying, "There is the sun of Austerlitz!" The artillery were employed in pushing forward the batteries which had been placed too far back. The Russians made no opposition; they seemed fearful of being the first to break the awful silence. While waiting for the sound of Poniatowski's fire on the right, Napoleon ordered Eugene to take the village of Borodino, on the left. The 106th regiment accordingly opened the attack; gained the village; rushed across the bridge, in the ardor of success, and would have been cut off had not the 92d come up to their relief. During this action, sounds on the right announced that Poniatowski had commenced his attack, and Napoleon immediately gave the signal of battle. "Then, suddenly," says Segur, "from the previously peaceful plain and silent hills, burst forth flashes of fire and clouds of smoke, which were instantly followed by a multitude of explosions and the whizzing of innumerable bullets which rent the air on every side. In the midst of this thunder, Davoust, with the divisions of Compans and Desaix, and thirty cannon, advanced rapidly upon the first redoubt of the enemy." The fusillade of the Russians now commenced, and was answered by the French cannon. The French infantry advanced at a quick pace, without firing; but General Compans, who headed the column, fell wounded with the foremost of his men, and the rest halted under the storm of balls. Rapp instantly took the post of Compans, and urged the troops forward at a running pace with charged bayonets, when he also fell. It was the twenty-second wound that he had received. He was conveyed to the Emperor, who exclaimed, "What! Rapp! always wounded! but how are they going on above there?" The aid-de-camp replied, that the guard was wanted to finish the business. "No," said Napoleon, "I will take good care of that; I will not have that destroyed. I will gain the battle without it." A third general, who succeeded Rapp, likewise fell; and Davoust himself was struck. At this moment, Ney, with his three divisions of ten thousand men, threw himself into the plain to support Davoust, and the Russian fire was thus diverted. Ney rushed on; Davoust's columns continued their advance with renewed confidence; and almost at the same time both of the French divisions scaled the heights; overthrew or killed their defenders, and obtained possession of both the redoubts of the Russian left. Napoleon then ordered Murat to charge and complete the victory. The king was on the heights in an instant; but the Russians, reinforced by their second line, now advanced with rapidity to regain their redoubts. The French were taken by surprise in the first disorder of their success, and retreated. Murat, endeavoring in vain to rally the troops, found himself nearly surrounded, and alone amidst the enemy's cavalry. They were even stretching out their arms to take him prisoner, when he escaped by throwing himself into one of the redoubts. There he found only a few soldiers in utter disorder. They were running backwards and forwards upon the parapet in consternation; but he seized the first weapon he could find, and fought with one hand, while he waved his plumed hat in the air with the other. His presence and his rallying calls to duty soon restored the courage of the men. Ney quickly re-formed his divisions; his fire threw the Russians into disorder; Murat was extricated; and the heights re-conquered. Murat was no sooner freed from this danger than he furiously and repeatedly charged the enemy at the head of the French cavalry, and in another hour the Russian left wing was entirely defeated.

In the meantime, a dreadful conflict had raged unceasingly on the French left. After Eugene had taken the village of Borodino, he had passed the Kalogha, in front of the great Russian redoubt, which was lined with eighty pieces of cannon, and protected by a ravine. General Bonnamy, at the head of eighteen hundred men of the 30th regiment, carried this strong position by one sudden charge, at six o'clock in the morning. But the Russians recovered from their first panic; and, rallying before their assailants could be supported, they were headed by Kutusoff and Yermdof in person, and made an attack in their turn. Bonnamy's regiment was surrounded, overwhelmed, and driven from the redoubt, with the loss of its commander and one-third of its numbers. Eugene, however, maintained his station on the sloping sides of the heights for four hours, under a terrific fire, and, until he was relieved by the turn of the battle, when Kutusoff was obliged to defend the left of his centre, now exposed in consequence of the defeat of his left wing by the divisions of Ney,

Davoust, and Murat as already detailed. The defence of Kutusoff was then carried on at two points. He poured a tremendous fire, with devastating effect, upon the troops of Ney and Murat, from the heights of the ruined village of Semenowska. It became necessary to carry that position. Maubourg swept the front of it with his cavalry; Friand and Dufour, with their infantry, mounted the acclivity, dislodged the Russians, and secured the position. The Russians had now lost every one of their intrenchments except the great redoubt, on which Prince Eugene was preparing for a decisive attack. He had already sent to Napoleon for assistance, but received the reply, that "he could give him no relief; it depended on him alone to conquer; that the battle was concentrated on that point." Murat and Ney, exhausted with their efforts, also sent for reinforcements; but Napoleon concluded that the presence of Friand and Maubourg on the heights would maintain them, and he saw that the battle was not yet won. Amidst all the excitement of these repeated and most urgent messages, he steadily refused to compromise his reserve.

The Russians now rallied *en masse*. Kutusoff commanded all his reserves, and even the Russian guard, to the assistance of his uncovered left. Infantry, artillery, and cavalry, all advanced for one grand and mighty effort. Ney and Murat, with intrepidity and firmness, sustained the rushing tempest. It was no time for them to think of following up their previous successes; all their strength was required to maintain their position. Friand's soldiers, ranged in front of the armed

MARSHAL MURAT.

heights of Semenowska, were swept off in whole ranks by a storm of grape-shot. The survivors were dismayed, and one of their brave commanders ordered a retreat; when Murat suddenly rode up to him, and catching hold of his collar, exclaimed,—"What are you doing?" The colonel, pointing to the ground on which half of his men lay dead or wounded, replied—"You see we can stay here no longer!" Murat hastily rejoined—"I can stay here very well myself!" The colonel looked steadily at him, and calmly replied—"It is right. Soldiers! let us advance to be slain!"

Murat had again sent to Napoleon for assistance, and he now gave it promptly and efficiently. The artillery of the guard were ordered to advance. Eighty pieces of cannon quickly crowned the heights, and discharged their contents at once. The Russian cavalry first charged against this tremendous barrier, but retired in confusion to escape destruction. The infantry exhibited a spectacle of stolid indifference to death, or devotion to their country and their leaders, perhaps unparalleled in the history of war,—affording a picture of the inherent powers of human nature, worthy of study, while most horrible to contemplate in their present misapplication. "The infantry," says Segur, "advanced in thick masses, in which our balls from the first made wide and deep openings; yet they constantly came on nearer and nearer, when the French batteries redoubling the rapidity of their fire, absolutely mowed them down with grape-shot. Whole platoons fell at once. Their soldiers struggled to preserve their compactness under this terrible fire; and, divided every instant by death, they still closed their ranks over it, trampling it with defiance under their feet. At last they halted, not daring to advance any farther, and yet resolved not to go back; whether they were appalled, and as it were petrified with horror in this tremendous gulph of destruction; or whether it was owing to Bagration being at that time mortally wounded; or whether it might be that a first arrangement being attended with failure, their generals felt incompetent to change it,—not possessing, like Napoleon, the art of moving such vast bodies at once, with unity, harmony, and order. In short, these heavy and stationary masses stood to be crushed and destroyed in detail for two entire hours, *without any other movement than that of the falling of the men.* It was in truth a deplorable and frightful massacre; and the intelligent valor of the French artillerymen admired the firm, resigned, but infatuated courage of their enemies." Scott describes the scene to the same effect. "Regiments of peasants, who till that day had never seen war, and who still had no other uniform than their grey jackets, formed with the steadiness of veterans, crossed their brows, and having uttered their national exclamation '*Gospodee pomiloui nas!*' (God have mercy upon us,) rushed into the thickest of the battle, where the survivors, without feeling fear or astonishment, closed their ranks over their comrades as they fell."

The problem, of whether that mass of men would have stood to be utterly destroyed to the last individual, was never worked out; for a fresh movement in the French army, bringing upon them a new form of peril, at last restored them to a sense of their human conditions, and put them to flight. Ney extended his right, pushed it rapidly forward, and, seconded by Davoust and Murat, turned the left of the Russian centre, and dispersed them. The battle still raged on the Russian right,—where Barclay, intrenched in the great redoubt, obstinately struggled with Prince Eugene,—and on their extreme left, where Poniatowski had as yet failed to make himself master of the great Moscow road. When another pressing demand for "the guard, to complete the destruction of the Russian army, was brought to Napoleon from Ney and Murat, who burned to follow up the retreat of the defeated infantry, he pointed in silence to those two conflicting bodies. The Emperor's words ought to be satisfactory as to the cause of his refusal to send his reserve, which has occasioned so many animadversions. "The case," he said, "was not sufficiently extricated and conclusive to induce him yet to part with his reserves; and that he must see more clearly the state of his chess-board." When Count Daru, at the pressing solicitation of Berthier, repeated the request, and said in a low tone "that on all sides the cry now was that the moment for the guard to act was come," Napoleon replied, "And if there should be a second battle on the morrow, what shall I have to carry it on with?"

Kutusoff was still unconquered. He rallied for the third time, and resting his right on the great redoubt, formed a fresh line in front of Ney and Murat; but it was a last effort. General Caulaincourt, at the head of the fifth French cuirassiers, made a desperate charge on the rear of the redoubt, while Eugene maintained his ground in the front. The last words of Caulaincourt, as he left Murat to open the attack, had been, "You shall see me there immediately, dead or alive!" He charged at the head of his regiment, overthrew all opposition, and was the first man who penetrated into the redoubt, where, almost at the instant, he fell mortally wounded; but that decisive charge determined the victory. The troops of Prince Eugene were pressing onwards, and had nearly reached the mouth of the battery, when suddenly its fire was extinguished, its smoke dispersed, and above the now silent engines of destruction appeared the moveable and polished brass which covered the French cuirassiers. The Russians had been driven from their last entrenchment. They returned with one more desperate effort to retake this position, as if determined to die rather than endure defeat. Their column advanced to the very mouths of the cannon, but at the terrible discharge of thirty pieces of artillery, which were directed against them, they appeared to be whirled round by the shock, and retired without being able to deploy. Officers now came in from every part of the field. Poniatowski, supported by Sebastiani, had conquered on the left, after a desperate struggle. The sounds of firing became weaker and less frequent. The Russians had retreated to a new position, where they appeared to be intrenching themselves. The day was drawing to a close, and the battle was ended.

Napoleon had remained nearly on the same spot throughout the whole of the battle, seated on the edge of a trench, or walking backwards and forwards on an elevated platform. He now mounted his horse, and slowly passed amidst the heaps of dead and wounded till he reached the heights of Semenowska. He said little; but the few words he uttered implied that he felt his victory had cost him too dear. He then repaired to his tent to write the bulletin of the battle, and made a point of announcing to France that neither himself nor his reserve had been subject to the least danger,—thus manifesting the confidence he felt in the opinion entertained of him by the French; and, at the same time, informing Europe that notwithstanding his distance from France, and while surrounded by enemies in a hostile country, he was still safe and powerful.

"It has been frequently asserted," says Count Mathieu Dumas, intendant general of the army, "that Napoleon did not display his customary activity on this day.

"His apparent indifference has excited astonishment; it has been intimated that he labored under bodily exhaustion; that he was not able to call into action all the resources of his genius; in short, that his star began to grow dim, even in the midst of victory. Napoleon certainly appeared to be indisposed; he had undergone excessive fatigue during the two preceding nights, which he had employed in person in reconnoitering the positions of the enemy, in placing the corps of the army, and in determining the point of attack. Having formed his plans to compel the enemy to abandon their strong position, he would not consent to make any change in the arrangements which he had resolved upon after profound consideration. He placed himself at a short distance from his right wing, against which it was probable that the Russian general would direct his principal effort, in order to take the attacking columns in the rear, while they should be stopped by the fire of the redoubts. The station which Napoleon had chosen, was, in fact, the best point of observation. It commanded a view of the whole field of battle, and if any manœuvre, any partial success of the enemy, had required new measures, the vigilance of Napoleon would not have failed to meet the urgency of the case. He would have gone to the spot in person, as he did at the battle of Wagram.

"About nine o'clock in the evening, Count Daru and myself were summoned to the Emperor. His bivouac was in the middle of the square battalion of his guard, a little behind the redoubt. His supper had just been served; he was alone, and made us sit down on his right and left hand. After having heard the account of the measures taken for the relief of the wounded, &c., he spoke to us of the issue of the battle; a moment afterwards he fell asleep for about twenty minutes; then, suddenly waking, he continued thus: 'People will be astonished that I did not bring up my reserves to obtain more decisive results; but it was necessary to keep them, in order to strike a decisive blow in the great battle which the enemy will offer us before Moscow: the success of the day was secured; I had to think of the success of the campaign, and it is for that I keep my reserves.'"

The Emperor was mistaken in supposing that there would be another great battle before Moscow; but in all other particulars, his sagacity was admirably displayed. Still, Borodino was far from decisive. Before day-break the next morning, there was an alarm among the French, which penetrated even to the tent of the Emperor, and the old guard was called to arms. This was mortifying after a victory, and carried with it an air of insult. As soon as morning dawned, the losses of the armies were ascertained by Napoleon.

Ten thousand men had been killed, and the wounded amounted to no less than twenty thousand. Forty-three generals had been killed or wounded. Among the Russians, there had been fifteen thousand killed, including the gallant Prince Bagration, and thirty thousand wounded. The French carried their wounded two leagues in the rear, to the large monastery of Kolotskoi. The chief surgeon, Larrey, had taken assistants from all the other regiments, and the hospital wagons had arrived —but all that could be done for the conveyance was insufficient. Larrey subsequently complained that not sufficient troops had been left to enable him to obtain the necessary articles from the surrounding villages.

When the Emperor inspected the field of battle, every thing concurred to increase its horrors. A gloomy sky, a cold rain, a violent wind, habitations in ashes, a plain absolutely torn up and covered with fragments and ruins, rendered the scene of carnage yet more appalling. The dark and funereal verdure of the north was seen all round the horizon. Soldiers were roaming like wild beasts among the bodies of their dead comrades, and emptying their knapsacks to procure subsistence for themselves. The wounds of the slain were of the most hideous description, occasioned by the large bullets used by the Russians. The bivouacs were mournful; no songs of triumph, no lively narrations,—all dreary and silent. Around the eagles were the rest of the officers and subalterns, and a few soldiers,—barely sufficient to guard the colours. Their uniforms were torn by the violence of the conflict, blackened with powder, and stained with blood; yet even amidst their rags, their misery, and destitution, they displayed a lofty bearing, and on the appearance of Napoleon welcomed him with acclamations.

Many wounded men were found in the bottom of ravines, where the French troops had been precipitated, or where they had dragged themselves for shelter from the enemy or the storm. Some of the younger soldiers in sighs and groans were calling upon the name of their country, or of their mother; but most of the veterans awaited death either with an impassive or a sardonic air, neither imploring or complaining. The anguish of some of the wounded made them beg of their comrades, as a mercy, to kill them instantly. Among the Russians, the enormous number of wounded presented on every side a spectacle of moving horrors. Many of these mutilated objects were seen dragging themselves with bloody trails along the ground, towards places where they might find shelter among a heap of dead bodies. Napoleon's horse chancing to tread upon the body of one apparently dead, a cry of anguish startled him, and excited his compassion. Somebody remarked that "it was only a Russian;"—upon which Napoleon angrily reproved the speaker, and observed that, "after a battle, none were enemies,—but all were men." The Emperor ordered the prisoners that had been taken, to be again numbered, and a few dismounted cannon to be collected. Between seven and eight hundred prisoners, and a score of unserviceable cannon, were the sole trophies of this most sanguinary and imperfect victory.

THE CAMP-FIRE AT MOSCOW.

THE Russians themselves kindled Napoleon's camp-fire at Moscow. They lighted his bivouacs with the flames of their ancient capital, and thus gave him an awful proof of their invincible opposition to the invader.

After the battle of Borodino, Napoleon found the road to Moscow open, and advanced rapidly towards the conquest he had so long desired. The city of his hopes has been thus described:

"Moscow was an immense and singular assemblage

of two hundred and ninety-five churches, and fifteen hundred splendid habitations, together with their gardens and offices. These palaces, built of brick, with the grounds attached to them, intermingled with handsome wooden houses, and even with cottages, were scattered over several square leagues of unequal surface, and were grouped around a lofty, triangular palace, whose vast and double inclosure, comprising two divisions, and about half a league in circumference, included—one of them—several palaces and churches, and a quantity of uncultivated and stony ground; the other, a vast bazaar—a city of merchants—exhibiting the opulence of the four quarters of the world. These buildings, shops as well as palaces, were all covered with polished and colored plates of iron. The churches, which were each of them surmounted by a terrace, and by several steeples terminating in gilded globes, the crescent, and finally the cross, recalled to mind the history of the people. They represented Asia and her religion, first triumphant, then subdued; and finally the crescent of Mahomet under the dominion of the cross of Christ. A single sunbeam made this superb city glitter with a thousand varied colors; and the enchanted traveller halted in ecstacy at the sight. It recalled to his mind the dazzling prodigies with which oriental poets had amused his infancy."

Count Rostopchin had been appointed governor of Moscow.

As the French army approached the capital, terror began to prevail among the inhabitants; and, after the taking of Smolensko, many of the wealthy classes removed their most valuable effects, and left the city. The governor secretly encouraged this gradual emigration, though he ostensibly maintained a complete confidence of success in the Russian cause, and kept up the spirits of the people by false reports and loyal declarations. Among other contrivances, he employed a number of females in the construction of an immense balloon, out of which, as he made the people believe, he would pour down a shower of fire upon the French army. Under this pretence, he is said to have collected a quantity of combustibles destined for a purpose widely different from this æronautic fiction. The panic at Moscow at length became general, and not only the nobility and higher classes in general, but tradesmen, mechanics, and even the poor, left it by thousands. The public archives and treasures were removed; the magazines emptied, as far as time permitted. The roads, especially those to the south, were covered with a long train of carriages of every description, and with successive crowds of fugitives on foot, the priests leading the way laden with the symbols of their religion, and singing mournful hymns of lamentation.

Kutusoff, with his retreating army, now appeared without the walls, and intrenched himself strongly in the position of Fili. He had ninety thousand men under his command, of whom six thousand were Cossacks, large numbers of recruits having been added to his ranks since the great battle; and it appears certain that he still entertained some intention of defending the capital. This purpose, however, was speedily relinquished. On the 14th of September, he broke up his camp, and his army continued its retreat, passing through Moscow, which was to be abandoned to its fate. The troops marched along the deserted streets with furled banners and silent drums; and passed out at the Kalomna gate. Some of the officers were observed to shed tears of rage and shame. With an army of ninety thousand men, in their own country, and with the constant power of retreating upon their resources, it is no wonder that all the braver spirits among the Russians felt this humiliating policy most deeply.

The long columns of retreat were followed by the garrison and all the remaining population, with the exception of one class, left there for a special purpose. Before his own departure, Rostopchin opened the prisons, and let loose their miserable and degraded inmates, to the number of three or four hundred, having given them a secret task to perform. The pumps of the city had all been removed or destroyed, and torches and combustibles in great quantities collected. Rostopchin then left the city.

Napoleon subsequently made the calculation that a hundred thousand of the inhabitants, thus abandoned and forced to fly from Moscow, perished in the woods of the neighborhood for want of food and shelter. In the midst of their despair at the very last, the multitude had been roused to an excitement of hope and confidence by the sight of a vulture caught in the chains which supported the cross of the principal church. This, they hailed as an omen that God was about to deliver Napoleon into their hands. "What," says Hazlitt, "can subdue a nation who can be thus easily deluded by the grossest appearances ; and whose whole physical strength, to inflict or to endure, can be wielded mechanically, and in mass, in proportion to their want of understanding ? Certainly, ignorance is power."

On the same day that the Russian army retreated through Moscow, and even before their rear-guard had cleared the city, Murat penetrated the suburbs, and Eugene and Poniatowski opened an attack at the gates. Napoleon himself with his guard gained the summit of the "Mount of Salvation," the last height which hid his long desired conquest from his view, about two o'clock in the afternoon, and saw the immense city glittering with a thousand colors in the sun,—a strange and magnificent sight in the midst of the desert. The troops halted involuntarily, struck with admiration, and loudly exclaimed,—" Moscow ! Moscow !" in a transport of joy. The marshals crowded with congratulations around the Emperor. He, also, had suddenly paused, in evident exultation. His first exclamation was,— " There at last, then, is that famous city !"—presently adding,—" It was high time !"

A flag of truce from Miloradowitch, who commanded the Russian rear-guard, met the Emperor at this point. He came to announce that his guard would set fire to Moscow if he were not allowed time to evacuate it. An armistice of two hours were granted him immediately. Napoleon's eager eye was fixed on the city, as on a vision he was just about to realise. He expected every moment to see a deputation issue from the gates to lay its wealth, its population, its senate, and its nobility at his feet. The troops of the two nations were intermingled for a few minutes. Murat was soon surrounded by a crowd of Cossacks, extolling his personal prowess by signs and gesticulations, and intoxicating him with their admiration. He distributed the watches of his officers among these barbarian warriors, one of whom denominated him his "Hetman." It began to look like an almost immediate peace; and Napoleon indulged in dreams of success and glory for two hours. In the mean time, the day was drawing to a close, and Moscow remained sad, silent, and death-like. Napoleon became anxious; the soldiers almost uncontrollably impatient. A few officers penetrated into the city, and a rumor began to spread that "Moscow was deserted!" Napoleon repelled the intelligence with irritation; he, however, descended the hill, and advanced towards the Dorogomilow gate. Here he again halted, but in vain; all remained motionless as before. Murat urged him to penetrate into the city; he refused for some time, shrinking perhaps from having the truth forced upon his conviction. At last he gave the order, "Enter then, since they will have it so!"—recommending, at the same time, the strictest discipline. Calling Daru to his side, he said aloud, "Moscow deserted! a most unlikely event! We must enter it, and ascertain the fact. Go and bring the *boyars* (landed proprietors) before me." Daru went, and returned. Not a single Muscovite was to be found:—"No smoke," says Segur, "was seen ascending from the meanest hearth; nor was the slightest noise to be heard throughout that populous and extensive city, its three hundred thousand inhabitants seeming all dumb and motionless as by enchantment. There was the silence of the desert.

After Daru, another officer, earnest to accomplish whatever the Emperor desired, appeared, driving before him five or six of those miserable beings who had been freed from prison, and left in Moscow for an important purpose. Then it was that Napoleon ceased to doubt the truth. Murat, with his long and close column of cavalry, had entered Moscow upwards of an hour since. They found it as yet uninjured, but without signs of life. Awed by the silence of this immense solitude, the troops passed onwards without uttering a word, listening to the hollow sound of their horses' feet re-echoed from the walls of these deserted palaces. They never appeared even to think of plundering. Suddenly the report of small arms was heard. The column halted. The discharge had been made from the walls of the Kremlin, the gates of which were closed. It was defended by a squalid rout of men and women of most disgusting and villanous aspect, who were in a state of bestial drunkenness, uttering savage yells and the most horrible imprecations. As they would listen to no terms, the gates were forced, and these ferocious miscreants were immediately driven away. Five hundred recruits, who had been forgotten, were left behind in the Kremlin, but they offered no resistance, and dispersed at the first summons. Several thousand stragglers and deserters also surrendered themselves voluntarily to the advanced guard. Murat scarcely bestowed a minute's delay on the Kremlin. After marching over so many leagues, and fighting so many battles to reach

Moscow, he passed through that magnificent city without once halting to notice it; and, ardent in his pursuit of the Russians, dashed forwards into the road to Voladimir and Asia. Several thousand Cossacks were retreating in that direction; and upon these Murat ordered a discharge of carbines.

Napoleon did not enter Moscow before night. He appointed Mortier governor of the city. "Above all," said he, "no pillage." During the night, many reports were brought him of the intended burning of the capital, but he would not credit the statements. He was, however, unable to sleep, and continually called his attendants to repeat to him what they had heard. About two o'clock in the morning he was apprised that the flames had broken out at the merchants' palace, or exchange, which was in the centre of the city. He gave orders, and dispatched messages with the greatest rapidity. At daylight, he hurried to Mortier, who showed him houses covered with iron roofs, and closely shut up, from which a black smoke was already issuing. They had not been broken into, but were evidently fired from the inside. Napoleon entered the Kremlin thoughtful and melancholy; yet when beholding this stupendous palace of the ancestral sovereigns of Russia, his ambition was gratified by the conquest, and he murmured after a pause—"I am at length then in Moscow!—in the ancient City of the Czars!—in the Kremlin!" In this brief moment of satisfaction, he wrote a pacific overture to the Emperor Alexander, and dispatched it by a Russian officer who had been discovered in the great hospital.

The flames had been checked by the exertions of the Duke of Treviso. Meantime, the incendiaries kept themselves so well concealed that their existence was much doubted. Regulations were now issued; order established; and officers and men proceeded to take possession of some convenient house, or sumptuous palace, wherein to rest and recruit themselves after so many hardships, dangers, and privations. Two officers, however, having taken up their quarters in one of the buildings of the Kremlin, were awoke about midnight by an overpowering glare of light in the room. Starting up, they looked out and saw palaces in flames. The wind was driving the flames directly towards the Kremlin. Presently the wind changed, and the devouring element was carried in an opposite direction. Observing this, the officers, rendered selfish by long fatigue and privation, fell asleep again. But they were once more aroused by a new burst of still fiercer light. They observed flames rising in a totally different quarter, which the changed wind was now urging directly towards the Kremlin. Three times the wind changed, and three times did new flames burst out from different quarters of the city, and blaze onwards towards the Kremlin.

The Kremlin contained a magazine of powder, of which the French were not aware, and the guards, overpowered by wine and fatigue, had left a whole park of artillery under the Emperor's windows. Soon the flames licked the palace from all sides, and the air was filled with flakes of fire. Mortier and his brother officers, exhausted by their efforts to subdue the conflagration, returned to the Kremlin, and fell down in despair. The real cause of the fire was soon placed beyond all doubt. The reports agreed that a globe of fire had been lowered upon the palace of one of the Russian princes, which had consumed it, on the first night of their entrance, and that this was a signal to the incendiaries.

Men of atrocious look and tattered garments, and frantic women, had been seen roaming amidst the flames, and thus completing a hideous resemblance of the infernal world. They were the malefactors whom Rostopchin had let loose from the prisons, and commissioned to execute this tremendous deed as the price of their liberation and pardon. Most thoroughly did they fulfil their trust: and, becoming delirious with intoxication, with excitement, and entire success, they no longer concealed themselves, but ran to and fro with diabolical yells, like furies, waving lighted brands round their heads. The French could not make them drop their torches, except by slashing at their naked arms with sabres. Orders were instantly given to shoot every incendiary on the spot. The army was drawn out. The old guard, which had been quartered in the Kremlin, took arms, and their horses and baggage quickly filled the courts. Masters of Moscow, they were obliged to seek their bivouac outside its gates.

Napoleon was awoke by the blaze and uproar of the conflagration. It was impossible for him any longer tc fortify himself with incredulity and scorn. On perceiving that the city was really on fire, in almost every quarter, he gave way to his first feelings of rage, and a passionate resolve to master the devouring element; but he presently recovered himself, and silently yielded to what he saw was inevitable. His inward agitation, however, was excessive. He seemed parched by the flames as he gazed at their fury. He continually sat down, and then abruptly started up, and traversed his apartments with rapidity. Again he seated himself, and began to transact most urgent business; yet every now and then he started up, and ran to the windows, uttering short and broken exclamations as he traced the progress of the flames: "What a frightful spectacle! To have done it themselves! Such a number of palaces! What extraordinary resolution!" There is something extremely fine in this power of standing apart from the scene, even while in the midst of such an excitement and danger, and admiring the forces brought into action, even though to his own utter destruction.

A report was now circulated that the Kremlin was undermined. Several Russian prisoners had affirmed this; certain writings attested it. Some of the attendants lost their senses with terror; the military awaited with firmness whatever Napoleon and their destiny should decide; but he noticed the alarm only by a smile of incredulity. Meantime, the conflagration raged with increasing violence, and they all began to inhale the smoke and ashes. Still Napoleon would not depart. He walked to and fro with convulsive energy.

Night was again approaching. The glare of the flames became more brilliant as the shades closed round, and he saw the devouring element seizing upon all the bridges, and all the accesses to the fortress which inclosed him, while the wind blew with redoubled violence. At this crisis, Prince Eugene and Murat arrived in breathless haste, most earnestly, and even on their knees, beseeching Napoleon to leave the palace. All their efforts, however, were in vain. Suddenly, a cry was heard,—"The Kremlin is on fire!" The words were echoed from every part of the building. The Emperor left his apartment that he might himself judge of the danger. A Russian soldier of police had been detected in the act. He had received a signal, and given the watchword. The exasperated grenadiers put an end to him with their bayonets. It was evident that there had been an organized plan to burn even the Kremlin. This incident decided Napoleon, and he rapidly descended the northern staircase.

A guide had been called to conduct Napoleon and his attendants through the Kremlin and out of the city. Segur has given a terrific description of the dangers which they had to encounter on their way. According to him, they were besieged in the midst of an ocean of flames, which enveloped all the gates of the citadel.

But the description is simply a piece of imagination. Napoleon proceeded slowly and calmly to the outer circuit of the city, and took up his quarters in the imperial castle of Petrowsky, situated about a league on the road to St. Petersburg. Count Dumas, who remained on duty within the walls until nightfall, says that he and Daru "left Moscow under a real rain of fire;" but he mentions nothing of such perils with regard to the Emperor.

On the following morning, September 17th, the

Emperor directed his first glances towards Moscow, hoping to find the fire subdued. It continued with all the violence of the previous night. The whole city now seemed to him "one vast fire-spout, ascending in awful whirls towards the sky." He was long absorbed in the contemplation of this scene of horror and ruin. Moscow had been the very centre of all his projects—the object of all his hopes in Russia. At length, he broke his melancholy silence merely by observing, "This forbodes us no common calamities."

The fire raged throughout the 18th and 19th of September, when it slackened for want of fuel. The greater part of the Kremlin, a few palaces, and all the churches built of stone, remained standing. All else was laid in ruins. The destruction of property was enormous. The flight of the nobility had been so sudden, that the French officers on their entrance found even the jewels of the ladies left behind. But there are other consequences of the burning of Moscow which are too horrible to dwell upon. Dumas states, that he found six thousand wounded Russians in the hospitals, which he examined by order of Napoleon, when the French army entered. Their fate cannot be doubtful. Napoleon returned to the Kremlin on the 20th. He passed towards the city through the camps of his army, which exhibited a very singular appearance. "They were situated," says Segur, "in the midst of fields, in a thick and cold mire; and contained immense camp-fires, fed by rich mahogany furniture, and gilded sashes and doors. Around these fires, with a litter of damp straw, sheltered only by a few miserable planks fastened together, his soldiers, with their officers, were to be seen, splashed with dirt, and stained with smoke, seated upon superb arm-chairs, or reclining on sofas covered with silk. At their feet, carelessly opened or thrown in heaps, lay Cashmere shawls, the finest furs of Siberia, the gold stuffs of Persia, and plates of solid silver, from which they had nothing to eat but a black dough baked in ashes, and half-broiled and bloody steaks of horse-flesh." The ground between the camps and the city was covered with marauders laden with booty. On his way through the ruined streets, Napoleon had passed heaps of furniture piled up for removal, and stalls where soldiers were exchanging showy and valuable commodities for common necessaries; and the richest wines, liquors, and bales of costly merchandise, for a loaf of bread. He had permitted this license at first; but hearing that the excesses increased, and that the peasantry who had formerly brought provisions were now prevented by fear, he issued severe orders, and commanded his guard to keep close to their quarters. He was obeyed at the first word. The plundering continued, but was conducted regularly, and every effort made to protect the peasants; nevertheless few appeared, and at length not one was to be seen.

CAMP-FIRE AT MALO-YAROSLAVETZ.

NAPOLEON had left the ruins of Moscow, like a funeral pyre, smouldering, behind him, and taken up the line of march for Kalouga. He had with him a hundred thousand effective men—troops in whom he still could place the deepest confidence. But the first snow had fallen! The ghostly terror of a Russian winter hovered over the army, and vexed the dreams of the Emperor. In a weaver's hut, where he passed the night of the 24th of October, he heard that

Kutusoff had anticipated him, and had taken up a position upon the road to Kalouga, which could not be assailed; that Prince Eugene, with only eighteen thousand troops had fought a bloody battle with fifty thousand Russians, and gained a dear but glorious victory. In the early part of the night, when the faithful troops were shivering round their fires, and the Emperor was seated in a comfortless hovel, divided into two apartments by a tattered cloth, came the intrepid Marshal Bessieres, with the terrible intelligence. The Emperor looked pale and worn with anxiety.

"Did you see rightly?" he exclaimed. "Are you sure? Will you vouch for what you say?"

"All that I have told you, sire, is truth," replied the marshal, calmly.

Napoleon crossed his arms upon his breast, his head fell, and for a few moments he seemed lost in thought. Bessieres respectfully retired. The Emperor seemed greatly agitated, but nothing except restless actions betrayed his feverish state of mind. He lay down and arose incessantly, called for his attendants, and when they came, had nothing to say to them. About four o'clock in the morning, while the camp-fires were still burning, the Prince D'Aremberg came into the hovel, and informed him that a horde of Cossacks, under cover of the night, and the woods, were gliding between him and the advanced posts. The Emperor, however, seemed to pay no attention to the intelligence, and as soon as the sun was above the horizon, mounted his horse and proceeded towards Malo-Yaroslavetz.

In crossing the plain, a confused clamor startled the

imperial party, and suddenly the Cossack Murat, Platoff, led his wild horsemen among the baggage and fires of the army, and overturning every thing in their course, they pressed onward with wild hourras. Rapp seized the Emperor's bridle, and exclaimed,—

"It is they! turn back!"

Napoleon's pride would not stoop to a retreat. His hand moved to his sword. Berthier and the grand equerry followed his example, and placing themselves on the left of the wood, the little party awaited the approach of the Cossacks. They came on rapidly, and were within forty paces of the Emperor. Rapp was wounded by one of their spears. About twenty horsemen and chasseurs then attacked the horde, and by their desperate bravery saved the Emperor. The cavalry of the guard then came up, and drove the Cossacks across the plain. The Emperor halted until the plain was cleared, and then rode forward to Maho-Yaroslavetz, in the neighborhood of which the main body of the army encamped. The Emperor occupied the afternoon in reconnoitering the position of Kutusoff, and as the shades of a sombre evening fell, returned to his head-quarters, the wretched hovel of an artisan. There he was joined by Murat, Berthier, Davoust, Bessieres, and the heroic Prince Eugene, who came to give Napoleon an account of the action of the day before. A cheerful fire was kindled on the hearth of the lowly hut, and an emperor, two kings, and three marshals sat down to the rough table. Without, the camp-fires of the soldiers were blazing; but the fierce wind was already blowing the requiem of the army. The Emperor sat, with his head resting in his hands, which concealed his features. Eugene was the first to speak.

"It is to be hoped that we shall not have many such conflicts as that of yesterday, sire, or however glorious the results, we shall only have a miserable remnant of the grand army to lead back to France."

"But it was a glorious battle, Prince; was it not? Tell me of it yourself," said the Emperor, without removing his hands from his face.

"Sire, it was briefly thus," replied Eugene. "On the night of the 23d, Delzons and his division were in possession of this place. At four in the morning, his bivouacs were surprised by Kutusoff. I heard the firing at three leagues distance, and hastened to his relief. As I drew near, a vast amphitheatre rose before me. The river Lonja marked its foot; from the opposite height, a cloud of Russian sharp-shooters and their artillery poured down their fire on Delzons. On the plain beyond, Kutusoff's whole army advanced rapidly by the Lectazowo road. A severe and desperate conflict ensued. Delzons and his brother were killed. We were enabled to maintain our ground by the wise manœuvres of Guilleminot, who threw a hundred grenadiers into a churchyard, in the walls of which they made holes for their muskets. Five times the Russians attempted to pass, and five times they were thrown into disorder and repulsed by a well-directed and murderous fire. The whole day the struggle wavered, and many times, I thought our troops could not be kept to the ground. But the fourteenth and fifteenth divisions held the Russians at bay, and maintained the bridge which was our road to retreat, against all assault. At length, being reduced to my last reserve, I came into battle myself, and by exerting myself to the utmost, rallied the troops and once more carried them up the heights. The Russians, wearied out, fell back, and concentrated themselves on the Kalouga road, between the woods and this place. We gained the victory, but we have lost many brave men, whom, in our present situation, we cannot with safety spare."

During this recital, Napoleon's eyes kindled with enthusiasm, and when Eugene had finished, he exclaimed,—

"Then you, Prince, with eighteen thousand men, huddled together in the bottom of a ravine, defeated fifty thousand Russians, posted above your heads, and seconded by every advantage which a town built on a steep acclivity could present! I have been over the ground, and know your difficulties, and appreciate the nature of your triumphs. Prince, the glory of this victory belongs entirely to you."

The Prince shook his head,—

"Sire, the French troops are brave—courage alone won this field. But leaving that affair, the question is, whether we shall march upon Smolensk by way of Kalouga, Medyn or Mojaisk."

"That is easily settled," said Murat, quickly. "The Russians are nothing. Let us pursue the route to Kalouga, and cut our way through them."

"Tut—tut! King of Naples, you speak rashly!" said Napoleon, quickly. "The course you counsel is the violent impulse of your heart."

"Entirely unwise!" said Bessieres. "The King of Naples is governed by his all-daring temper."

"With deference, Sire," said the stern Davoust, "I would recommend that we proceed to Medwysick. We can reach that point without loss; and permit me to remark, sire, that our present circumstances, every man is of almost indispensable value."

"But," interrupted Murat, "it is certain that we shall have to lose men; and it is better to lose them now, in beating the Russians, than to drop them upon a march, without having effected any thing. Marshal Davoust is ever recommending timid, half-way measures."

A quarrel between Murat and Davoust had occurred some time previous, and it was only by the interposition of the Emperor himself, that bloodshed had been prevented. They were always ready to renew the contest.

"Timid and half-way measures!" exclaimed the harsh voice of Davoust. "I recommend the measures of a general who cares for the safety of his army, as well as victory. The King of Naples counsels like a mere hot-headed, inexperienced conscript."

Here Napoleon, raising his head, extinguished all this fire by saying that "we had exhibited temerity enough, already; that we had done but too much for glory, and it was now high time to give up thinking of any thing but how to save the rest of the army."

Bessieres, either because his pride revolted at the idea of being put under the command of the King of Naples, or from a desire to preserve uninjured the cavalry of the guard, which he had formed, and for which he was answerable to Napoleon, and which he exclusively commanded, then ventured to add, that "neither the army nor even the guard had sufficient spirit left for such efforts. It was already said in both, that, as the means of conveyance were wholly inadequate, henceforth the victor, if overtaken, would fall a prey to the vanquished; that of course every wound would be mortal. Murat would therefore be but feebly seconded. And in what a position! its strength had just been but too well demonstrated. Against what enemies! had they not remarked the field of the previous day's battle, and with what fury the Russian recruits, only just armed and clothed, there fought and fell!" The marshal concluded by giving his opinion in favor of retreat, which the Emperor approved by his silence.

The Prince of Eckmuhl then immediately said that, "as a retreat had been decided upon, he proposed that it should be by Medyn and Smolensk." But Murat here interrupted him; and, whether from enmity, or from that discouragement which usually succeeds the rejection of a rash measure, he declared himself astonished "that any one should dare propose so imprudent a step to the Emperor. Had Davoust sworn the destruction of the army? Would he have so long and so heavy a column trail along in utter uncertainty, without guides, and on an unknown track, within reach of Kutusoff, presenting its flank to all the attacks of the enemy? Would he, Davoust, defend it? When in our rear Borowsk and Vereria would lead us without danger to Mojaisk, why reject that safe route? There provisions must have been already collected, there everything was known to us, and we could not be misled by any *traitor*."

At these words, Davoust, burning with a rage which he could scarcely repress, replied that "he proposed a retreat through a fertile country, by an untouched, plentiful, and well-supplied route, where the villages were still standing, and by the shortest road, that the enemy might not be able to cut us off, as on the route by Mojaisk to Smolensk, recommended by Murat. And what a route! a desert of sand and ashes, where convoys of wounded would increase our embarrassment, where we should meet with nothing but ruins, traces of blood, skeletons, and famine!

"Moreover, though he deemed it his duty to give his opinion when it was asked, he was ready to obey orders contrary to it, with the same zeal as if they were consonant with his suggestions; but that the Emperor alone had a right to impose silence on him, and not Murat, who was not his sovereign, and never should be!"

The quarrel growing warm, Bessieres and Berthier interposed. As for the Emperor, still absorbed and in the same attitude, he appeared insensible to what was passing. At length he broke up the council with the words, "Well, gentlemen, I will decide."

"Enough, it is well, sirs. I will decide," said Napoleon calmly, and the King of Naples resumed his seat, biting his lips from the effects of passion. "Sirs," continued the Emperor, "I decide to retreat." Here he paused, as if such a decision was costing him a dreadful effort. "I decide to retreat by way of Mojaisk. We cannot afford to fi ht, and that is the road which will lead us most speedily from the enemy." This decision was extremely distasteful to Murat; but not more so than it was to the Emperor, who, after he had announced it, looked as though he wished that it had not been uttered. However, the resolution, fatal as it proved, was taken, and nothing could induce the Emperor to revoke it. Had he but known, that at the moment when this decision was made, Kutusoff, stunned by the defeat at Malo-Yaroslavetz, was retiring with his forces by the bridge over the Oka, offering a fair mark for the French, he might have changed his design, and delivered such a crushing blow to the enemy, as would have secured his retreat unmolested. But this knowledge came not to the Emperor's mind; and as he stretched himself for repose amid his faithful generals, and by the side of the blazing fire, he had nothing to relieve the prospect of a disastrous retreat.

THE CAMP-FIRE IN THE SNOW.

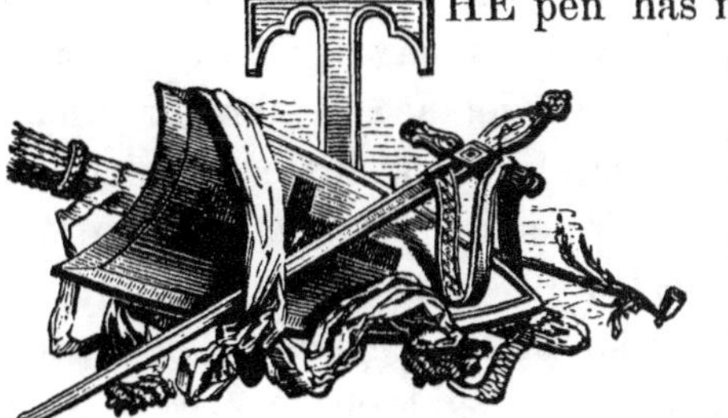

THE pen has no colors to depict the horrors of the grand army's retreat amid the fierce storms of a Russian winter. Though "horrors upon horror's head" accumulate, there is always lacking something which shall picture to the heart the full truth of that disastrous march.

The Emperor reached Wiazma in two days' march from Gjatz. Here he halted for the arrival of Prince Eugene and Davoust; and to reconnoitre the road from Medyn and Juknof. Hearing no tidings of the Russians, he set off after thirty-six hours' stay, leaving Ney at Wiazma to relieve Davoust, who was accused of dilatoriness; but he said that the artillery and wagons were constantly precipitated into deep ravines which crossed the road, and that it was nearly impossible to drag them up the opposite icy slope, the horses' shoes not having been turned. Nevertheless, both he and the Viceroy arrived within two leagues of Wiazma on the 2d of November, and might have passed through it; but neglecting to do so, the Russian advanced-guard under Miloradowich (called the Russian Murat) turned their bivouacs in the night, and posted themselves along the left bank of the road, between the French generals and Wiazma. On the 3d of November, Prince Eugene was preparing to take the road to that town, when the first dawn of day showed him his situation, his rear-guard cut off, and Ney, who was to have come to his assistance, fighting in his own defence in the direction of Wiazma. He immediately took his resolution. He stopped, faced about, formed in line along the main-road, and kept the foremost of the enemy's troops in check, till Ney marched up one of his regiments, and attacking them in the rear, compelled them to retire. At the same time, Compans, one of Davoust's generals, joined his division to the Italian guard; and while they fought together, Davoust passed, and got between Wiazma and the Russians. The battle was not over, but begun. The French amounted to thirty thousand, but were in great disorder. The Russian artillery, superior in number, advanced at a gallop, and mowed down their lines. Davoust and his generals were still surrounded with many of their bravest men. Several of the officers who had been wounded at the Mosqua were still seen, one with his arm in a sling, another with his head covered with bandages, encouraging the soldiers, keeping them together, throwing themselves upon the enemy's field-pieces and seizing them, and thus preventing the effects of bad example by good. Miloradowich saw that his prey would escape him, and sent the Englishman Wilson to summon Kutusoff to his aid; but the old general laughed at him. The fight had already lasted seven hours; when night approached, the French began to retire. This retrogade movement encouraged the enemy; and had it not been for a signal effort of the 25th, 57th, and 85th regiments, Davoust's corps would have been turned, broken, and destroyed. Prince Eugene made good his retreat to Wiazma; Davoust followed, but Morand's division, which entered first, found a number of Russians there before them, and had to cut their way through them. Compans, who brought up the rear, put an end to the affair by facing about, and making a furious assault upon Miloradowich. The bivouacs were set up by the light of the burning of Wiazma, and amidst repeated discharges of artillery. During the night the alarm continued. Several times the troops thought they were attacked, and groped about for their arms. On the following morning, when they returned to their ranks, they were astonished at the smallness of their numbers.

Nevertheless, the example of the chiefs and the hope of finding rest at Smolensk kept up the men's spirits. Besides, so far they had been cheered by the sight of the sun; but on the 6th of November, the snow came on, and every thing underwent a total change. The consequences were most disastrous. The troops marched on without knowing where, and without distinguishing any object; and while they strove to force their way through the whirlwinds of sleet, the snow drifted in the cavities where they fell, and the weakest rose no more. The wind drove in their faces not only the falling snow, but that which it raised in furious eddies from the earth. The Muscovite winter attacked them in every part, penetrated through their thin dress and ragged shoes. Their wet clothes froze upon them; this covering of ice chilled their bodies, and stiffened all their limbs. A cutting and violent wind stopped their breath or seized upon it as it was exhaled, and converted it into icicles, which hung from their beards. The unhappy men crawled on with trembling limbs and chattering teeth till the snow, collecting round their feet in hard lumps, like stones, some scattered fragment, a branch of a tree, or the body of one of their companions, made them stagger and fall. Their cries and groans were vain; soon the snow covered them, and small hillocks marked where they lay. Such was their sepulture. The road was filled with these undulations, like a burying-place. A number of them froze as they stood still, and looked like posts, covered with snow. The most intrepid or obdurate were affected; they hurried past with averted eyes. But before them, around them, all was snow; the horizon seemed one vast winding-sheet, in which nature was enveloping the whole army. The only objects which came out from the bleak expanse were a few gloomy pines skirting the plain, and adding to the horror of the scene with their funeral green and the motionless erectnesss of their black trunks! Even the weapons of the soldiers were a weight almost insupportable to their benumbed limbs. In their frequent falls they slipped out of their hands and were broken or lost in the snow. Many others had their fingers frozen on the musket they still grasped. Some broke up into parties; others wandered on alone. If they dispersed themselves in the fields, or by the cross-paths, in search of bread or a shelter for the night, they met nothing but Cossacks and an armed population, who surrounded, wounded, and stripped them, and left them with ferocious laughter to expire naked upon the snow. Then came the night of sixteen hours. But on this universal covering of snow, they knew not where to stop, where to sit, where to lie, where to find a few roots for food, or dry sticks to light their fires. At length fatigue, darkness, and repeated orders induced a pause, and they tried to establish themselves for the night; but the storm scattered the preparations for the bivouacs, and the branches of the pines covered with ice and snow only melted away, and resisted the attempts of the soldiers to kindle them into a blaze. When at length the fire got the better, officers and soldiers gathered round it, to cook their wretched meal of horse-flesh, and a few spoonfuls of rye mixed with snow-water. Next morning, circles of stiffened corpses marked the situation of the bivouacs, and the carcasses of thousands of horses were strewed round them. From this time disorder and distrust began to prevail. A few resisted the strong contagion of insubordination and despondency. These were the officers, the subalterns, and some of the soldiers, whom nothing could detach from their duty. They kept up each other's spirits by repeating the name of Smolensk, which they were approaching, and looked forward to as the end of their sufferings.

At the lake of Semlewo, it was found necessary to sacrifice the spoils of Moscow. Cannon, armor, the ornaments of the Kremlin, and the cross of the Great Iwan, all sunk at once in the waters of the lake. On the 6th of November, just as the snow was beginning to fall, Napoleon had reached Mikalewska. There he took up his quarters in a palisaded house. He had scarcely arrived, before news of Mallet's conspiracy in Paris reached him, and added new trouble to his already perturbed spirit. Under all the gloomy circumstances of the time, when the fabric of his power, which he had reared with so much skill, and maintained with such vast energy, seemed to "totter to its fall," the fortitude of the Emperor was remarkable. He preserved a firm countenance, and strove to induce those around him to believe that his star had not yet begun to decline.

As the Emperor sat in his cheerless hut, with the

white storm nowling far around, he was aroused by the entrance of Dalbignac, one of Ney's aid-de-camps.

From Wiazma that general had commenced protecting the retreat, which, though fatal to so many others, conferred immortal renown upon him. As far as Dorogobouje, he had been molested only by some bands of Cossacks, troublesome insects, attracted by the dying, and the forsaken carriages, flying away the moment a hand was lifted against them, but still annoying from their continual return.

It was not these that were the subject of Ney's message. On approaching Dorogobouje, he was shocked at the traces of disorder left behind them by the corps which had preceded him, and which it was not in his power to efface. He had made up his mind to leave the baggage to the enemy; but he blushed with shame at the sight of the first pieces of cannon abandoned before Dorogobouje.

The marshal had halted there. After a dreadful night, during which snow, wind, and famine had driven most of his men from the fires, the dawn, which is always waited for with so much impatience in a bivouac, brought with it at once a tempest, the enemy, and the spectacle of an almost general defection. In vain he fought in person at the head of what men and officers he had left; he had been obliged to retreat precipitately behind the Dnieper; and of this he now sent to apprise the Emperor.

He wished him to know the worst. His aid-de-camp, Colonel Dalbignac, was instructed to say that "the first movement of retreat from Malo-Yaroslawetz, for soldiers who had never yet fallen back, had greatly dispirited the army; that the affair at Wiazma had shaken its firmness; that the deluge of snow, and the increased cold which it had brought with it, had completed its disorganization; and that a multitude of officers, having lost everything, their platoons, battalions, regiments, and even divisions, had joined the roving masses; so that generals, colonels, and officers of all ranks were seen mingled with the privates, and marching at random, sometimes with one column, sometimes with another; that, as order could not exist in the midst of disorder, this example was seducing even the veteran regiments, which had served through all the wars of the revolution; and that, accordingly, the best soldiers were heard asking one another why they alone were required to fight to secure the escape of the rest; and how it could be expected that they should keep up their courage, when they heard the cries of despair issuing from the neighboring woods, in which the large convoys of their wounded, who had been dragged to no purpose all the way from Moscow, had just been abandoned? Such, no doubt, was the fate which awaited themselves; what had they, then, to gain by remaining with their colors? Incessant toils and combats by day, and famine at night, with shelterless bivouacs, still more destructive than battle; hunger and cold effectually drove sleep from their eyes; or if, perchance, fatigue got the better of these for a moment, the repose which should refresh them put a period to their lives. In short, the eagles had ceased to protect them—they only destroyed. Why, then, remain around them to perish by battalions, by masses? It would be better to disperse; and, since there was no other course than flight, to try who could run the fastest. It would not then be the bravest and best that would fall; the poltroons behind them would no longer have a chance to eat up the relics of the high road." Lastly, the aid-de-camp was commissioned to explain to the Emperor all the horrors of the marshal's situation, the responsibility of which that commander absolutely refused to assume.

But Napoleon saw enough around himself to judge of the rest. The fugitives were that moment passing by him; he was sensible that nothing could now be done but to sacrifice the army successively, part by part, beginning at the extremities, in order to save the head. When, therefore, the aid-de-camp was beginning to state farther particulars, he sharply interrupted him with these words: "Colonel, I do not ask you for these details." The colonel said no more; aware that, in the midst of these terrible disasters, now irremediable, and in which every one had occasion for all his energies, the Emperor was afraid of complaints, which could have no other effect than to discourage as well those who indulged in them as those who listened to them.

He remarked the attitude of Napoleon, the same as he retained throughout the whole of this dismal retreat. It was grave, silent, and resigned; suffering much less in body than others, but far more in mind, and brooding with speechless agony over his misfortunes. At that moment General Carpentier sent him from Smolensk a convoy of provisions. Bessieres wished to take possession of them; but the Emperor instantly ordered them to be forwarded to the Prince of Moskwa, saying that "those who were fighting ought to eat before the rest." At the same time, he sent word to Ney to "defend himself long enough to allow him some stay at Smolensk, where the army should eat, rest, and be reorganized."

But if this hope kept some still to their duty, many others abandoned every thing to hasten towards that promised goal of their sufferings. As for Ney, he saw that a sacrifice was required, and that he was marked out as the victim; he nobly resigned himself, therefore, prepared to meet the whole of a danger great as his courage; and thenceforward he neither attached his honor to baggage, nor to cannon, which the winter alone wrested from him. An elbow of the Borysthenes stopped and kept back part of his guns at the foot of its icy slopes: he sacrificed them without hesitation, passed that obstacle, faced about, and made the hostile river, which crossed his route, serve him as the means of defence.

The Russians, however, advanced under favor of a wood and of the forsaken carriages, whence they kept up a fire of musketry on Ney's troops. Half of the latter, whose icy arms froze their stiffened fingers, became discouraged; they gave way, excusing themselves by their want of firmness on the preceding day, and fleeing because they had before fled, which, but for this, they would have considered as impossible. But Ney, rushing in among them, seized one of their muskets, and led them back to action, which he was himself the first to renew; exposing his life like a private soldier, with a firelock in his hand, the same as though he had been neither possessed of wealth, nor power, nor consideration; in short, as if he had still every thing to gain, when in fact he had every thing to lose. But, though he had again turned soldier, he ceased not to be general: he took advantage of the ground, supported himself against a height, and covered his approach by occupying a palisaded house. His generals and colonels, among whom he particularly remarked Fezenzac, strenuously seconded him; and the enemy, who had expected to pursue, was obliged to retreat.

By this action Ney afforded the army a respite of twenty-four hours; and it profited by it to proceed towards Smolensk. The next day, and every succeeding day, he displayed the same heroism. Between Wiazma and Smolensk he fought ten whole days.

On the 13th of November, Ney was approaching that city, which he was not to enter till the ensuing day, and had faced about to beat off the enemy, when all at once the hills upon which he intended to support his left were seen covered with a multitude of fugitives. In their terror, these unfortunate wretches fell, and rolled down to where he was, upon the frozen snow, which they stained with their blood. A band of Cossacks, which was soon perceived in the midst of them, sufficiently accounted for this disorder. The astonished marshal, having caused this horde of enemies to be dispersed, discovered behind it the army of Italy, returning completely stripped, without baggage and without cannon.

Platoff had kept it besieged, as it were, all the way

from Dorogobouje. Near that town Prince Eugene had quitted the high road, and, in order to proceed towards Witepsk, had taken that which, two months before, had brought him from Smolensk; but the Wop, which, when he had crossed it before, was a mere brook and had scarcely been noticed, he now found swollen into a river. It ran over a muddy bed, and was bounded by two steep banks. It was found necessary to cut a passage in these precipitous and frozen banks, and to give orders for the demolition of the neighboring houses during the night, for the purpose of building a bridge with the materials. But those who had taken shelter in them opposed their being destroyed; and, as the viceroy was more beloved than feared, his instructions were not obeyed. The *pontonniers* became disheartened, and when daylight, with the Cossacks, appeared, the bridge, after being twice broken down, was at last abandoned.

Five or six thousand soldiers still in order, twice the number of disbanded men, the sick and wounded, upward of a hundred pieces of cannon, ammunition wagons, and a multitude of vehicles of every kind, lined the bank and covered a league of ground. An attempt was made to ford the river, through the floating ice which was carried along by its current. The first guns that were attempted to be got over reached the opposite bank; but the water kept rising every moment, while at the same time the bed of the stream at the place of passage was continually deepened by the wheels and by the efforts of the horses, and at length the stoppage became general.

Meanwhile the day was advancing; the men were exhausting themselves in vain efforts; hunger, cold, and the Cossacks became pressing, and the viceroy finally found himself compelled to order his artillery and all his baggage to be left behind. A distressing spectacle ensued. The owners were allowed scarcely a moment to part from their effects; while they were selecting from them such articles as they most needed, and loading their horses with them, a multitude of soldiers came rushing up; they fell in preference upon the vehicles of luxury; these they broke in pieces and rummaged every part, avenging their poverty on the wealth, and their privations on the superfluities they here found, and snatching them from the Cossacks, who were in the meantime looking on at a distance.

But it was provisions of which most of them were in quest. They threw aside embroidered clothes, pictures, ornaments of every kind, and gilt bronzes for a few handfuls of flour. In the evening it was a strange sight to behold the mingled riches of Paris and of Moscow, the luxuries of two of the largest cities in the world, lying scattered and despised on the snow of the desert.

At the same time, most of the artillerymen spiked their guns in despair, and scattered their powder about. Others laid a train with it as far as some ammunition wagons, which had been left at a considerable distance behind the baggage. They waited till the most eager of the Cossacks had come up to them, and when a great number, greedy of plunder, had collected about them, they threw a brand from a bivouac upon the train. The fire ran, and in a moment reached its destination; the wagons were blown up, the shells exploded, and such of the Cossacks as were not killed on the spot, dispersed in dismay.

A few hundred men, who were still called the 14th division, were opposed to these hordes, and sufficed to keep them at a respectful distance till the next day. All the rest, soldiers, sutlers, women, and children, sick and wounded, driven by the enemy's balls, crowded the bank of the river. But at the sight of its swollen current, of the sharp and massive fragments of ice floating down its stream, and the necessity of aggravating their already intolerable sufferings from cold by plunging into its chilling waves, they all started back.

Colonel Delfanti, an Italian, was obliged to set the example and cross first. The soldiers then moved, and the crowd followed. The weakest, the least resolute, and the most avaricious, stayed behind. Such as could not make up their minds to part from their booty, and to forsake fortune which was forsaking them, were surprised in the midst of their hesitation. The next day, amid all this wealth, the savage Cossacks were seen still covetous of the squalid and tattered garments of the unfortunate creatures who had become their prisoners: they stripped them, and then, collecting them in troops, drove them along over the snow, hurrying their steps by hard blows with the shafts of their lances.

The army of Italy, thus completely dismantled, soaked in the waters of the Wop, without food, without shelter, passed the night on the snow near a village where its officers expected to have found lodgings for themselves. Their soldiers, however, beset its wooden houses. They rushed like madmen, and in swarms, on every habitation, profiting by the darkness, which prevented them from recognising their officers or being known by them. They tore down every thing, doors, windows, and even the woodwork of the roofs, feeling but little compunction in compelling others, be they who they might, to bivouac like themselves.

Their generals attempted in vain to drive them off: they took their blows without a murmur or the least opposition, but without desisting—even the men of the royal and imperial guards; for, throughout the whole army, such were the scenes that occurred every night. The unfortunate fellows kept silently but actively at work on the wooden walls, which they pulled in pieces on every side at once, and which, after vain efforts, their officers were obliged to relinquish to them, for fear they would fall upon their own heads. It was an extraordinary mixture of perseverance in their design and of respect for the anger of their superiors.

Having kindled good fires, they spent the night in drying themselves, amid the shouts, impre ations, and groans of those who were still crossing the torrent, or who, slipping from its banks, were precipitated into it, and drowned.

It is a fact by no means creditable to the enemy, that during this disaster, and in sight of so rich a booty, a few hundred men, left at the distance of half a league from the viceroy, on the other side of the Wop, were sufficient to curb for twenty hours not only the courage, but even the cupidity of Platoff's Cossacks.

It is possible, indeed, that the hetman made sure of destroying the viceroy on the following day. In fact, all his measures were so well planned, that at the moment when the army of Italy, after an unquiet and disorderly march, came in sight of Dukhowtchina, a town yet uninjured, and was joyfully hastening forward to shelter itself there, several thousand Cossacks sallied forth from it with cannon, and suddenly stopped its progress; while at the same time Platoff, with all his hordes, came up and attacked its rear guard and both flanks.

Several eye-witnesses assert that a complete tumult and confusion then ensued; that the disbanded men, the women, and the attendants ran headlong over each other, and broke quite through the ranks; that, in short, there was a moment when this unfortunate army was but a shapeless mass, a mere rabble rout hurrying to and fro. All seemed to be lost; but the coolness of the prince and the efforts of his officers, saved all. The best men disengaged themselves, and the ranks were again formed. They advanced, and, firing a few volleys, the enemy, who had every thing on his side excepting courage, the only advantage yet left the French, opened and retired, confining himself to a useless demonstration.

The army occupied his quarters still warm in that town, while he went beyond to bivouac, and to prepare for similar surprises to the very gates of Smolensk. For this disaster at the Wop had made the viceroy give up the idea of separating from the Emperor, near to whom these hordes became still bolder; they surrounded the 11th division. When Prince Eugene would have gone to its relief, his men and officers, stiffened with a cold of twenty degrees, which the wind rendered most piercing, remained stretched on the warm ashes of the fires. To no purpose did he point out to them their comrades surrounded, the enemy approaching, the bullets and balls which were already reaching them; they refused to rise, protesting that they would rather perish where they were than any longer endure such cruel hardships. The videttes themselves had abandoned their posts. Prince Eugene nevertheless contrived to save his rear guard.

It was in returning with it towards Smolensk that his stragglers had been driven back on Ney's troops, to whom they communicated their panic; all hurried confusedly towards the Dnieper, where they crowded together at the entrance of the bridge, without thinking of defending themselves, when a charge made by the 4th regiment stopped the advance of the enemy.

Its colonel, young Fezenzac, contrived to infuse fresh life into these men, who were half perished with cold. There, as in every thing that can be called action, was manifested the triumph of the sentiments of the soul over the sensations of the body; for every physical feeling tended to encourage despondency and flight; Nature advised it with her hundred most urgent voices; and yet a few words of honor alone were sufficient to produce the most heroic devotedness. The soldiers of the 4th regiment rushed like furies upon the enemy, against the mountains of snow and ice of which he had taken possession, and in the teeth of the northern hurri cane, for they had every thing against them. Ney himself was obliged to moderate their impetuosity.

Such fighting could only be the work of heroes, who were determined to triumph or perish. Ney proved himself worthy to command the rear guard, upon which the safety of the army depended. He was equal to a host, and around his stalwart form the troops rallied, as they would around a rock of salvation. He seemed even determined to conquer the Russian storm.

At length the army once more came in sight of Smolensk: it had reached the goal so often announced to it of all its sufferings. The soldiers exultingly pointed it out to each other. *There* was that land of promise where their hunger was to find abundance, their fatigue rest; where bivouacs in a cold of nineteen degrees would be forgotten in houses warmed by good fires. *There* they would enjoy refreshing sleep; there they might repair their apparel; there they would be furnished with new shoes, and clothing adapted to the climate.

But Smolensk was a heap of blackened ruins, and the commissary found there, was compelled to own that he had not enough provisions to supply half the army for the required time, fifteen days. If any thing was wanted to increase the wretchedness of this doomed army it was this disastrous disappointment. Napoleon himself displayed a consciousness of the terrors by which he was surrounded, and seemed to apprehend the destruction of his entire army.

THE CAMP-FIRE AT KRASNOE.

UPON the retreat from Smolensk, the grand army, reduced to thirty-six thousand effective men, had been divided into four columns, commanded by Napoleon, Eugene, Davoust and Ney. These were separated by the march of a few days from each other. The Emperor reached the town of Krasnoe without diffi culty; but the second division, under Prince Eugene, was compelled to fight against forces immensely superior in numbers.

It was the night of the 16th of November. The weather was bitter cold; and though Krasnoe fairly blazed with camp-fires, the soldiers of the guard shivered in spite of the sternest efforts of their wills.

The Emperor had waited for the viceroy during the whole of the preceding day. The noise of an engagement had agitated him. An effort to break through the enemy, in order to join him, had been ineffectually attempted; and when night came on without his making his appearance, the uneasiness of Napoleon was at its height. "Eugene and the army of Italy, and this long day of baffled expectation, had they then terminated together?" Only one hope remained, and that was, that the viceroy, driven back towards Smolensk, had there joined Davoust and Ney, and that on the following day they would, with united forces, attempt a decisive effort.

In his anxiety, the Emperor assembled the marshals who were with him. These were Berthier, Bessieres, Mortier and Lefebvre; they were safe; they had cleared the obstacles; they had only to continue their retreat through Lithuania, which was open to them; but would they abandon their companions in the midst of the Russian army? No, certainly; and they determined once more to enter Russia, either to deliver or to perish with them.

No sooner was this resolution taken, than Napoleon coolly made his arrangements to carry it into effect.

He was not at all shaken by the great movements which the enemy was evidently making around him. He saw that Kutusoff was advancing in order to surround and take him prisoner in Krasnoe. The very night before he had learned that Ojarowski, with a vanguard of Russian infantry, had got beyond him, and taken a position at Maliewo, a village on his left. Irritated instead of being depressed by misfortune, he called his aid-de-camp Rapp, and told him "that he must set out immediately, and during the darkness attack that body of the enemy with the bayonet; this was the first time of his exhibiting so much audacity, and that he was determined to make him repent it, in such a way that he should never again dare approach so near to his head-quarters." Then instantly recalling him, he exclaimed, "But no: let Roguet and his division go alone. As for you, remain where you are; I don't wish you killed here; I shall have occasion for you at Dantzic."

Rapp, as he was carrying this order to Roguet, could not help feeling astonished that his chief, surrounded by eighty thousand of the enemy, whom he was going to attack the next day with nine thousand, should have so little doubt about his safety as to be thinking of what he should have to do at Dantzic, a city from which he was separated by the winter, two hostile armies, famine, and a hundred and eighty leagues of distance.

The nocturnal attack on Ojarowski at Chirkowa and Maliewo proved successful. Roguet formed his idea of the enemy's position by the direction of their fires:

they occupied two villages, connected by a causeway, defended by a ravine. He disposed his troops into three columns of attack: those on the right and left were to advance silently, as close as possible to the Russians; then, at the signal to charge, which he himself would give them from the centre, they were to rush into the midst of the hostile corps without firing a shot, and make use only of their bayonets.

Immediately the two wings of the young guard commenced the action. While the Russians, taken by surprise, and not knowing on which side to defend themselves, were wavering from their right to their left, Roguet, with his column, rushed suddenly upon their centre, and into the midst of their camp, which he entered pell-mell along with them. Thus divided, and in utter confusion, they had barely time to throw the best part of their cannon and small arms into a neighboring lake, and to set fire to their tents, the flames of which, instead of saving them, only gave light to their destruction.

This check stopped the movements of the Russian army for four-and-twenty hours, put it in the Emperor's power to remain at Krasnoe, and enabled Eugene to rejoin him during the following night. He was received by Napoleon with the greatest joy; whose uneasiness, however, respecting Davoust and Ney, now became proportionably greater.

Around the French, the camp of the Russians presented a spectacle similar to what it had done at Vinkowo, Malo-Yaroslawetz, and Wiazma. Every evening, close to the general's tent, the relics of the Russian saints, surrounded by an immense number of wax tapers, were exposed to the adoration of the soldiers. While these, according to their custom, were giving proofs of their devotion by endless crossings and genuflexions, the priests were employed in exciting their fanaticism with exhortations that would have been deemed barbarous and absurd by a civilized nation.

It is asserted that a spy had represented to Kutusoff, Krasnoe as being filled with an immense number of the imperial guard, and that the old marshal was afraid of hazarding his reputation by attacking it. But the sight of the distress emboldened Bennigsen ; this officer, who was chief of the staff, prevailed upon Strogonoff, Gallitzin, and Miloradowitch, with a force of more than fifty thousand Russians, and one hundred pieces of cannon, to venture to attack at daylight, in spite of Kutusoff, fourteen thousand famished, enfeebled, and half-frozen French and Italians.

This was a danger, the imminence of which Napoleon fully comprehended. He might have escaped from it, for the day had not yet appeared. He was still at liberty to avoid this fatal engagement; by rapid marches along with Eugene and his guard, he might have gained Orcha and Borizoff; there he could have rallied his forces, and strengthened himself with thirty thousand French, under Victor and Oudinot, with the corps of Dombrowski, Regnier, and Schwartzenberg, been within reach of all his depots, and, by the following year, have made himself as formidable as ever.

On the 17th, before daylight, he issued his orders, armed himself, and going out on foot at the head of his

Old Guard, began his march. But it was not towards Poland, his ally, that he directed it, nor towards France, where he would still be received as the head of a new dynasty, and the Emperor of the West. His words on grasping his sword on this occasion were, "I have sufficiently acted the emperor; it is time I should become the general." He turned back upon eighty thousand of the enemy, plunging into the thickest of them, in order to draw all their efforts against himself, to make a diversion in favor of Davoust and Ney, and to rescue them from a country, the gates of which were closed against them.

Daylight at last appeared, exhibiting on the one part the Russian battalions and batteries, which on three sides, in front, on the right, and in the rear, bounded the horizon, and on the other Napoleon, with his six thousand guards, advancing with a firm step, and proceeding to take his place in the centre of that terrible circle. At the same time, Mortier, a few yards in front of the Emperor, deployed, in the face of the whole Russian army, with the five thousand men still remaining to him.

Every moment strengthened the enemy and weakened Napoleon. The noise of artillery, as well as Claparede, apprized him that in the rear of Krasnoe and his army, Bennigsen was proceeding to take possession of the road to Liady, and entirely cut off his retreat. The east, the west, and the south were flashing with the enemy's fires; one side alone remained open, that of the north and the Dnieper, towards an eminence, at the foot of which were the high road and the Emperor.

The French fancied they saw the enemy already covering this eminence with their cannon. In that situation they would have been just over Napoleon's head, and might have crushed him at a few yards' distance. He was apprized of his danger, cast his eyes for an instant towards the height, and uttered merely these words, "Very well, let a battalion of my chasseurs take possession of it!" Immediately afterward, without giving farther heed to it, his whole attention was directed to the perilous situation of Mortier.

Then, at last, Davoust made his appearance, forcing his way through a swarm of Cossacks, whom he dispersed by a precipitate movement. At the sight of Krasnoe this marshal's troops disbanded themselves, running across the fields to get beyond the right of the enemy's line, in the rear of which they had come up; and Davoust and his generals could only rally them at that place.

The first corps was thus preserved; but it was learned at the same time that the rear guard could no longer defend itself at Krasnoe; that Ney was probably still at Smolensk, and that they must give up waiting for him any longer. Napoleon, however, still hesitated: he could not determine on making this great sacrifice.

But at last, as all were likely to perish, his resolution was taken. He called Mortier, and pressing his hand sorrowfully, told him "that he had not a moment to lose; that the enemy were overwhelming him in all directions; that Kutusoff might already reach Liady, perhaps Orcha, and the last elbow of the Borysthenes before him; and that he would therefore proceed thither rapidly, with his Old Guard, in order to occupy that passage. Davoust would relieve him, Mortier, but both of them must endeavor to hold out in Krasnoe until night, after which they must advance and rejoin him." Then, with his heart full of Ney's misfortune, and of despair at abandoning him, he withdrew slowly from the field of battle, traversed Krasnoe, where he again halted, and thence cleared his way to Liady.

THE CAMP-FIRE AT BORYSTHENES.

NEY, "the bravest of the brave," the commander of the rear-guard of the grand army, had been given up as lost by most of his heroic brethren in arms. But Napoleon could not believe it. He knew that the chances were those of desperation, but he expected all things from the lion-hearted marshal. The Emperor had reached Orcha, on the Borysthenes, with ten thousand men. He found there abundance of provisions and his troops encamped by ample fires. But his anxiety for the fate of Ney rendered him very much dejected. He could not bring his mind to the idea of quitting the Borysthenes.

It appeared to him that this would be like a second abandonment of the unfortunate Ney, and a final casting off of his intrepid companion in arms. There, as at Liady and Dombrowna, he was calling every hour of the day and night, and sending to inquire if no tidings had been received of that marshal. But nothing was heard of him through the intervening Russian army; and four days this fatal silence had lasted, and yet the Emperor still continued to hope.

Being at length, on the 20th of November, compelled to quit Orcha, he left there Eugene, Mortier, and Davoust, and halted after a march of two leagues from that place, still inquiring for Ney, and still expecting him. The same feeling of grief pervaded the portion of the army remaining at Orcha. As soon as the most pressing wants allowed a moment's rest, the thoughts and looks of every one were directed towards the Russian bank. They listened for any warlike sounds which might announce the arrival of Ney, or, rather, his last desperate struggle with the foe; but nothing was to be seen but parties of the enemy, who were already menacing the bridges of the Borysthenes. One of the three marshals now proposed to destroy them, but the others would not consent, as this would be separating themselves still more widely from their companion in arms, and acknowledging that they despaired of saving him, an idea which, from their unhappiness at the thought, they could not bear to entertain.

But with the fourth day all hope had vanished, and night only brought with it an agitated repose. They blamed themselves for Ney's misfortune, forgetting that it was utterly impossible to have waited longer for him in the plains of Krasnoe, there to fight for another twenty-four hours, when they had scarcely strength and ammunition left for one.

Already, as is always the case in such painful losses, they began to seek for some soothing recollections. Davoust was the last who had quitted the unfortunate marshal, and Mortier and the viceroy were inquiring of him what were his last words. At the first reports of the cannonade of the enemy on the 15th, it would seem that Ney was anxious to evacuate Smolensk immediately, in the suite of the viceroy; but Davoust refused, pleading the orders of the emperor, and their obligation to destroy the ramparts of the town. The two chiefs became warm; and Davoust insisting to remain until the following day, Ney, who had been appointed to bring up the rear, was compelled to wait for him.

It is true that on the 16th, Davoust sent to warn him of his danger; but Ney, either from change of opinion, or from feelings of resentment against Davoust, returned for answer "that all the Cossacks in the universe should not prevent him from executing his instructions."

After exhausting these recollections and all their conjectures, they had relapsed into a gloomy silence, when suddenly they heard the steps of horses, and then the joyful cry, "Marshal Ney is safe! here are some Polish cavalry come to announce his approach!" One of his officers now galloped in, and informed them that the marshal was advancing on the right bank of the Borysthenes, and had sent him to ask for assistance.

Night had just set in; and Davoust, Eugene, and Mortier were allowed only its short duration to revive and animate the soldiers, who had hitherto constantly bivouacked. For the first time since they left Moscow, these poor fellows had received a sufficient supply of provisions; and they were about to prepare them and to take their rest, warm and under cover. How was it possible, then to make them resume their arms, and turn them from their comfortable asylums during that night of rest, whose inexpressible sweets they had just begun to taste! Who could persuade them to interrupt it, to trace back their steps, and once more, in the midst of darkness, return into the frozen deserts of Russia?

Eugene and Mortier disputed the honor of making this effort, and the first carried it only in right of his superior rank. Shelter and the distribution of provisions had effected that which threats would have failed to do. The stragglers were rallied, and the viceroy again found himself at the head of four thousand men; all were ready to march at the idea of Ney's danger; but it was their last effort.

They proceeded in the darkness, by unknown roads, and had marched two leagues at random, halting every few minutes to listen. Their anxiety instantly increased. Had they lost their way? Were they too late? Had their unfortunate comrades fallen? Was it the victorious Russian army they were about to meet? In this uncertainty Prince Eugene directed some cannon-shot to be fired. Immediately after, they fancied they heard signals of distress on that sea of snow: they were not mistaken; they proceeded from the third corps, which having lost all its artillery, could answer the cannon of the fourth only by some volleys of platoon firing.

The two corps were thus directed towards their meeting. Ney and Eugene were the first to recognise each other: they ran up, Eugene the most eagerly, and threw themselves into each other's arms. Eugene wept, but Ney only let fall some angry words. The first was delighted, melted, and elevated at the sight of the chivalrous hero whom he had just had the happiness to save. The latter still heated from the combat, irritated at the dangers which the honor of the army had run in his person, and blaming Davoust, whom he wrongfully accused of having deserted him.

Some hours afterwards, when the latter sought to justify himself, he could draw nothing from Ney but a severe look and these words, "Monsieur le Marechal, I have no reproaches to make you: God is our witness and your judge!"

As soon as the two corps had fairly recognised each other, they could no longer be kept in their ranks. Soldiers, officers, generals, all rushed forward together. The soldiers of Eugene, eagerly grasping the hands of those of Ney, held them with a joyful mixture of astonishment and curiosity, and embraced them with the tenderest sympathy. They lavished upon them the refreshments which they had just received, and overwhelmed them with questions. Then they proceeded in company towards Orcha, all burning with impatience, Eugene's soldiers to hear, and Ney's to relate, their story. There they were soon gathered around the cheerful camp-fire, and resting from their toils.

The officers of Ney stated that on the 17th of November they had quitted Smolensk with twelve cannon, six thousand infantry, and three hundred cavalry, leaving there five thousand sick to the mercy of the enemy; and that, had it not been for the noise of Platoff's artillery and the explosion of the mines, their marshal would never have been able to draw from the ruins of that city seven thousand unarmed stragglers who had taken shelter among them. They dwelt upon the attentions which their leader had shown to the wounded, and to the women and their children, proving upon this occasion that the bravest are also the most humane.

Ney's officers continued to speak in the most enthusiastic terms of their marshal; for even his equals could not feel the slightest jealousy of him. He had, indeed, been too much regretted, and his preservation had excited emotions far too grateful to allow of any feelings of envy; besides, Ney had placed himself completely beyond its reach. As for himself, he had in all this heroism gone so little beyond his natural character, that, had it not been for the eclat of his glory in the eyes, the gestures, and the acclamations of every one, he would never have imagined that he had performed an extraordinary action.

And this was not an enthusiasm of surprise, for each of the few last days had had its remarkable men: that of the 16th, for instance, had Eugene, and that of the 17th, Mortier; but from this time forward Ney was universally proclaimed the hero of the retreat.

When Napoleon, who was two leagues farther on, heard that Ney had again made his appearance, he leaped and shouted for joy, exclaiming, "Then I have saved my eagles! I would have given three hundred millions from my exchequer sooner than have lost such a man."

Such a man! Where else in history shall we find such a man? Davoust, Mortier, Junot, Murat, and other celebrated officers of that army were brave—wonderful men, indeed—but Ney towered above them all, in a courage which was full of sublimity—a courage which found resource when others saw nothing left for them but a resignation to death.

That night the marshal slept beside the camp-fire of his beloved Emperor—the sweet sleep which grows from the consciousness of duty performed.

THE LAST CAMP-FIRES IN RUSSIA.

AT Malodeczno, Napoleon suddenly determined to leave the wretched remnant of his army, and, accompanied by a few faithful officers, to return to France. Murat was left to command the army, and the greatest hopes of speedy relief and fresh triumph were excited by the Emperor before he departed. He journeyed very rapidly, and reached Paris on the 19th of December, two days after his memorable twenty-ninth bulletin had told France the disasters of the campaign. But the remains of the grand army—what was their fate?

On the 6th of December, the very day after Napoleon's departure, the sky exhibited a more dreadful appearance. Icy particles were seen floating in the air, and the birds fell stiff and frozen to the earth. The atmosphere was motionless and silent; it seemed as if every thing in nature which possessed life and movement, even the wind itself, had been seized, chained, and, as it were, congealed by a universal death. Not a word or a murmur was then heard; there was nothing but the gloomy silence of despair, and the tears which proclaimed it.

"We flitted along," says Segur, "in the midst of this empire of death like doomed spirits. The dull and monotonous sound of our steps, the crackling of the frost and the feeble groans of the dying, were the only interruptions to this doleful and universal silence. Anger and imprecations there were none, nor any thing which indicated a remnant of warmth; scarcely was strength enough left to utter a prayer; and most of them even fell without complaining, either from weakness or resignation, or because people complain only when they look for kindness, and fancy they are pitied.

"Such of our soldiers as had hitherto been the most persevering here lost heart entirely. Some times the snow sunk beneath their feet, but more frequently, its glassy surface refusing them support, they slipped at every step, and tottered along from one fall to another. It seemed as though this hostile soil were leagued against them; that it treacherously escaped from under their efforts; that it was constantly leading them into snares, as if to embarrass and retard their march, and to deliver them up to the Russians in pursuit of them, or to their terrible climate."

And, in truth, whenever, for a moment, they halted from exhaustion, the winter, laying his icy hand upon them, was ready to seize his victims. In vain did these unhappy creatures, feeling themselves benumbed, raise themselves up, and, already deprived of the power of speech, and plunged into a stupor, proceed a few steps like automatons; their blood froze in their veins, like water in the current of rivulets, congealing the heart, and then flying back to the head; and these dying men staggered as if they had been intoxicated. From their eyes, reddened and inflamed by the constant glare of the snow, by the want of sleep, and the smoke of the bivouacs, there flowed real tears of blood; their bosoms heaved with deep and heavy sighs; they looked towards heaven and on the earth, with an eye dismayed, fixed, and wild, as expressive of their farewell, and, it might be, of their reproaches against the barbarous nature which was tormenting them. It was not long before they fell upon their knees, and then upon their hands; their heads still slowly moved for a few minutes alternately to the right and left, and from their open mouth some sounds of agony escaped; at last, in its turn, it fell upon the snow, which it reddened with livid blood, and their sufferings were at an end.

Their comrades passed by them without moving a step out of their way, that they might not, by the slightest curve, prolong their journey, and without even turning their heads; for their beards and hair were so stiffened with ice that every movement was painful. Nor did they even pity them; for, in fact, what had they lost by dying? who had they left behind them? They suffered so much, they were still so far from France, so much divested of all feelings of country by the surrounding prospect and by misery, that every dear illusion was broken, and hope almost destroyed. The greater number, therefore, had become careless of dying, from necessity, from the habit of seeing death constantly around them, and from fashion, sometimes even treating it with contempt; but more frequently, on seeing these unfortunates stretched upon the snow, and instantly stiffened, contenting themselves with the thought that they had no more wants, that they were at rest, that their sufferings were over. And, indeed, death, in a situation quiet, certain, and uniform, may be felt as a strange event, a frightful contrast, a terrible change; but in this tumult, this violent and ceaseless movement of a life of action, danger, and suffering, it appeared nothing more than a transition, a slight alteration, an additional removal, which excited little alarm.

Such were the last days of the grand army: its last nights were still more frightful. Those whom they surprised marching together, far from every habitation, halted on the borders of the woods: there they lighted their fires, before which they remained the whole night, erect and motionless, like spectres. They seemed as if they could not possibly have enough of the heat;

they kept so close to it as to burn their clothes, as well as the frozen parts of their body, which the fire decomposed. The most dreadful pain then compelled them to stretch themselves on the ground, and the next day they attempted in vain to rise.

In the meantime, such as the winter had almost wholly spared, and who still retained some portion of courage, prepared their melancholy meal. It had consisted, ever since they left Smolensk, of some slices of horseflesh broiled, and a little rye meal made into a sort of gruel with snow water, or kneaded into paste, which they seasoned, for want of salt, with the powder of their cartridges.

The sight of these fires was constantly attracting fresh spectres, who were driven back by the first comers. Many of them, destitute of the means and the strength necessary to cut down the lofty fir trees, made vain attempts to set fire to them as they were standing; but death speedily surprised them, and they might be seen in every sort of attitude, stiff and lifeless about their trunks.

Under the vast pent-houses erected by the sides of the high road in some parts of the way, scenes of still greater horror were witnessed. Officers and soldiers all rushed precipitately into them, and crowded together in heaps. There, like so many cattle, they pressed upon each other around the fires, and as the living could not remove the dead from the circle, they laid themselves down upon them, there to expire in their turn, and serve as a bed of death to some fresh victims. In a short time additional crowds of stragglers presented themselves, and, being unable to penetrate into these asylums of suffering, they completely besieged them.

It frequently happened that they demolished their walls, which were formed of dry wood, in order to feed their fires; at other times, repulsed and disheartened, they were contented to use them as shelters to their bivouacs, the flames of which very soon communicated to the buildings, and the soldiers who were within them, already half dead with the cold, perished in the conflagration.

At Youpranoui, the same village where the Emperor only missed by an hour being taken by the Russian partisan Seslawin, the soldiers burned the houses as they stood, merely to warm themselves for a few minutes. The light of these fires attracted some of those miserable wretches, whom the excessive severity of the cold and their sufferings had rendered delirious; they ran to them like madmen, they threw themselves into these furnaces, where they perished in horrible convulsions. Their famished companions looked on unmoved; and there were some who drew out these bodies, blackened and broiled by the flames, and, shocking to relate, they ventured to pollute their mouths with this dreadful food!

This was the same army which had been formed from the most civilized nation of Europe; that army, formerly so brilliant, which was victorious over men to its last moment, and whose name still reigned in so many conquered capitals. Its strongest and bravest warriors, who had recently been proudly traversing so many scenes of their victories, had lost their noble bearing;

covered with rags, their feet naked and torn, and supporting themselves with branches of fir, they dragged themselves painfully along; and the strength and perseverance which they had hitherto put forth in order to conquer, they now made use of only to flee.

In this state of physical and moral distress, the remnant of the grand army reached the city of Wilna, the Mecca of their hopes. There food and shelter were obtained; but the Russians soon came up and told, in the thunder of their artillery, that Wilna was not a place of rest for the French. They were driven from the town, and Ney, with a handful of men, could scarcely protect their flight. Who can ever do sufficient honor to the lion-hearted marshal? This was the order of retreat which he adopted:

Every day, at five o'clock in the evening, he took his position, stopped the Russians, allowed his soldiers to eat and take some rest, and resumed his march at ten o'clock. During the whole of the night, he pushed the mass of the stragglers before him, by dint of cries, of entreaties, and of blows. At daybreak, which was about seven o'clock, he halted, again took position, and rested under arms and on guard until ten o'clock; the enemy then usually made his appearance, and he was compelled to fight until the evening, gaining as much ground in the rear as possible. This depended at first on the general order of march, and at a later period upon circumstances.

For a long time this rear guard did not consist of more than two thousand, then of one thousand, afterward of about five hundred, and finally it was reduced to sixty men; and yet Berthier, either designedly, or from mere routine, made no change in his instructions. These were always addressed to the commander of a corps of thirty-five thousand men; in them he coolly detailed all the different positions which were to be taken up and guarded until the next day, by divisions and regiments which no longer existed. And every night, when pressed by Ney's urgent warnings, he was obliged to go and awake the King of Naples, and compel him to resume his march, he testified the same astonishment.

In this manner did Ney support the retreat from Wiazma to Eve, and a few wersts beyond it. He attempted in vain to rally a few of them; and he who had hitherto been almost the only one whose commands had been obeyed, was now compelled to follow it.

He arrived along with it at Kowno, which was the last town of the Russian empire. Finally, on the 13th of December, after marching forty-six days under the most terrible sufferings, they once more came in sight of a friendly country. Instantly, without halting or looking behind them, the greater part plunged into, and dispersed themselves in, the forests of Prussian Poland. Some there were, however, who, on their arrival on the friendly bank of the Niemen, turned round, and there, when they cast a last look on that land of horrors from which they were escaping, and found themselves on the same spot whence, five months before, their countless legions had taken their victorious flight, tears gushed from their eyes, and they broke out into exclamations of the most poignant sorrow.

Two kings, one prince, eight marshals, followed by a few officers, generals on foot, dispersed, and without attendants; finally, a few hundred men of the old guard, still armed—these were its remains—these alone represented the grand army.

The camp-fires of the invaders in Russia were at an end. From Moscow to the Niemen they could be traced in circles of death. Every bivouac had its throng of victims, conquered more by the climate than the troops of Russia. Like a vast stream, which gradually disappears in the ground as it flows, the grand army of four hundred thousand men had vanished amid the snows of Russia. Upon the banks of the Niemen, it lived only in Marshal Ney.

THE CAMP-FIRE AT LUTZEN.

WE have seen Napoleon, with the wreck of an army, a fugitive amid the frozen plains of Russia. A few months have scarcely elapsed. It is April, 1813; and the Emperor of the French has taken the field at the head of three hundred and fifty thousand men, to beat back the enemies who have arisen against him in the hour of his adversity. Once more, in spite of the retreat from Moscow, Europe trembles at his name.

The allies have posted themselves between Leipsic and Dresden. Napoleon, with a hundred and fifteen thousand men under his immediate command, advances to the attack with his customary confidence and decision. Skirmishes took place at Weissenfels and Posen on the 29th of April, and the first of May. On the last day, the French approached the town of Lutzen, where Gustavus Adolphus had gained his final victory. The foremost column came upon the advanced guard of the allies, posted on the heights of Posen, and commanding a defile through which it was necessary to pass. Marshal Bessieres, the commander of the Old Guard—the companion of Napoleon in so much glory—dashed forward to reconnoitre the enemy's position, when a cannon ball struck one of his aids, and killed him upon the spot. The marshal reined in his fiery charger.

"Inter that brave man," said he, coolly; but scarcely had the words passed his lips, when he was struck by a spent cannon ball, and he fell from his horse, a corpse. A white sheet was thrown over him to conceal his features from the soldiers whom he had so often led to glory. The body was conveyed to a neighboring house, and there it lay during the battle of the next day, when the Guard looked in vain for the manly form of their commander. Napoleon deeply regretted Bessieres. He ordered the body to be embalmed and sent to the Hotel des Invalides, whence he designed to have it interred with great honors; but his fall prevented the execution of his intention.

On the night of the first of May, the army under Napoleon encamped in order of battle, within sight of the camp-fires of the allies, near Lutzen. The centre was at a village called Kaya, under the command of Ney. It consisted of the young conscripts, supported by the Imperial Guard, with its new parks of artillery drawn up before the well known town of Lutzen. Marmont commanded the right. The left reached from Kaya to the Elster. The silence of night settled down upon the camp of the French. But the allies, encouraged by the presence of the Czar and the King of Prussia, had determined to take the offensive—a very unusual course for any enemy in the face of Napoleon. While the French were reposing around their camp-fires, the Prussian general, Blucher, crossed the Elster. At daybreak, before Napoleon was stirring in his quarters, the French, in the centre, were startled by the furious assault of the enemy, who pushed their way through all obstacles, and were on the point of gaining possession of Kaya. The crisis was imminent. Napoleon, roused from slumber by intelligence of the attack, hurried in person to bring up the Guard to sustain the centre, while he moved forward the two wings, commanded by Macdonald and Bertrand, and supported by the tremendous batteries, so as to outflank and surround the main body of the allies. Thus began the battle of Lutzen. The struggle was fierce, and it endured for several hours. The village of Kaya was taken and retaken a number of times, but at length it remained in the hands of General Gerard. The students who were in the ranks of the allies, fought with desperate courage, and fell in great numbers. Schavnhort, a noted Prussian general, was killed, and Blucher was wounded. The artillery of the French carried immense destruction into the ranks of the enemy, and, at length, fearing from Napoleon's manœuvres, that they would be taken in flank, they beat a retreat, which they effected safely, but with much difficulty. They left twenty thousand dead upon the field. The loss of the French was not more than ten or twelve thousand men. The victory was not decisive, but it was glorious, and once more Napoleon's star shone with brilliant lustre, free from the shadow of defeat.

The French army was ordered to encamp on the field of battle in squares, by divisions, in order to provide against any sudden return of the enemy. Couriers were immediately sent off with the news of the victory to every friendly court in Europe. That night there was rejoicing around the camp-fires of the French. Napoleon once more received the congratulations of his generals upon a victory, and he began to dream of a peaceful occupation of his imperial throne.

THE CAMP-FIRE AT BAUTZEN.

AFTER the victory of Lutzen, Napoleon proposed a cessation of hostilities. But those allies who continually accused him of being always for war, rejected his conciliatory proposals, and resolved to try the sword again. They entrenched their camps at Bautzen, and far from attempting the offensive, which they had found so perilous, they anxiously awaited reinforcements. In the meantime, Napoleon had entered Dresden in triumph. There he remained a week. Finding that all attempts at conciliation were fruitless, he then determined to prosecute the campaign vigorously. On the 18th of May, he commenced the march upon Bautzen, and on the 21st, he reached the position of the allies. They were posted in the rear of Bautzen, with the river Spree in front; a chain of wooded hills and various fortified eminences to the right and left were occupied.

The action at this place commenced by the movement of a column of Italians, who were intended to turn the Prussian flank. This body, however, was attacked and dispersed before Marshal Ney could support them. The remainder of the day was spent by the French in passing the Spree, which was effected without molestation. The Emperor bivouacked in the town of Bautzen for the night. While the camp-fires of the French and their adversaries blazed near each other beyond the Spree, Napoleon called a council of his principal marshals, and after much deliberation, it was resolved to turn the camp of the enemy, instead of storming it. Day had just peeped in the east, and the fires had died out, when the dauntless Ney made a wide circuit to the right of the Russians, while Oudinot engaged their left, and Soult and the Emperor attacked the centre. The battle was fiercely fought. The Prussians, under the lead of the bold and pertinacious Blucher, kept their ground for four hours against the repeated charges of Soult. The slaughter was dreadful on both sides. At length, the Prussians were driven back, and the French were left in undisputed possession of the heights. Ney had now gained the rear of the allies, and he poured in murderous volleys of shot on their dispirited ranks. Panic stricken at this furious assault, they commenced their retreat, with such celerity as to gain time to rally on the roads leading to Bohemia. As night descended, the French shouted lustily for another victory. And there was revelry around the camp-fires of Napoleon's army. But the Emperor's heart was sorely touched.

General Bruyeres, a gallant officer, had been stricken down in the joyous moment of victory, at the head of the Imperial Guard. But it was not for him that the Emperor wept. About seven in the evening, the grand marshal of the palace—the devoted Duroc—he who was dearer to Napoleon than even Lannes or Bessieres—was mortally wounded. He was standing on a slight eminence, and at a considerable distance from the firing, conversing with Marshal Mortier and General Kirgener, all three on foot, when a cannon ball, aimed at the group, ploughed up the ground near Mortier, ripped open Duroc's abdomen, and killed General Kirgener. The grand marshal was conveyed to a lowly house as the victors encamped for the night. Napoleon was deeply affected when informed of the mournful event. He hastened to Duroc, who still breathed, and exhibited wonderful self-possession. Duroc seized the Emperor's hand and pressed it to his lips. "All my life," he said, "has been devoted to your service, and I only regret its loss for the use which it might still have been to you."

"Duroc," replied the Emperor, "there is another life. It is there that you will await me, and that we will one day meet."

"Yes, sire; but that will be in thirty years, when you shall have triumphed over your enemies, and realized the hopes of our country. I have lived an honest man; and have nothing to reproach myself with. I leave a daughter; your majesty will be a father to her."

Napoleon was deeply affected. He felt that the time was coming when he should need friends like Duroc. He took the right hand of the grand marshal in his own, and remained for a quarter of an hour with his head resting on the left hand of his old comrade, without being able to proffer a word.

Duroc was the first to break the silence. He did so, in order to spare Napoleon any further laceration of mind. "Ah, sire," said he, "go hence! This spectacle pains you!"

Napoleon paused a moment, and then rose and said:

"Adieu, then, my friend!" and he required to support himself on Marshal Soult and Caulaincourt, in order to regain his tent, where he would receive no person the whole night. He was again victorious. But he had lost his most faithful friends. His enemies were every day increasing in numbers, while he was only growing weaker by the gradual diminution of his forces; but some of the generals, upon whom he was most accustomed to rely, were of doubtful fidelity. Victorious or not, he saw that the struggle was to be continued against fearful odds, and a cloud approached his star.

THE CAMP-FIRE AT MONTEREAU.

A DISTINGUISHED historian, (Alison,) expresses the opinion that the greatest displays of Napoleon's genius were made during his first campaign in Italy, and the next to the last in his career, in France. In spite of his triumphs at Lutzen, Bautzen and Leipsic, he was compelled to retreat upon France, into which he was followed by the overwhelming forces of the allies. His throne was threatened on all sides. His army was but a handful compared with that of his enemies. Yet by his lightning movements, masterly combinations and indomitable resolution, he gained a succession of dazzling victories, and for a time seemed likely to drive his foes from France. We can only show this astonishing man during one portion of this unparalleled campaign.

It was the 16th of February, 1814. Having conquered the Russians at Montmirail, Napoleon had left the Duke of Ragusa—the Judas of the Emperor—in command of that portion of the army, and flown to the army of the Seine, commanded by the Dukes of Belluno and Reggio. He proceeded to Guignes by way of Crecy and Fontenay.

The inhabitants lined the road with carts, by the help of which the soldiers doubled their distances; and the firing of cannon being heard, the artillery drove on at full speed. An engagement had been obstinately maintained since noon by the Dukes of Belluno and Reggio, in the hope to keep possession of the road by which Napoleon was expected; an hour later the junction of the forces would have been difficult. The arrival of the Emperor restored full confidence to the army of the Seine. That evening he contented himself with checking the allies before Guignes; and the next morning the troops were seasonably reinforced by General Treilhard's dragoons, who had been detached from the army in Spain. Couriers dispatched to Paris entered the suburbs escorted by crowds of people who had anxiously assembled at Charenton. On the 17th the troops quitted Guignes and marched forward. The allies instantly knew that Napoleon was returned. General Gerard's infantry, General Drouet's artillery, and the cavalry of the army of Spain did wonders. The enemy's columns were driven back in every direction, and left the road between Mormars and Provins covered with the slain. The Duke of Belluno had orders to carry the bridge of Montereau that same evening; and the imperial guard lit their camp-fires round Nangis, the Emperor sleeping at the castle.

In the course of the evening, one of those lures by which he was too often inveigled arrived in the shape of a demand for a suspension of hostilities, brought by Count Parr from the Austrians. He availed himself of this opportunity of transmitting a letter from the Empress to her father, and of writing one himself. Napoleon at the same time, however, had spirit to write to Caulaincourt to revoke his *carte blanche*, saying it was to save the capital, but the capital was now saved; that it was to avoid a battle, but that the battle had been fought, and that the negotiations must return to the ordinary course. The allies had the assurance to reproach Buonaparte with this, as a receding from his word according to circumstances, when they themselves encroached upon him with every new advantage and every hour, as fast as the drawing aside the veil of hypocrisy would let them.

In the meantime, the Duke of Belluno was encamped at the bridge of Montereau. Early on the morning of the 18th, Napoleon was vexed to hear that the bridge was not yet captured; but that the camp-fires of the duke were burning amidst troops at rest, when great efforts were demanded of them. The Emperor hurried to that point. But the Wurtemberg troops had established themselves there during the night.

Napoleon ordered forward the Bretagne national guard and General Pajol's cavalry. General Gerard came up in time to support the attack, and Napoleon himself arrived to decide the victory. The troops took possession of the heights of Surville, which command the confluence of the Seine and the Yonne; and batteries were mounted which dealt destruction on the Wurtemberg force in Montereau. Napoleon himself pointed the guns. The enemy's balls hissed like the wind over the heights of Surville. The troops were fearful lest Napoleon, giving way to the habits of his early life, should expose himself to danger; but he only said, "Come on, my brave fellows, fear nothing; the ball that is to kill me is not yet cast." The firing redoubled; and under its shelter the Bretagne guards established themselves in the suburbs, while General Pajol carried the bridge by so vigorous a charge of cavalry, that there was not time to blow up a single arch. The Wurtemberg troops, inclosed and cut to pieces in Montereau, vainly summoned the Austrians to their aid. This engagement was one of the most brilliant of the campaign. Their success encouraged the troops, roused the country people, and stimulated the ardor of the young officers; but nothing could revive the spirits of the veteran chiefs. Hope does not return twice to the human breast. Several of the most distinguished officers were deeply depressed.

Napoleon could no longer repress his dissatisfaction. He reproached General Guyot in the presence of the troops, with having suffered the enemy to surprise some pieces of artillery the preceding evening. He ordered General Digeon to be tried by a council of war for a failure of ammunition on the batteries: but afterwards tore the order. He sent the Duke of Belluno, who had suffered the Wurtembergers to surprise the bridge of Montereau before him, permission to retire; and gave the command of his corps to General Gerard, who had greatly exerted himself during the campaign. The Duke repaired to Surville to appeal against this decision; but Napoleon overwhelmed him with reproaches for neglect and reluctance in the discharge of his duties. The conduct of the Duchess was also made a subject of complaint; she was Lady of the Palace, and yet had withdrawn herself from the Empress, who, indeed, seemed to be quite forsaken by the new court. The Duke could not for some time obtain a hearing; the recollections of Italy were appealed to in vain; but, mentioning the fatal wound which his son-in-law had received in consequence of his delay, the Emperor was deeply affected at hearing the name of General Chateau, and sympathized sincerely in the grief of the marshal. The Duke of Belluno resuming confidence, again protested that he would never quit the army. "I can shoulder a musket," said he: "I have not forgotten the business of a soldier. Victor will range himself in the ranks of the Guard." These last words completely subdued Napoleon. "Well, Victor," he said, stretching out his hand to him, "remain with me. I cannot restore the command of your corps, because I have appointed General Gerard to succeed you; but I give you the command of two divisions of the Guard; and now let every thing be forgotten between us."

The Emperor was victorious. But victory only served to fill him with false hopes. He triumphed again and again. But it was of no avail. The forces of the enemy were overwhelming; and at the moment when it seemed most likely that he could save France, the disgusting treachery of Marmont and Augereau, two men whom he had raised from the dust, as it were, brought about his ruin. He found, like many other great characters of history, in their hour of adversity, that the men who were most indebted to him were the men upon whom it were most unsafe to rely.

THE CAMP-FIRE AT ARCIS.

WHILE the allies held anxious councils, and were filled with apprehensions at almost every movement of Napoleon in his mighty struggle for his throne, he continued to strike vigorous blows at his thronging enemies. He triumphed at Craonne, and took possession of Rheims. The Austrians, under Schwartzenberg, were compelled to retreat. On the 17th of March, Napoleon broke up his head-quarters at Rheims, and advanced by Epernay to attack the rear of the Austrian army. On the 20th, his advanced guard encountered an Austrian division at Arcis-sur-Aube. The conflict became fierce. The Austrians brought up fresh battalions, supported by cannon; and Napoleon found that instead of attacking a rear guard in retreat, he was in front of the whole of the grand army in its advance on Paris.

This was unfortunate for the Emperor's calculations. He conceived himself to be acting upon the retreat of the allies, and expected only to find a rear guard at Arcis; he was even talking jocularly of making his father-in-law prisoner during his retreat. If, contrary to his expectation, he should find the enemy, or any considerable part of them, still upon the Aube, it was, from all he had heard, to be supposed his appearance would precipitate their retreat towards the frontier. It has also been asserted, that he expected Marshal Macdonald to make a corresponding advance from the banks of the Seine to those of the Aube; but the orders had been received too late to admit of the necessary space being traversed so as to arrive on the morning of the day of battle.

Napoleon easily drove before him such bodies of light cavalry, and sharp-shooters, as had been left by the allies, rather for the purpose of reconnoitring than of making any serious opposition. He crossed the Aube at Plancey, and moved upwards, along the left bank of the river, with Ney's corps, and his whole cavalry, while the infantry of the guard advanced upon the right; his army being thus, according to the French military phrase, *a-cheval,* upon the Aube. The town of Arcis had been evacuated by the allies upon his approach, and was occupied by the French on the morning of the 20th March. That town forms the outlet of a sort of defile, where a succession of narrow bridges cross a number of drains, brooks, and streamlets, the feeders of the river Aube, and a bridge in the town crosses the river itself. On the other side of Arcis is a plain, in which some few squadrons of cavalry, resembling a reconnoitring party, were observed manœuvring.

Behind these horses, at a place called Clermont, the Prince Royal of Wurtemberg, whose name has been so often honorably mentioned, was posted with his division, while the elite of the allied army was drawn up on a chain of heights still farther in the rear, called Mesnil la Comptesse. But these corps were not apparent to the vanguard of Napoleon's army. The French cavalry had orders to attack the light troops of the allies; but these were instantly supported by whole regiments, and by cannon, so that the attack was unsuccessful; and the squadrons of the French were repulsed and driven back on Arcis at a moment, when, from the impediments in the town and its environs, the infantry could with difficulty debouch from the town to support them. Napoleon showed, as he always did in extremity, the same heroic courage which he had exhibited at Lodi and Brienne. He drew his sword, threw himself among the broken cavalry, called on them to remember their former victories, and checked the enemy by an impetuous charge, in which he and his staff officers fought hand to hand with their opponents, so that he was in personal danger from the lance of a Cossack, the thrust of which was averted by his aid-de-camp, Girardin. His Mameluke, Rustan, fought stoutly by his side, and received a gratuity for his bravery. These desperate exertions afforded time for the infantry to debouch from the town. The Imperial Guards came up, and the combat waxed very warm. The superior numbers of the allies rendered them the assailants on all points. A strongly situated village in front, and somewhat to the left of Arcis, called Grand Torcy, had been occupied by the French. This place was repeatedly and desperately attacked by the allies, but the French made good their position. Arcis itself was set on fire by the shells of the assailants; and night alone separated the combatants by inducing the allies to desist from the attack.

The French remained masters of the field, which they had maintained against nearly treble their number. They had not gained a victory, but they had fought one of their most glorious battles, and Napoleon had displayed not only the full blaze of his genius, but had shown the allies that he was still the valorous hero of Arcola. Many of the houses of Arcis were blazing when the wearied heroes kindled their camp-fires along the Aube. Upon the distant heights of Mesnil la Comptesse, the watch-fires of the enemy were to be seen, and the sky was redly illumined as far as the eye could penetrate. Napoleon had retired to his head-quarters, to rest his weary body, but not to sleep. He had but twenty-seven thousand men, and he was before a strong position, occupied by eighty thousand troops. He was busy in examining his maps, when an aid, Girardin, entered and announced the arrival of Marshals Macdonald and Oudinot, and General Gerard, with their detachments. A few moments afterwards, those brave commanders entered. Napoleon received them with much apparent gratification. Others of his generals also arrived, and a council was held to determine upon the course to be pursued. Macdonald was the most influential of the Emperor's advisers at this time. His great good sense, cool, steady courage, and honest heart, had won upon Napoleon's favor, and he listened to his counsel with much attention and consideration. In a former part of his career, he had treated Macdonald very unjustly. In his darker hours, he found the marshal's great worth, and ever afterwards spoke of him in the highest terms.

The character of Macdonald could be read in his broad, Scotch countenance. His expression was honest, penetrating and determined. He was above all meanness. He lacked enthusiasm; but he had a mind that could calmly work in the midst of the most terrible excitement. He never appeared to be ruffled. The tone of his voice was always dry, even, and steady, as if it was out of the power of the ordinary human emotions to gain an influence over him. Napoleon eagerly asked the advice of the renowned marshal, and received a prompt reply—that retreat was necessary; and it would be well if it could be effected in the face of an overwhelming enemy. Oudinot and Gerard concurred in Macdonald's opinion; indeed, there seemed to be a prevailing idea, that immediate retreat was necessary, and Napoleon acquiesced. But the manner of it was not so easy to determine. The army was in a difficult position. The line of retreat on either side of the Aube was rendered dangerous by the numerous defiles, where an enemy might attack with advantage. Finally, it was decided to retreat on both sides of the Aube, as a method of presenting a smaller mark to an enemy in pursuit, and of hurrying through the dangerous defiles. The council then dissolved into a conversational party, but the spirits of the generals seemed under the shadow of a cloud. There was scarcely one of them who did not apprehend a speedy termination of the fearful struggle in which they were engaged. To all Napoleon's expressions of his grand designs, for which he had no means, they gave the reply of a shake of the head, or indicated the obstacles. Napoleon could see that their enthusiasm and confidence had been dissipated by the disasters which their glorious efforts had been unable to avert from the French arms. The demeanor of the Emperor was calm and dignified. He was Emperor of France and at the head of an army still. He was even victorious. But there was no lightness in his look or speech.

At daybreak the camp-fires of the army were extinguished, and the order of retreat given. It was a masterly exploit. With his small army, the Emperor retreated through the difficult defiles, in the face of a whole Austrian army; and though pursued and annoyed, sustained but little loss.

But what availed these miracles of generalship? The

struggle was quickly decided, by irresistible numbers and sickening treachery.

Paris was surrendered by Marmont, while still capable of defence, and the enemy gained possession of Lyons by the same means. All hope was lost, and the Emperor was advised by Macdonald and others of his most faithful friends, to comply with the terms of the allies and abdicate his throne. He resisted as long as there was a shadow of hope, and then obeyed stern necessity. The enemies of France were supreme. The sovereign of her choice was consigned to the little island of Elba, and the detested Bourbons were restored in the person of Louis XVIII.

We will not dwell upon the leave-taking of the Emperor—how he kissed the eagles, and embraced the veterans of Fontainebleau. It is not within our scope. It is enough to know, that such victories as Montereau, Arcis and Montmirail, won in the last hours of his imperial power, sustained the glory of Napoleon's genius, and proved that no treason, "coming like a blight over the councils of the brave," could annihilate his title to immortal remembrance.

THE CAMP-FIRE AT WATERLOO.

NAPOLEON had returned to France. He had landed at Cannes with but a few soldiers as a guard; but he had been swept up to the imperial throne of Paris upon a mighty wave of popular enthusiasm. All Europe had arisen in arms against the choice of the nation. The campaign of the Hundred Days had commenced. At the head of a hundred and twenty thousand men, the Emperor had advanced to attack Wellington and Blucher, with two hundred and fifty thousand.

In order to escape from the danger which might result from too great an inferiority of numbers, Napoleon strove, from the commencement of the campaign, to separate the English from the Prussians, and manœuvred actively to throw himself between them. His plan was strikingly successful on the 16th at the battle of Ligny; Blucher, being attacked alone, was completely beaten, and left twenty-five thousand men on the field of battle. But this enormous loss did not materially enfeeble an army which had such masses of soldiers in line, and behind, still more numerous reserves. In the position in which the Emperor found himself, he required a more decisive advantage, a victory which should annihilate the army of Blucher, and allow him to fall upon Wellington next, in order to crush him in his turn. This successive defeat of the English and Prussians had been most skilfully prepared by the orders and instructions he dispatched on all sides. But, we cannot too often repeat it, his destiny was accomplished; and fatal misunderstandings deceived the calculations of his genius. Moreover, he had himself a presentiment that some unforeseen incident would disarrange his combinations, and that fortune had more disasters in store for him. "It is certain that in these circumstances," he said to his suite, "I had no longer in myself that definitive feeling; there was nothing of former confidence." His presentiments were too soon realized.

At daybreak on the 17th, Grouchy, at the head of

thirty-four thousand men, was dispatched in pursuit of the enemy, who had fled in two columns by way of Tilly and Gembloux, with orders to proceed to Wavres. About seven in the morning, the Emperor galloped forward with Count Lobau's cavalry towards Quatre-Bras, which place he expected to find in possession of Ney; the latter, however, had not been able to retrieve his error of the 16th, and remained facing the position of the British, although now occupied only by their rear-guard, which made off as soon as its commander perceived the approach of Lobau's horsemen. Pursuit was immediately given, Napoleon hoping that he might yet be able to overtake and defeat the English. In consequence of the state of the roads, from the heavy rains, it was near four o'clock before the retreating column reached the plain of Waterloo, and nearly seven before the troops were in position on the rising ground in front of Mount St. Jean.

That night the English bivouacked on the field they were to maintain in the battle of the morrow. Between six and seven, Napoleon reached Planchenois; and perceiving the enemy established in position, fixed his head-quarters at the farm of Cailloux, and posted his followers on the heights around La Belle Alliance. The reinforcements received by the Duke of Wellington during the 16th and 17th, had raised his army to seventy-five thousand men, who were supported by two hundred and fifty pieces of cannon. Napoleon's forces have been estimated at seventy thousand men, and about two hundred and forty pieces of cannon; it must, however, be borne in mind, that the Duke could not depend on the Belgian, Nassau, and Hanoverian troops.

"Never," says Alison, "was a more melancholy night passed by soldiers than that which followed the halt of the two armies in their respective positions on the night of the 17th of June, 1815.

"The whole of that day had been wet and cloudy, but towards evening the rain fell in torrents, insomuch that, in traversing the road from Quartre-Bras to Waterloo, the soldiers were often anklo doep in water. When the troops arrived at their ground, the passage of the artillery, horse, and wagons over the drenched surface had so completely cut it up, that it was almost every where reduced to a state of mud, interspersed in every hollow with large pools of water. Cheerless and dripping as was the condition of the soldiers, who had to lie down for the night in such a situation, it was preferable to that of those battalions who were stationed in the rye-fields, where the grain was for the most part three or four feet high, and soaking wet from top to bottom. The ground occupied by the French soldiers was not less drenched and uncomfortable. But how melancholy soever may have been their physical situation, not one feeling of despondency pervaded the breasts either of the British or French soldiers. Such was the interest of the moment, the magnitude of the stake at issue, and the intensity of the feelings in either army, that the soldiers were almost insensible to physical suffering. Every man in both armies was aware that the retreat was stopped, and that a decisive battle would be fought on the following day. The great contest of two-and-twenty years' duration was now to be brought to a final issue: retreat after disaster would be difficult, if not impossible, to the British army, through the narrow defile of the forest of Soignies: overthrow was ruin to the French. The two great commanders, who had severally overthrown every antagonist, were now for the first time to be brought into collision; the conqueror of Europe was to measure swords with the deliverer of Spain. Nor were sanguine hopes and the grounds of well-founded confidence wanting to the troops of either army. The French relied with reason on the extraordinary military talents of their chief, on his long and glorious career, and on the unbroken series of triumphs which had carried their standards to every capital in Europe. Nor had recent disasters weakened this undoubting trust, for the men who now stood side by side were almost all veterans tried in a hundred combats: the English prisons had restored the conquerors of Continental Europe to his standard, and for the first time since the Russian retreat, the soldiers of Austerlitz and Wagram were again assembled round his eagles. The British soldiers had not all the same mutual dependence from tried experience, for a large part of them had never seen a shot fired in battle. But they were not on that account the less confident. They relied on the talent and firmness of their chief, who they knew, had never been conquered, and whose resources the veterans in their ranks told them would prove equal to any emergency. They looked back with animated pride to the unbroken career of victory which had attended the British arms since they first landed in Portugal, and anticipated the keystone to their arch of fame from the approaching conflict with Napoleon in person. They were sanguine as to the result; but, come what may, they were resolute not to be conquered. Never were two armies of such fame, under leaders of such renown, and animated by such heroic feelings, brought into contact in modern Europe, and never were interests so momentous at issue in the strife."

The field of Waterloo, rendered immortal by the battle which was fought on the following day, extends about two miles in length from the old chateau, walled garden, and inclosures of Hougoumont on the right, to the extremity of the hedge of La Haye Sainte on the left. The great *chaussee* from Brussels to Charleroi runs through the centre of the position, which is situated somewhat less than three quarters of a mile to the south of the village of Waterloo, and three hundred yards in front of the farm-house of Mount St. Jean. This road, after passing through the centre of the British line, goes through La Belle Alliance and the hamlet of Rossomme, where Napoleon spent the night. The position occupied by the British army, followed very nearly the crest of a range of gentle eminences, cutting the high road at right angles, two hundred yards behind the farm-house of La Haye Sainte, which adjoins the highway, and formed the centre of the position. An unpaved country road ran along this great summit, forming nearly the line occupied by the British troops, and which proved of great use in the course of the battle. Their position had this great advantage, that the infantry could rest on the reverse of the crest of the ridge, in a situation in great measure screened from the fire of the French artillery; while their own guns on the crest swept the whole slope, or natural glacis, which descended to the valley in their front. The French army occupied a corresponding line of ridges, nearly parallel, on the opposite side of the valley, stretching on either side of the hamlet of La Belle Alliance. The summit of these ridges afforded a splendid position for the French artillery to fire upon the English guns; but their attacking columns, in descending the one hill and mounting the other, would of necessity be exposed to a very severe cannonade from the opposite batteries. The French army had an open country to retreat over in case of disaster; while the British, if defeated, would in all probability lose their whole artillery in the defiles of the forest of Soignies, although the intricacies of that wood afforded an admirable defensive position for a broken array of foot soldiers. The French right rested on the village of Planchenois, which is of considerable extent, and afforded a very strong defensive position to resist the Prussians, in case they should so far recover from the disaster of the preceding day as to be able to assume offensive operations and menace the extreme French right.

This is an admirable picture of the position and condition of the respective armies which were to decide the fate of Europe. It could not be improved.

The farm-house of Cailloux, in which the Emperor was busy with his maps and plans, and surrounded by his celebrated marshals, was surrounded with the meagre fires which the guard had kindled; but the rain frequently extinguished them and drove many of the veterans to seek the shelter of sheds.

Napoleon displayed all his usual activity and dispatch. He dictated orders to be conveyed to the different commanders of columns with the rapidity of lightning. Every body near him was kept in a state of feverish excitement, except the calm and steady Soult, whom it seemed impossible to move. There, too, was the stalwart Ney, whom the storms of battle could not even scar—ready for any duty, no matter how hopeless the performance. There also was the brave but reckless Jerome, who was destined to earn a high fame on the morrow. Berthier, who had so long been a fixture by the side of Napoleon, was not there, he had deserted the man from whose glory he had borrowed beams But there was Maret, Bertrand, the steady Drouot, of the Old Guard, Gorgaud and Labedoyere—a galaxy of bravery and talent—such as was wont to surround the Emperor. All were busy noting down instructions, and replying to the swift questions of the tireless man whom they obeyed. Without, the rain was heard dripping incessantly. Drouot let fall an expression of opinion that, in consequence of the deluge, the ground would be impracticable for artillery.

"We shall see, it is not yet morning," replied the Emperor. Then he leaned his head upon his hand, and thought—perhaps in the way of presentiment of disaster—but no expression of apprehension escaped his lips. Grouchy would keep Blucher in check, and Wellington would be crushed. Fortune might yet be favorable. But the heavens had quenched the last camp-fire of Napoleon.

About ten o'clock at night, Napoleon sent a dispatch to Grouchy, to announce that the Anglo-Belgian army had taken post in advance of the forest of Soignes, with its left resting on the hamlets of La Haye and Ohain, where Wellington seemed determined on the next day to give battle; Grouchy was, therefore, required to detach from his corps, about two hours before daybreak, a division of seven thousand men, and sixteen pieces of artillery, with orders to proceed to St. Lambert; and, after putting themselves in communication with the right of the grand army, to operate on the left of the British.

Meanwhile, the Duke of Wellington being in communication with Blucher, was promised by him that the Prussian army should advance to support the British on the morning of the 18th.

The rain, which had not ceased during the night, cleared off about five o'clock in the morning; and at eight it was reported by the officers who had been sent to inspect the field, that the ground was practicable for artillery. The Emperor instantly mounted his horse, and rode forward towards La Haye Sainte, to reconnoitre the British line.

By half-past ten o'clock the two armies were arrayed, and impatient for orders to commence the battle. The Emperor proceeded to the heights of Rosomme, where he dismounted to obtain a clear view of the whole field; and there stationed his guard, as a reserve, to act where emergency might require. Meanwhile, the English remained silent and steady, waiting the commands of their chief; who, with telescope in hand, stood beneath a tree, near the cross-road, in front of his position, watching the movements of his opponents.

The village clock of Nivelles was striking eleven when the first gun was fired from the French centre. Then followed a tremendous rattle of musketry, as the brave Jerome led the column on the left to the attack on Hougomont, and drove the Nassau troops before him. The chateau and gardens, however, were bravely defended by a division of English guards, who were not to be dislodged. The fight, raged here more or less during the day, till at length the chateau was set on fire by the shells of the French, and it was found necessary to abandon it.

Napoleon, who was anxiously watching the first movement of his troops, was interrupted by an aid-de-camp, sent by Ney, who had been charged to attack the enemy's centre, arriving at full gallop to announce that every thing was in readiness, and the marshal only waiting the signal to attack. For a moment the Emperor glanced round the field, and perceived in the direction of St. Lambert, a moving cloud advancing on the left of the English: pointing it out to Soult, he asked whether he conceived it to be Grouchy or Blucher? The marshal being in doubt, Generals Domont and Subervie were dispatched with their divisions of light cavalry, with orders to clear the way in the event of its being Grouchy, and if Blucher, to keep him in check.

Ney was then ordered to march to the attack of La Haye Sainte; after taking that post with the bayonet, and leaving a division of infantry, he was to proceed to the farms of Papelotte and La Haye, and place his troops between those of Wellington and Bulow. With his usual promptitude, the Prince of the Moskowa had in a few moments opened a battery of eighty cannon upon the left centre of the English line. The havoc occasioned by this deadly fire was so immense, that Wellington was obliged to draw back his men to the reverse slope of the hill on which they had stood, in order to screen them from its effects. The Count d'Erlon, under cover of the fire, advanced along the Genappe road; but as they ascended the position of La Haye Sainte, the Duke of Wellington directed against them a charge of cavalry, which speedily drove one column back into the hollow.

The English guards were in turn repulsed by a brigade of Milhaud's cuirassiers, and galloping onwards, attacked the infantry; the horsemen not being able to make an impression on the squares formed for their reception, while they were themselves exposed to an incessant fire of musketry. One of D'Erlon's unbroken columns pushed forward, meanwhile, beyond La Haye Sainte, upon which it made no attack, and charging one Belgian and three Dutch regiments, drove them from their posts in disorder, and took possession of the heights. Sir Thomas Picton was now sent to dislodge the enemy, and being supported by a brigade of heavy cavalry, the French, after firing a volley, paused, wheeled, and fled in confusion. Many were cut down by the guards; while seven guns, two eagles, and about two thousand prisoners were taken. The British, however, pursued their success too far; and becoming involved among the infantry, were attacked by a body of cuirassiers, in their turn broken, and forced to retire with great loss.

Although for the time, Ney was deprived of his artillery, he continued to advance upon La Haye Sainte. For three hours, this important position, and the part of the field which it commanded, was hotly contested by both parties, the hill being now held by the English, and now by the French. The contest, which shortly extended itself along the whole front of the British line, became of the most desperate character. Whole battalions fell as they stood in line; and the cries and groans of the wounded and dying were heard even above the incessant roll of the musketry, and the thunder of the artillery.

Napoleon, who had returned to the rising ground to watch the progress of the battle, fancying he beheld indications of the enemy's retreat, ordered Kellerman to advance with all his cuirassiers immediately, to support the cavalry between Mount St. Jean and La Haye-Sainte. The dragoons galloping forward, drove the English from their guns, and furiously charged the squares of infantry behind. Notwithstanding the deadly shower which thinned their ranks, the cuirassiers appeared determined to succeed in their purpose; and returned again and again, riding round the squares, and penetrating even to the second British line; the infantry, however, was immovable: and after sustaining frightful carnage, the cuirassiers were compelled to retire. The conflict now rather abated, until near six o'clock, and the chiefs of each army were anxiously expecting rein forcements. Domont, Lobau, and Subervic had effectually checked Bulow on the French right; but there was no sign of Grouchy making his appearance, and it was soon discovered that Blucher had come up with the main body of his army, and that the French opposed to him could not long maintain their ground. News was received from Grouchy, that instead of leaving Gembloux at day-break, according to his previously stated intentions, he had delayed there till half-past nine, and then pursued the road to Wavres, being unacquainted with the Emperor's engagement at Waterloo. The crisis of the battle now approached, and Napoleon saw that nothing but the most consummate skill and desperate valor could save his army from ruin. His preparations were, therefore, commenced for the final struggle. A series of movements, changing the whole front of his army, so as to face both Prussians and English, was the result of his first orders. Napoleon next formed the infantry of the Imperial Guard, which had not yet been brought into action, at the foot of the position of La Belle Alliance, into two columns, and led them forward in person, to a ravine which crossed the Genappe road, in front of the British lines. Here he relinquished the command to Ney, at the entreaty of his officers; the Marshal, who had had five horses shot under him during the day, advanced on foot. A heavy discharge of artillery announced that they were in motion; the British guns soon commenced a most destructive firing on the troops, which committed dreadful havoc. Although their numbers were thinned at every step, the guards continued to advance, and soon gained the rising ground of Mount St. Jean, where the English awaited their assault. The French bands played the Imperial march, and the troops ruched on with loud shouts of "*Vive l' Empereur!*" The Belgian, Dutch, and Brunswick troops gave way instantly, and the Duke of Wellington was compelled to rally them in person. Before the Imperial Guard could deploy, he gave the word for the British infantry to advance; the men, who had been lying prostrate on the hill, or resting on their arms on the slope, sprang forward, and closing around Ney, and his gallant followers, poured into their ranks a continuous stream of bullets. The guard attempting to deploy, were thrown into confusion, and rushed in a crowd to the hollow road in front of La Haye Sainte, whence they were speedily driven. In this desperate charge, Ney's uniform and hat were riddled with balls. In the meantime, Blucher had pressed forward, and driven the few French from the hamlet of La Haye; and his advanced guard already communicated with the British left. Bulow, who had been repulsed from Planchenois, but was now reinforced, was again advancing. Wellington, having assumed the offensive, was advancing at the head of his whole army. It already grew dusk; the French had every where given way: the guard, never before vanquished, had been routed by the stern troops of Britain; and night brought with it terror and despair. It having been reported that the Old Guard had yielded, a panic suddenly spread throughout the French lines, and the fatal cry of "*Sauve qui peut!*" was raised, and becoming universal discipline and courage were forgotten, and a wild flight ensued. The cavalry and artillery of the English and Prussians now scattered death on all sides. The vengeance of the latter was unsatiated, and these scoured the field, making fearful carnage, and giving no quarter. The Old Guard was yet unbroken, and Napoleon lingered on the ground. Prince Jerome, who had fought bravely throughout the day, urged him to an act of desperation. "Here, brother," said he, "all who bear the name of Bonaparte should fall!" Napoleon, who was on foot, mounted his horse, but his soldiers would not listen to any proposal involving his death: and at length, an aid-de-camp seizing his bridle, led him at a gallop from the field. He arrived at Genappe shortly before ten o'clock at night, where he again attempted to rally; but the confusion was so great as to be utterly irremediable.

The pursuit of the French was continued far into the night by the Prussians. Nine times, the wearied fugitives halted, kindled fires and prepared to bivouac. Nine times they were startled by the dreadful sound of the Prussian trumpet, and obliged to continue their flight. The star that had arisen at Toulon, and shone resplendent over Lodi, Marengo, Jena, Wagram, Borodino, and a throng of other sanguinary fields—had sunk forever. It is painful to trace the career of fallen greatness. We will not follow the Emperor, shorn of his purple, to his prison at St. Helena, where a deadly climate did the work that the leaden storms of a hundred fights had refused to perform. We will not go to that bed of death, from which, while the elements were at terrible war, that stormy spirit was carried away. Leave Hannibal at Zama, and Napoleon at Waterloo.